D0681284

GLOBAL ORDER

GLOBAL ORDER

VALUES AND POWER
IN INTERNATIONAL POLITICS

Lynn H. Miller

Westview Press • Boulder and London

Copyright © 1985 by Westview Press, Inc.

Published in 1985 in the United States of America by Westview Press, Inc., 5500 Central Avenue, Boulder, Colorado 80301; Frederick A. Praeger, Publisher

Library of Congress Cataloging in Publication Data
Miller, Lynn H.
  Global order.
  Includes bibliographies.
  1. World politics—1975–1985. 2. International relations. I. Title.
D849.M542 1985   327′.09′047   84-17203
ISBN 0-8133-0068-1
ISBN 0-8133-0069-X (pbk.)

Printed and bound in the United States of America

10   9   8   7   6   5   4   3

To Nancy and Jim,
with hope for all their generation

Contents

Preface

This book is the product of a consciously normative and value-oriented perspective on world order problems. Often neglected in the standard texts on international politics, such an approach seems to me essential for a number of reasons. First, the normative framework is that in which the game of international politics is played. It provides the parameters within which international actors compete for power and influence. That framework is not an accident of nature but a human invention, created to rationalize and order the relevant social and technological capabilities of increasingly sovereign actors more than 300 years ago and consciously enlarged and adapted to respond to changes in those capabilities ever since. It therefore should not be regarded as merely a footnote or an afterthought in the analysis of international politics, but as the ordering ideal structure that both shapes international behavior and makes its evaluation possible.

Second, the value-oriented perspective also encourages analysis of the strengths and weaknesses of the international normative system itself, which is particularly important now that its ability to maintain needed order seems more strongly threatened than at any time in the past. Politics shape the normative structure, but the normative structure also shapes politics, increasingly with potentially disastrous consequences in a world of sovereign nuclear capability. The structural reasons for our current peril need to be addressed in ways that are seldom possible in state-based analysis alone.

Third, this approach provides us as students with a critical orientation toward policy as well, for we are encouraged to judge international political phenomena on the basis of world order criteria. We are forced to examine our own values in the process and to consider their congruence or incongruence with what other individuals or groups in the world desire, and why. We are forced to think about global ethics as a result, and no doubt with more objectivity than is usually possible when our analysis is heavily state based or oriented toward the outlook of particular decision makers.

The basic purpose of this book is to provide a kind of normative guide to the examination of the most important issues on today's international agenda. That is the major substantive component of the book in Chapters 5 through 8, in which the principal agenda items are considered. Chapters 2 and 3, meanwhile, constitute an excursion into the historical basis of our present condition. There the development and logic of the Westphalian system of sovereign nation-states is examined, from its creation at the end of the Thirty Years' War to the present. This component is intended to demonstrate the interplay between value and power in the creation and growth of the world's political system and to suggest what is mutable and what immutable in the way in which humanity historically has organized itself on the planet. Chapters 1 and especially 4 attempt to provide the reader with the basic tools for exploring the chaotic world of competing social and political forces as a world order system. They include discussion of the world order process in the contemporary period, the relationship between power and values and between power and authority, the relativity of both anarchy and order in the international system, and distinctions and connections between politics and law in society.

The manuscript has profited from the comments of a number of people, among whom Peter Bachrach, Robert W. Hansen, Lloyd Jensen, Robert C. Richter, and Burns Weston have provided particularly valued advice. David Bonnell was my committed and helpful assistant for one phase of my research. Among the many whose ideas have influenced me, Richard A. Falk has been my principal mentor. His work and that of a number of his associates at the World Policy Institute have left their imprint on these pages. Had it not been for my students, finally, it is unlikely that this book would have been written. Certainly they have had far more to do with its shape and contents than they can possibly imagine. None of those mentioned need share any of the blame for what follows.

Lynn H. Miller

1
The Best and Worst of Times

It was the best of times, it was the worst of times,
it was the age of wisdom, it was the age of foolishness,
it was the epoch of belief, it was the epoch of incredulity,
it was the season of Light, it was the season of Darkness,
it was the spring of hope, it was the winter of despair,
we had everything before us, we had nothing before us.
—Charles Dickens, *A Tale of Two Cities*

These famous lines first appeared in 1859, and they have captured the imagination of readers ever since for the way in which they evoke the almost fantastic range of possibilities available in every human experience. Men and women have an enormous capacity for wisdom and enlightenment, an ability to learn all sorts of complex and useful things about the wondrous universe of which they are a part. From the time members of our species learned to domesticate plants and animals until their descendants first journeyed to the moon, humanity's progress in making the physical universe serve its commands has been remarkable, giving rise to hope, happiness, and the sense that we have everything before us. These are among the emotions and the experiences that provide every generation with its own best of times.

Yet humans are not gods, nor, as they generally have thought, are they destined to become them, for they are flawed by ignorance and misunderstanding and behave despicably toward each other in their quest for mastery over a confusing and chaotic world. They often inflict misery and death upon many while building marvelously complex societies. Still, the oppressors, like their victims, ultimately are vanquished by their own mortality, which has guaranteed to weak and strong alike their own worst of times.

These are brief descriptions of what appear to be the two extremes of the human condition. Not every human being who has ever lived would describe those extremes in exactly the same way. Some generations have lived at times when the darker prospects for the species seemed to dominate the possibilities for happiness or human progress; others have been born into a world in which the opposite perception had fertile ground in which to take root and spread. Yet the appeal of Dickens's opening words to *A Tale of Two Cities*—words written in a time and society that we today tend to see as particularly optimistic— is that they seem an accurate depiction of what every man or woman has at some time known to be true.

PESSIMISTIC VERSUS OPTIMISTIC VISIONS OF HUMAN CAPABILITY TODAY

As we enter the waning years of the twentieth century, what sorts of things constitute the best and worst of these particular times? We should not expect them to be exactly those that would have occurred to Dickens's readers in Victorian England. When we look about for what we might list, we are likely to be struck by the sense that never before in human history have the best and worst seemed as extreme as they do today and for the near future. We may even wonder if the extremes are not now so great that we must redefine in fundamental ways what traditionally have been thought of as the nature and place of humanity on earth.

The best visions of what is possible for human life today actually seem to challenge the notion that our mortality is a boundary that we cannot cross. We live in a time when it is possible to save and prolong life through the use of wonder drugs and other medical and surgical techniques that were unknown a generation or two ago. Hearts and lungs and other vital organs, some artificially created, can now be transplanted routinely into the bodies of patients to make continued life possible where not long ago it would have been unimaginable. Not yet routine, but even more dramatic in their challenge to death itself, are the various developments in genetic engineering that could soon permit the cloning of any species—including human beings— so as to produce offspring that are exact genetic copies of their parents. In such a situation, does it make much sense to continue to think in terms of the "death" of a parent, when its carbon copy lives and can itself be cloned and so on, presumably forever? Or consider the geneticist's ability to transfer genes from an organism of one species to another. That power can only be considered godlike, for it suggests incredible possibilities for modifying species in ways that could turn humankind's natural enemies into benign creatures, thereby eliminating much disease, increasing our food supply severalfold, and, no doubt, accomplishing many other miracles as well. The imagination staggers.

These and other developments in the science of genetics may seem the most dramatic challenges to the very mortality of living things, but in other areas, too, we are frequently assured that no problem faces us that cannot be overcome through some new or potential scientific advance. Granted, for example, that the day is fast approaching when no significant reserves of oil will be left underground to keep the world's industrial machine in operation, we shall develop alternative energy resources that are truly renewable so not to have to face the problems of resource scarcity again. The sun's energy can be harnessed for our benefit, as can the wind, the waves of the earth's oceans, and even the decaying organic matter, which is the waste of the entire life process. The sensible harnessing of such resources seems certain to provide future generations with virtually unlimited amounts of power to ensure the indefinite advance of material progress for the species. If these and a myriad of other technological advances do not grant immortality to each of us, they at least seem to promise that our descendants will live and flourish in ways we cannot yet imagine.

The worst of times? After these considerations, what a jolt it is to realize today's potential for the worst imaginable future for humanity that the species has ever had to face! The worst imaginable is, of course, no future at all—or at least none of a sort that we would recognize as truly human. At any moment we could end with the "bang" of a massive nuclear exchange that, if prolonged for days or possibly only hours, could annihilate outright much of the globe's human population and kill countless millions more in the aftereffects of radiation, the poisoning of the earth's food and water supply, and the devastating disruption of social organization everywhere. Now that we are several decades into this Age of Overkill, a handful of governments possess enough explosive power to bring death to every man, woman, and child on earth. Or, barring all-out nuclear war, we could end with the "whimper" of gradual ecological collapse, perhaps starting from an accident at a nuclear plant, the release of chemical or bacteriological weapons in some limited military conflict, the irreversible pollution of major portions of the oceans, or numerous other possible causes. Perhaps the whimpering end may result from factors already at work—booming growth in populations, desertification of the world's arable lands, the silent extinction of a growing number of animal species—all of which, or a host of other possibilities, already may be leading us toward our doom.

Whatever the form and duration of the forces that could end human life as we have known it, those of us alive today must live with the fact that in our lifetimes, as never before in the history of the planet, one species has the capacity to make the globe we share with thousands of other living species uninhabitable for us all, with the possible exception of the most primitive forms of plant and animal life. That capacity, too, is a godlike power, although one we traditionally would attribute only to a satanic god.

So there is something unique about our sense of the best and worst possibilities for humanity today. Never before have those opposites extended nearly so far toward the unlimited; never have they been so unbounded by our physical weakness, which for earlier generations limited what was possible; never before have human beings had the power at their disposal to act in ways that our ancestors would have regarded, not as human, but as godlike, with all the terrible responsibilities such power inevitably brings.

THE ETHICAL AND POLITICAL CHALLENGE OF OUR POWER

This uniqueness in our condition today reminds us of another distinctive quality of the extreme prospects in our time. As we think about both our best and worst capabilities, we are likely to find that our discomfort—horror even—at the satanic power we now hold looms larger than whatever comfort or satisfaction we might find in our capacity for good. What, we may ask, is the point of being awed at medical advances if tomorrow vastly more of us may be wiped out in the burst of a few terrible explosives than have been killed in all the plagues of history? Why should we exult in our ability to voyage through interplanetary space when we constantly risk making our home planet largely uninhabitable? Why should we take comfort in the prospect that limitless supplies of energy may soon be available when we consider the destructive potential of such massive amounts of energy?

The more we consider, the more likely we are to see that the worst possibilities we face are more hypnotizing and commanding than the best. If headlong disaster engulfs us, we shall no longer have the leisure to accomplish those marvelous advances in civilized life that otherwise seem to be within our grasp. We shall then have to cope, if we are able, with a human society that has retrogressed so drastically that basic survival values must take precedence over other, more advanced or "civilized" concerns.

But that is not our only or even our most troubling consideration. We increasingly suspect that the worst possibilities for humanity's continuation on the planet are themselves the direct result of the same forces that have produced what we think of as the best prospects. If the Western world had not undergone its industrial revolution during the past two centuries—a phenomenon that brought dramatic increases in the general standard of living in mature industrial societies before it began to spread to other regions—it would not today have the technology to build atomic bombs as well as automobiles, to poison rivers and streams with pollutants while enabling a single farmer to produce vastly more food than his peasant ancestors, or to create the conditions for totalitarian political systems while producing computers and television sets.

We begin to notice that *all* the developments we list as characteristic of the "best of times" and the "worst of times" are somehow related to accomplishments in science and technology. None can be traced to advances in ethics, humanistic studies, and the arts, or what philosophers call metaphysics. No one would dream of suggesting that the 1980s are the best of times because of breakthroughs we have made in getting human beings to live together peaceably, or in producing the greatest art the world has ever known, or in discovering how to rear children so that they all are smarter, happier, and better citizens than their parents, or because we have exhibited greater love for our neighbors than humans did in the past.

Conversely, when we think about the worst of human behavior, we may note that our century has brought forth some of history's greatest tyrants. But we would not say, when we considered it, that a Hitler or a Stalin established such grim records because they were inherently more evil than certain people in an earlier period. The scope of their evil deeds was possible because of the availability of technologies that permitted greater or more far-reaching ruthlessness, technologies that have refined spying to a high degree, controlled the movement of people, and made possible mass murder on a scale unknown to the ancients.

These examples of the power of modern tyrants should remind us of two fundamental facts about the world we live in. First, all our modern technologies are instruments of power. They serve to supplement the comparatively puny ability of even the strongest or most intelligent human being to have an impact on the material world. Every time we call sounds and pictures from the airwaves by turning on a television set or travel in an airplane or switch on an electric light, or do any of the countless other things that draw upon modern technology, we are asserting our mastery over some aspect of the material universe that far exceeds our natural ability. What separates us more than anything else from our primitive ancestors is this vastly greater power that we have acquired.[1]

Second, the technologies themselves are morally neutral: They can be used either for good or for evil and themselves contain no guidelines, no instructions, to tell us which is which. The technologies that enable us to communicate almost instantly with other people throughout the globe can also be used to invade our privacy and otherwise control us in a myriad of ways; the technologies that let us travel faster than the speed of sound can also carry instruments of mass destruction to rain fire down from heaven; and the technologies that run the vast industrial machine that gives us wealth and power over so much of the physical world are also those that make possible both genocide and ecocide—terms that describe two ultimate, cataclysmic events that, not coincidentally, have entered the language only in our time.

Now we have come full circle as we see that those technological developments that today give promise of our best of times are also those that can provide the very worst. Not long ago many Americans would have placed upon their best list the apparent promise that nuclear power soon would provide a virtually limitless, cheap, and nonpolluting source of energy for future generations. After the accident at Three Mile Island in 1979, many ceased to view that particular technology with such optimism. If the possibilities inherent in genetic engineering excite our imaginations today, we should remember that in addition to their beneficial prospects, they also have a dreadful potential to interfere in the life process with consequences no one can yet anticipate.[2] Little imagination is needed to grasp the possible dire consequences in the misapplication of virtually any technology that might also contribute to our list of wonderful developments. Moreover, we should by now begin to see that the unique capacity both our best and our worst lists have to push human capability toward godlike extremes in our time is the direct result of the very nature of technological development; i.e., it is cumulative and irreversible. As long as technology does not lead eventually to the destruction or radical retrogression of the human race, which we all know is more than a small possibility, it proceeds to build upon itself in directions that give its creators ever greater power, for good or evil, over the physical universe.

We have not learned to deal adequately with this situation; for many of us, much of the time, our response is no response at all. We try not to think about it while we go about the pressing business of daily living, which normally does not force us to treat matters of eschatology. Or we regard these matters as too weighty and important for anyone but an expert to treat (the fact that most people see themselves as nearly powerless in the face of the godlike possibilities open to the human race is an interesting paradox, whose implications we shall explore). We tend to be so much the children of a scientific age that we are tempted to say, when confronted with the dangers of our time, "Well, the scientists will discover something." If we use up fossil fuels, then someone will find replacements. If the metal ore necessary to keep the industrial machine going is all mined, then we will substitute plastics or other synthetics. If the earth's arable land has about reached the limit of what it can support, then we will develop aquaculture. If the planet gets too crowded, then, of course, we will colonize space. And if nuclear weapons threaten to annihilate us, then we will simply spend billions of dollars more on other high-technology weapons to protect us.

THE INADEQUACY OF SCIENTIFIC "SOLUTIONS"

These may not be impossible scenarios, though many of the best minds among us have their doubts. The problem with relying on such developments as solutions is that they are not solutions at all—not, at least, to the problems that really matter for the future of humanity on the planet, because these are above all political and economic problems, problems related to the ways human beings live and prosper as individuals and in their relations with one another throughout the globe. Whatever power technological solutions may provide us for further mastery and control over our nonhuman environment will also give us additional power to destroy that environment and all the species, including *Homo sapiens*, that draw life from it. Every technological capability we may develop to do greater good for our own and future generations carries with it a capability for evil. What is worse, as we have realized, is that we have arrived at a point in our development when we realistically can expect that the dire, if unforeseen, consequences of these new powers will far outweigh their benefits.

Good and evil. We cannot seem to avoid using these terms whenever we consider the applications of our modern technologies. These terms have no meaning outside the realm of human thought and action, for they relate exclusively to how human beings live or try to live. Moreover, they are not concepts that have a place within the postulates of the scientific method, which proceeds from the assumption that the material world is paramount, that it must be studied and understood by one who proceeds agnostically, that is, without a priori prejudices or values to color what may be learned from the facts under investigation. This is not to say, of course, that scientists are more immoral than the rest of us; the greatest of them have been profoundly concerned with the moral issues of their time and often have shown a real sensitivity to the implications of their discoveries for good and evil in human life.[3] Yet when a scientist is concerned with issues of human value, he or she has entered a realm outside that of science, one that encompasses politics and includes metaphysics.

That realm needs the attention of us all—scientists and nonscientists alike—and in a far more rigorous and serious way than typically is given if we are to save ourselves from the Faustian capabilities we now have at our command. If, in fact, humankind has a future worth hoping for—one in which we are no longer threatened by nuclear explosions, whether accidental or deliberately planned; one in which the genetic material of the species is not irreparably damaged by radiation or other poisoning; one in which mass murder, economic deprivation, and the most extreme forms of political oppression are at least considerably reduced, if not eliminated—it will be because, and only because, we have turned away from the mindless expectation that science will somehow save us and have moved seriously to try to save ourselves through the only means we have at our disposal: the careful examination of public policy choices, followed by action calculated to advance our chosen values.

The overriding need today is to learn to make ethically informed decisions about the nature and direction of our lives together on the planet. This task cannot be left to experts—although the views of philosophers, humanists, theologians, and, yes, scientists should help to guide us—for in an important sense, every human being must develop the expertise in these matters that together can make the better possibilities inherent in our situation prevail over the worst. This task is perhaps not as hopeless as it sounds for, although not all of us are geneticists or physicists, every intelligent human being must make ethical choices every day, choices that affect the individual's relationship to others in society. Yet in another sense, *expertise* is the wrong word to choose here because it implies an end product that a specialist strives for, and particularly a specialist whose arcane knowledge comes through the pursuit of science; it suggests directives for action built upon a complex body of knowledge, acquisition of which points the expert ever more sharply in particular, specified directions discovered through a rigorous, value-free reading of the facts. Yet such expertise leads us no nearer our goal of a safer, more humane world; its orientation allows us perpetually to avoid coming to grips with the questions of human value priorities that we have determined are at the root of our current problems.

THE RECONCILIATION OF CONFLICTING VALUES

If the approach of science alone will not save us from ourselves, what then? How do we go about the business of making ethically informed decisions? Our first task is to understand that a fundamental difference exists between what for simplicity's sake we may call scientific and nonscientific problems, and that each requires a distinctive kind of mental effort. E. F. Schumacher has made the difference and its consequences wonderfully clear. As he pointed out, the problems of science call into play the mode of logical thought, of reasoning from one fact or finding to the next, of "working out a problem" in mathematics or in science, whether inductively or deductively. Problems of this type constitute "man's most useful invention; they do not as such exist in reality, but are created by a process of abstraction. When they have been solved, the solution can be written down and passed on to others, who can apply it without needing to reproduce the mental effort necessary to find it."[4] These are known as *convergent* problems because the kind of intellectual process involved in treating them leads one to examine a variety of factors that ultimately converge in a solution. Science has advanced so dramatically in recent centuries because of this human invention of looking for convergent solutions.

The other basic kind of problem in human life is the sort with which we are faced every time human values enter the picture. It is not possible to provide nearly so clear-cut a description of the basic mode of thinking needed to resolve issues of this type. That is no doubt because these problems cannot, by definition, be solved by logic, although logic is needed to help define them and their consequences. They are *divergent* in nature, requiring us to reconcile conflicting goals and interests in ways that can be lived with. If the reconciliation works, it is a more or less temporary solution, limited to a particular historical or social situation and subject to being upset when the particularities of the situation change. Divergent problems require us to balance conflicting wants and needs and, where other human beings are involved, as they typically are, their wants and needs become part of the equation. These divergent problems, which are "the true problems of living," in Schumacher's words, "demand of man not merely the employment of his reasoning powers but the commitment of his whole personality,"[5] which is to say that ethical as well as rational decisions must be made.

Many examples can be given of the divergent problems that face human beings in their political lives, whenever and wherever they live. Their inherent opposition is apparent in such questions as the following: Is the loss of freedom in a highly centralized, authoritarian state worth the greater security to a greater number of individuals that may come with it? Does wide participation in making political decisions in a liberal democracy compensate for a lessened efficiency in government? Does the so-called right of national self-determination have any limits as, for example, when those who identify themselves as a subject nation are scattered, or constitute a very small group, or are not educated for self-government? Can the desire to achieve political independence ever justify the use of force against innocent civilians?

Each of these and similar perennial questions about what is good, bad, acceptable, or unacceptable in political life obviously relates to matters of different human values around which choices must be made, choices that will not be the same for everyone but will be influenced by one's perspective, one's place within the relevant social situation under discussion, one's particular view of what is better and what worse for society. Each of these questions asks some variation about two opposing concepts, anarchy and order, which may be what makes them characteristically political questions. These questions have no scientific answers; they cannot be resolved for all people in all times and places. All we can be sure of is that people will always search for an answer within the range in which opposing tendencies can be balanced in some way; each abstract right or value cited must be limited in practice, or else it destroys a different or opposing right.[6] Problems of metaphysics simply cannot be resolved like those in the convergent world of science, and in that sense, no comparable kind of progress for humanity can take place in the realm of public policy.

Of course, it does not follow that, because human values are obviously involved in all matters of human choice, we must ignore the human-made techniques of convergent problem-solving altogether in the study of human behavior. We can learn many things about the way we act by using the scientific method. If that were not the case, we would not have developed the academic disciplines of sociology, economics, anthropology, psychology, and political science—all of which are founded upon the assumption that some kinds of human issues can be treated as convergent problems. Rather, we must understand clearly how far the convergent mode can be used and when it must give way to divergent considerations.

For example, if I have enough relevant data at my command, I may be able to explain and even predict the likely outcome of a U.S. presidential election some days or weeks before it takes place and within a small margin of error—pollsters have become remarkably accurate at forecasting by adhering rigorously to scientific techniques—but I cannot give a scientific rationale for directing an individual citizen to vote for one candidate rather than another. In making that decision every voter faces divergent issues, requiring him or her to balance a variety of values and then try to determine which candidate's victory will most likely advance those currently most important to that individual. Now I may, of course, become an advocate for a particular candidate or political party, and my advocacy may have some impact on other voters. That influence will depend upon such things as the extent to which they accept my own reading of the likely outcome and whether they view my value goals as congruent with their own, which initially requires that I am clear about them myself and can communicate them to others. But obviously, the moment I become an advocate, I cease to behave within the framework of the scientific method, although science may have informed my advocacy, and concern myself, broadly speaking, with matters of metaphysics.[7]

Much of what will follow in this book will relate to questions of advocacy, or more specifically, to the effort to clarify certain important policy choices as these relate to particular social, political, and economic goals of men and women in our time. For such advocacy to be meaningful, however, it must be built upon as rigorous an analysis as possible of various social trends and patterns, especially those most relevant to the state of world order today. The convergent mode of analysis will let us focus upon, and ideally make intelligent and informed decisions about, some of the great divergent issues that we face.

HUMAN BEHAVIOR AND VALUE PRIORITIES

The second matter that arises at this point relates to the complex nature of human values themselves and the ways in which they find social implementation. Clearly, some needs are biologically derived: Every living person needs food and shelter at a minimum and therefore places a basic value on securing them. Beyond the bare survival values come a host of those intended to provide the greater and greater realization of human potential.[8] Some of these are clearly prerequisites to the realization of others: The higher values—such as that which some hold for creative expression through the writing of poetry— obviously cannot be obtained if the value of literacy through education has not first been reached. Political organization certainly has always had as its basic task making the survival values attainable to the individuals within the polity; however, it characteristically must do more than that because its general function is the allocation of a whole range of competing values within the system in ways that provide a measure of order for all. That order can never entirely satisfy all who submit to it, although some societies, those we typically regard as comparatively just, do a better job of that than others, which may maintain order through terror and intimidation rather than consent.

Even though all values are at root the goals of individual human beings, we may define some of them as social or political if their implementation can only be sought through the given social or political system. Dominant political values (which are not the same, except perhaps in democratic societies, as those held by a majority of the population) shape particular political systems which in turn help mold and modify other values. The process is one of continual interaction between the system and the interests held and expressed by the individuals or groups of individuals that live within it.

For instance, most contemporary Americans may naturally suppose that any political system that permits adult citizens a fair amount of participation in the allocation of important values affecting all their lives is superior to a polity where the huge mass of citizens have almost no say in these matters. Yet the contemporary U.S. view has probably been the minority view through most of history—not because men and women have somehow evolved more democratic natures over the course of centuries (after all, democracy is an ancient political invention), but because the polity in which we live today generally reinforces democratic values in a way that other polities have not. The doctrine of the divine right of kings clearly supported the power and values of monarchs within certain European societies in an earlier time. Its real importance was not simply that kings may have been prone to believe it for self-serving reasons: the mass of common people also must have accepted that doctrine as true, which of course reinforced their disinclination to challenge the rule of kings.

CHANGING SOCIAL VALUES

We see now that the basic normative choices that govern social groups are sociologically derived; i.e., particular dominant values are the product of particular historical configurations. This relationshp is evident when we look for examples such as the one above. Yet that is something most of us too seldom do, for there are widespread confusion and misunderstanding about which kinds of political behavior and belief are time-bound and which, if any, are inherent in human nature.

For instance, many people appear to believe that *Homo sapiens* is inherently an aggressive animal and that war therefore is an inevitable feature of relations among human groups. But upon further examination, that assertion does not tell us very much that is useful, even if it can be said to be generally true. Certainly it cannot explain how we have managed to create societies that are successful in preventing whatever aggressive instincts we may have from embroiling its own members in constant civil war. Most members of civil societies are by definition at peace with each other most of the time. But perhaps the assertion is meant to apply only to the relationship between and not within social groups (and if so, we already suspect that simply to define those who do not usually go to war as members of the same group, or tribe, or nation does not explain anything at all; it merely gives a label to that which is excluded from the generalization, however important the relationship to the excluded entity may be to an understanding of the real issue). In that case, what explanation have we for the fact that competing groups (tribes, nations, and so on) are not perpetually at war? Even if we regard war as one of the characteristic features of what, for lack of more precise terminology, we call international politics, we must acknowledge that it is not a perpetual or even the only feature.[9]

Already we have explored one particular truism far enough to suspect that social organization and the values that are and are not advanced therein play a crucial role in determining whether an aggressive instinct in humans produces war or nonviolent outlets for humanity's energies. We also may have noted that types and forms of acceptable violence, even within societies, are not constant in all times and places. Blood feuds, personal vendettas, and dueling were once accepted forms of violence between persons within a larger social group that now are almost universally condemned. Even in intersocietal conflict—that domain admittedly characterized by toleration of much higher levels of violence than is typically acceptable domestically— what was thought to be the acceptable treatment of one's enemy has shifted over the centuries. When Rome defeated Carthage in the third Punic War, Roman generals destroyed the city completely, even spreading salt about the ruins so that nothing would grow there again. Prisoners in ancient times were routinely murdered, conquered cities were plundered, and the civilian population was enslaved. Whatever abominable practices we still engage in in wartime, they generally differ from those of the ancients.

Slavery has been one of the dominant features of social life through most of human history. Not until the twentieth century was it largely eliminated everywhere on earth. It is easy, and no doubt satisfying, to conclude that slavery has at last ceased to be a major social problem because at long last "good" men and women have made their opposition to it prevail through an appeal to conscience. That undoubtedly has had some influence, since appeals to our higher motives can be extremely powerful, but a close examination tells us that appeals to conscience are never enough when social conditions combine to encourage perpetuation of a social evil. In modern times, the abolition of slavery in societies where it still existed followed the industrial revolution and the growth of capitalism; these new forces provided economically dominant classes with more of the world's material goods and services than they ever could have had through the mere physical enslavement of people. Hence, complex changes in social and economic forces combined to shift values away from those that once had dominated. Once slavery finally was abolished, the abolitionist ethic became a part of the dominant normative order, so that what had been accepted by earlier generations as an economic necessity and therefore excluded from the moral agenda became unthinkable to their descendants.

The processes at work in fundamental social changes of this kind are obviously enormously complex. Only the tip of the iceberg involved in ending slavery has been exposed above. At least it should be clear that political behavior is shaped by the dominant values of a society, which in turn are the product of complex historical forces, and value priorities shift in relation to perceived needs. A group that is physically isolated from its nearest neighbor will develop a very different foreign policy from one constantly subject to attack and subjugation. A society emerging from feudalism into capitalism will likely free its serfs.

But this general rule has an opposite face as well, which is that large social organizations are slow to change—and generally, the larger and more complex, the slower they are to change. Even when the factors that caused them to advance certain values over others begin to fade, they may continue to behave in the traditional way, long past the time that it is rational to do so. A state whose traditional isolationism has served it well may cling to such a doctrine even when a greater exercise of its influence in the world might better serve its interests. A society may preserve the feudal class structure even when such stratification runs counter to the logic of the new economic organization. This phenomenon is the product of structural lethargy in which the reluctance to change gains support from the social system itself. The vested interests of once dominant groups or classes are reflected in the laws the society has produced and in the culture more generally, all of which tend to legitimize old values and to shun new ones. In extreme cases, structural lethargy may lead to a sclerotic condition in which the resistance to change is so great that violent revolution becomes the only alternative possible.

THE SLOWNESS OF SOCIAL CHANGE

Perhaps we may now add a third explanation for our perception that the worst prospects for humanity today seem more imperative than the best. The structural lethargy of large-scale social organizations inhibits them from the kinds of rapid adaptations that would let them respond more effectively to the challenges of our time, and they may be ill equipped to prevent the worst from happening. Traditional ways of dealing with problems of military security remain firmly in place even though today they may, paradoxically, make us not more but vastly less secure. Energy self-sufficiency remains a goal of some nations although such a policy encourages not the conservation but the more rapid depletion of nonrenewable resources. Even when, thanks to the modern network of communication, we are made aware of flagrant violations of human rights as we could not have been in the past, we find that we are unable to take effective action to stop such abuses.

These examples point to a fourth reason for our pessimism about the world's future. When confronted with these kinds of contrahuman facts of our sociopolitical life, we are inclined to respond to them much as we do to the technological imperative, as regrettable, no doubt, but beyond our reach—a natural state of things that is impervious to human judgment and action. It is all very well to make ethically informed choices about social problems, but even when we do we seem not to have the power to advance our goals.

There is no magic formula for overcoming that frustration. The best we can do is to keep trying, informing ourselves about the likely consequences for the whole society if our value choices were implemented, recognizing that we will no doubt have more failures than successes in moving society, learning as best we can through trial and error what possibilities for change exist at a given time, remaining open and receptive to the goals of others; in short, behaving with conviction tempered by toleration, knowledge balanced by recognition of our own ignorance, and awareness that the effort is the greatest, most typically human effort of our lives.

A basic thesis of this book is that the fundamental reason for our frequent failure to make the right kinds of policy choices in the world today stems from our continued refusal to see the planetary social system as a whole. We know, or should know, that all human beings are members of a single species, with far more similarities in their needs and wants than differences. Yet we behave in most aspects of our political lives as if our separate nations housed separate species. This age-old habit is an increasing anachronism at best and may in fact lead to our undoing within the foreseeable future, for it prevents us from effective treatment of most of the life-threatening issues in our worst of times scenario. The preceding discussion of values and their implementation applies equally to any social system, including the single global one. In succeeding chapters we will engage in just such an application, for only when we adopt such a perspective do we begin to see the issues that confront the species for what they are—human problems, not simply those of particular tribes or nations.

The fact that most of us are still accustomed to thinking of these matters almost exclusively in parochial terms has far less to do with any inherent limitations on our perception than it does with the ways our views of the world have been structured historically—for all our knowledge is sociologically derived. The structural bias of global political and social organization has long emphasized and reinforced all those things, including values, that divide us rather than those that strengthen our species commonality. In the past, that encouragement of divisions and boundaries may have had much to recommend it. Certainly it was a far less dangerous way of organizing the world politically than it appears to be today. We need to understand what gave rise to this organizational scheme and sustained it if we are to assess how it does and does not serve us in today's world. Therefore, we shall begin by surveying the evolution of the world's basic principles for political organization during the past several hundred years, that of sovereign nation-states coexisting in a normative framework of mutual equality—the Westphalian international system.

NOTES

1. Typically, we rejoice in the powers we have acquired through science and technology and assume they mark our own advance over earlier modes of living. But Sigmund Freud, among many others, reminded us that our modern way of life does not necessarily bring happiness but may instead merely provide greater obstacles to its achievement by creating new problems. In *Civilization and Its Discontents* he asked, "Is there, then, no positive gain in pleasure, no unequivocal increase in my feeling of happiness, if I can, as often as I please, hear the voice of a child of mine who is living hundreds of miles away . . . ?" His answer was to note that "if there had been no railway to conquer distances, my child would never have left his native town and I should need no telephone to hear his voice" ([New York: W. W. Norton, 1960], p. 35).

2. The dangers are truly incalculable, perhaps especially when the experimentation is intended to be entirely beneficial. David Ehrenfeldt described a case in which experiments were undertaken with genetic transplants into *E. coli* bacteria, the organisms that normally inhabit the human intestine and are needed for our good health, for making the enzyme cellulase. Since cellulase is absent in humans, researchers thought that an ability to manufacture it within the human body would give us the capability to break down cellulose, the basic material of plant fiber, and thereby provide humankind with access to food supplies never before available to the species. Yet the experiments were ended when the scientist conducting them discovered that in making digestion of this new material possible, carbon dioxide gas would be released within the gut, which could cause us to swell like balloons whenever we ate

fibrous products. *The Arrogance of Humanism* (New York: Oxford University Press, 1978), p. 95.

3. To take two well-known examples of scientists who played particularly important roles in the development of atomic weapons, Albert Einstein was a lifelong pacifist who agonized over the issue of whether or not the United States should try to develop such a weapon during World War II, and Robert Oppenheimer, who directed the Los Alamos project that eventually produced such a bomb, later found himself in considerable political trouble in Washington for his opposition to the development of the "H-bomb," as it was known at the time, or fusion weapon. Oppenheimer's view was that such a weapon could serve no useful political purpose because of its destructive power and therefore should not be produced.

4. E. F. Schumacher, *Small Is Beautiful* (New York: Harper and Row, 1973), p. 97.

5. Ibid., p. 99.

6. The unending need to balance anarchy and order in social life has its counterpart in Freudian psychology within every human personality, in which it is expressed as the conflict between the individual's claim to unrestrained freedom (in the working of the id) and the demands of society (upon the superego) for restraints upon that freedom for the general social good. See especially Freud, *Civilization and Its Discontents.*

7. For a much fuller exploration of this and other issues involved in the philosophy of science, see Carl Gustav Hempel, *Aspects of Scientific Explanation and Other Essays in the Philosophy of Science* (New York: Free Press, 1965); and Thomas S. Kuhn, *The Structure of Scientific Revolutions,* 2d ed. enl. (Chicago: University of Chicago Press, 1970).

8. Abraham Maslow has developed this idea in *Toward a Psychology of Being* (Princeton, N.J.: Van Nostrand, 1962; revised ed., 1968), *Motivation and Personality* (New York: Harper and Bros., 1954; revised ed., 1970), and *The Farther Reaches of Human Nature* (New York: Viking Press, 1971). Maslow's theory on the hierarchy of human development suggests that basic needs must generally be satisfied before meta needs can be realized. The former range from the physiological requirements to sustain life through those for love, respect, and self-esteem. Meta needs entail self-actualization through the quest for truth, goodness, beauty, justice, peace, and so on.

9. Moreover, Freud and his followers have argued that the aggressive "instinct" is by no means an unmitigated human and social evil, for they view it as the source of energy and creativity in human life, without which most of what we regard as human accomplishment would not have been possible. If that is so, then we are clearly confronted with one of life's divergent problems: How do we control the destructive capability of human aggression and at the same time give encouragement to its creative potential?

2
The Growth of the Westphalian System

The natural state of nations . . . is . . . one of equality and independence, which establishes an equality of right among them, and pledges them to have the same regard and respect for one another.

—Jean Jacques Burlamaqui
Principes du droit naturel

The power of declaring war is . . . especially necessary to a state for the purpose of constraining wrongdoers; wherefore, just as the sovereign prince may punish his own subjects when they offend others, so may he avenge himself on another prince or state.

—Francisco Suarez
De Triplici Virtute Theologica, Fide, Spe, et Charitate

Analysis of the world order system in which we live confronts us at every turn with divergent problems. The essential purpose of any social order is to provide enough regularity in relationships among the individuals within it so that values supporting the common good can be achieved, maintained, and advanced, while those most damaging to the common interest are controlled. The common interest almost always lies in a reasonable assurance that individuals will interact peaceably and predictably in important ways, behavior encouraged by the agreed-upon rules that govern human interaction. When a man leaves his house to enter a dangerous world, he needs some assurance that his neighbors are not likely to attack him, that he may safely cross a busy street when the light is green. Yet that same man, if he is oblivious to all considerations of the common good—if he fails, in the words of one of the world's most fundamental ethical precepts, to do unto others as he would have them do unto himself—may have the physical strength to rob his neighbor of his wallet and almost certainly will be tempted to cross a street against a red light if he deems it safe to do so.

The need for social order, for law to govern our relationships, lives in constant tension with the individual will to exercise power, which is identical with a desire for freedom. Both needs arise directly from the human condition, and balancing their divergent demands is the central task of organized political life.

THE PEACE OF WESTPHALIA

The international legal system that has dominated the way in which ever more numerous groups of human beings have ordered global politics down to the current generation is European in origin. It dates for the most part from the Peace of Westphalia of 1648, one of the important points demarking the medieval from the modern period in Europe's development. Like all such historical benchmarks, Westphalia is in some respects more a convenient reference point than the source of a fully formed new normative system. Some elements that characterize the modern world, separating us from the Middle Ages, were well established long before 1648; others did not emerge until many years after. Still, the Peace of Westphalia created at least the foundations of a new European system—and one that, in our day, was to become truly a world system—out of the ruins of the political structures and the idealized rationale for them that had existed more or less unchanged in Europe for the preceding thousand years.[1]

It is significant, first, that the Peace of Westphalia was created by the many belligerents in the last and most devastating of the great wars of religion that had wracked Europe for more than a century, the Thirty Years' War. That conflict had been complex, with a bewildering number of participants all with different interests at stake over its long course, and anomalous, with Catholic France aligned late in the war with German Protestant princes against Catholic Austria. But above all, it had exacted a terrible toll in human life, particularly throughout Germany and Bohemia, where for three decades rival armies roamed the land, plundering, killing, and devastating those societies on a scale that has perhaps never been equaled. The civilian populations suffered the most, and from the indirect even more than the direct effects of war, from famine, disease, and destruction of property. At least one-third and perhaps as much as half of the population of those regions perished. An area that had provided religious and cultural leadership throughout northern Europe in the previous century was largely ground into the dust, setting back its development at least a hundred years.

The result was the collapse of the medieval structures that had promoted the common good and the unrestrained contest of individual actors for power. Out of that chaos came a revolutionary change in the way the states of Europe were to order their mutual relations in the future. Indeed, the state system then created still looks so familiar to us today that Westphalia's revolutionary quality may not be immediately apparent. Put most directly, the Westphalia treaties created the basis for a *decentralized system of sovereign and equal nation-states.* Nothing quite like it had ever existed on the earth before. Although some of its component features had long been familiar, none of those features had been continuously present from the beginning of recorded history.

At first glance, the one unvarying fact of humanity's political life on a global scale has been its *decentralization,* its fragmentation into separate groups without centralized authority. As far into the past as we can see, the human species has been politically divided. But that separation is more apparent from our point of view than it often has been for people living in other times and places.

In the year A.D. 120, an Aquitanian grape grower may have known very little about the life of a shepherdess in the hills of Cyprus; yet both owed their allegiance to the same government, that of Rome, and, more important, each no doubt perceived herself and imagined the other as living within a single world society, the Roman one. At about the same time, a resident of Loyang in central China also must have viewed the world as containing a single, overarching political system, although in his case, it would have been Chinese. Although we are able to look back today and see the Roman and Han empires as separate political units coexisting on the globe, from the subjective outlook of the inhabitants of either empire, the existence of the other mattered not at all. Each was a self-contained universe, a single, "global" system. Clearly, the whole concept of decentralized or pluralistic decision making is meaningless when applied to groups that do not interact at all or that know nothing of each other's existence. The fact that ancient Romans and Chinese did coexist on the same planet is irrelevant in terms of social consequences for either polity; it is a nonfact. Nothing in the behavior of either of those communities can be ascribed to it. Erroneous perceptions, when they form the basis for behavior, are more true in their explanatory value than true facts that have no bearing on the way people act and view the world.

In any case, we may suppose that this situation for two ancient civilizations has been exceptional in human history, or at least that as populations have grown and cultures made slow contact over the centuries, the misperception of political unity where none exists has become less and less likely and those who hold it, less relevant to the real world of politics. For example, what about Europe in the centuries prior to Westphalia? A great many political actors made decisions independent of each other, a process that frequently brought them into such conflict that they warred among themselves. Their political system surely was decentralized if any ever has been; its chief characteristic seems to have been anarchy, i.e., the absence of central rule.

THE MEDIEVAL CONCEPTION OF ORDER

Yet the anarchy of the Middle Ages was not the theoretical equivalent of anarchy in the modern world. Westphalia made the absence of central rule the basic condition around which the new international system would be organized, whereas the medieval normative system tried to overcome it by idealizing central rule. The medieval Europeans' conception of the kind of world they lived in was that it was bounded by a unified Christendom, defined by the supreme authority of emperor and pope, the one the final arbiter in matters secular and the other the highest spiritual authority. The medieval person's cosmology was of a hierarchical system of order in all aspects of human life, as well as in the universe as a whole, in which every individual had an ordained place that carried with it appropriate rights and obligations. All knew precisely where they were in such a social system in relation to everyone else, to whom one owed allegiance, from whom allegiance was due. One's place in the system was determined almost entirely by the circumstances of his or her birth; peasants were born to till the fields and princes to rule. Yet in theory even the relatively much greater power of princes over peasants was always circumscribed by the prince's obligation to obey whomever had even greater authority within the system, ultimately, the emperor or the pope, who spoke for all of Christendom.[2]

Although this principle is familiar to us in such hierarchical systems as the Church of Rome (which remains virtually unchanged in its organization since the Middle Ages) or any modern army, we may still be unconvinced of its importance in medieval political thought, for we rightly regard the time as a violent and anarchic epoch of human history. But the anarchy and the violence in fact help to explain the force of the notion of the unity of Christendom as an organizing ideal, for it guided Europeans for centuries even though it was seldom more than very imperfectly realized. The political disintegration of Europe after the fall of Rome in A.D. 476 must rank as one of the most traumatic social upheavals of all time. The highly centralized "world state," which was the only political condition within historical memory, came crashing down at the hands of those who had been subjugated within it and who had no comparable political system of their own waiting to replace it. Successive generations of Europeans looked back upon the fallen empire as the ideal to be recreated, or more accurately, revived, since they did not even concede that the empire itself had been ended, but merely suspended, with the abdication of the last emperor. Reality may have been so divorced from the political ideal that it made the latter no more than an illusion—may have been except that the illusion itself was so strong it shaped reality in important ways. A political universe was created that is knowable only in the light of the historical memory and the ideal of unity.

The ancient world empire *was* revived, although for little longer than his lifetime, by Charlemagne in A.D. 800. It was revived again, much more imperfectly in terms of the extent of its authority, more than a century later. This time it lasted well into the modern age as the Holy Roman Empire and, before it finally met its end in modern times, the original underlying dream that it should maintain continuity with an ancient past was forgotten. That the Holy Roman Empire persisted as long as it did into the modern age, however, was testimony to the power and durability of the dream of a unified Christendom.[3]

In spite of the illusion, the Christianized Holy Roman Empire of the Middle Ages and the peripheral political authorities around it bore almost no resemblance to the older namesake. The basic difference between the political worlds of Rome and the Middle Ages was that in the earlier time, power had been highly centralized, whereas in the latter, comparable centralization was never possible. Even at its height, the Holy Roman Empire never achieved more than a fraction of the territorial scope of its model, while within almost all of Europe, actual political unity was almost nonexistent by our own standards. The interlocking and complex patterns of allegiance known as feudalism often failed to check the freedom of self-help through violence.[4] Yet considered as a normative arrangement, feudalism's complex evolution was an ingenious long-term effort to reconcile the fact of a radical dispersal of political power with the ideal of political unity. The feudal order gave that vision of unity a potency for centuries that appears with hindsight to have been a remarkable collective delusion.

The delusion finally was recognized as such in the Peace of Westphalia. Since then, the reality of decentralized, scattered power has been regarded as the legitimate mode of organization, first, for the European, and finally, for the global international system. The thousand-year-old dream of Christian unity expressed through something like a world state (never really more than a European state, of course) was seen to be outmoded, i.e., no longer an effective legitimizing ideal for the behavior of princes. The separateness that replaced it could only be made legitimate by insisting that the fragmentation of authority now carried with it a new concept, that of the sovereign equality of territorial states.

THE SOVEREIGNTY OF NATION-STATES

The term *sovereignty* had begun to achieve some currency several decades before the outbreak of the Thirty Years' War, most notably in the writings of Jean Bodin.[5] Bodin insisted upon the absolute authority, or sovereignty, of the monarch within his realm, limited only by the laws of God and nature. Bodin began an argument that virtually every political philosopher of modern times has been forced to join, although most of the debate since Westphalia has focused upon the *internal* dimension of sovereignty, e.g., limitations on absolutism, justifications for various forms of republican government, for revolution, and so on. In short, much of the most familiar side of the debate has proceeded from the perspective that equates the individual state with the social system under analysis. What is more relevant to our discussion of the single international social system is sovereignty's *external* dimension that for Bodin was shaped by his determination to deny the continued authority of an imperial or hierarchical conception of world order and to replace it with a legitimized system of sovereign equals.

Since sovereignty may be defined as supreme authority, unhampered by any other, to act within a particular sphere, it follows logically that when the concept is applied to more than one unit or actor—as was the case from Bodin's day onward—then all those defined as sovereigns must be regarded as having equal rights and duties in their interactions. If they are considered to be unequal, then they coexist in a system of dominance and subordination and the supreme authority of the constituent unit is a fiction. Sovereignty, then, begets equality where more than one actor is defined as a sovereign just as imperialism cannot exist without political inequality and hierarchical organization of the social units, whether in the form of medieval feudalism or modern colonialism.[6]

Why did Westphalia create a new normative system of sovereign equal actors when the territorial units that have been governed by it ever since are so manifestly unequal in any material standards of measurement? The answers are complex, but they begin to be apparent when we see the ways in which the then-new material capabilities of political actors came to be reflected in this principle. The invention of gunpowder and the growing ability of kings to raise conscripted armies (itself a mark of the gradual dominance of monarchs over the private military power of their own feudal barons) made it increasingly possible for them to defend the borders of their territorial units and to provide a reasonable assurance of control and therefore security over an area where the claim to such control before had been largely pretense. This new capability had its obvious limits in that of similar rulers to control and defend their territories as well. When that emerging fact of life was widely ignored, the result could be the costly retrogression of the Thirty Years' War. So common sense suggested that a defensible or largely impermeable territory should reasonably be considered the sovereign equal of other like units.[7] The alternative would be more or less perpetual violence by competing actors all vainly intent on reimposing hierarchy, with themselves presumably at the pinnacle of the political structure.[8]

This new impermeability of the territorially based state was and has remained a relative matter. During the modern period, some states have been overrun and a lesser number destroyed. Boundaries have shifted as a result of coercion. Yet this era has been characterized by the general ability of sovereigns to defend the core of the territorial unit and those living within it and, as a result, to command the allegiance of the subjects in return. Conversely, the last three centuries have been just as strongly characterized by the refusal of sovereign actors to allow imperial domination to be reimposed over them. For very practical reasons the creation of a nonhierarchical normative system made sense to European statesmen by the mid-seventeenth century; in simplest terms, its appeal lay in its feasibility and in the hope that, to the extent sovereign actors lived by its rules, violence among them could be reduced to tolerable levels. In that equation, Westphalia sought to reconcile new material capabilities with an essential social value.

The sovereign equality of decentralized units is an abstract conception that theoretically could be applied to any social system's interacting components. But the final characteristic of the Westphalian construct, that the units in question be *nation*-states, is far more timebound. True, the kinds of powerful attachments to an exclusive social group that we think of as characteristic of modern nationalism appear to have existed throughout human history. But that attachment is only one of the characteristics of nationalism, which is distinguished above all by the scale of the communities encompassed by it, which are larger and more socially complex than extended families, tribes, cities, castes, or other social classes, all of which have served in premodern times as the basic units of allegiance. The most important fact for our consideration is that the nation is now firmly wedded to the state as the sovereign unit of international politics.[9] The nation-state purports to make the community's sense of a common history, culture, and language the legitimizing force of its sovereignty and therefore the source of its equal standing with other such units.

As usual, the real world situation is more ambiguous than that generalization would imply; in today's world a great many of the some hundred and fifty state actors do not appear to be single nations in any clear-cut sense. By some definitions, both the United States and the Soviet Union are anomalies, for both are composed of a variety of nationality groups, largely as the result of immigration in the first case, and through centuries-old conquest and assimilation in the second. Yet as with the idea of sovereign equality, the "fiction" of nationhood as the legitimate source of statehood has led to a powerful self-fulfilling prophecy: Out of many nations, one, in the case of the United States, whereas within the Soviet Union russification of non-Russian peoples has proceeded so far that the current government is even able to support the maintenance of the cultures and languages of non-Russian minorities since these things no longer threaten the larger Russian state with their separateness.[10]

Just as the attainment of sovereignty has become the predictable goal of subordinated social groups in the modern world, so has the fostering of nationhood become their principal weapon for reaching and maintaining that goal. To take two of many current examples, the black majority of a white-ruled colony achieved independence for Zimbabwe by subordinating historical divisions and antipathies between the majority Shona and minority Ndebele peoples in a united struggle for majority rule. If Zimbabwe is to survive as a state in its original form, it almost certainly must succeed in transforming that successful coalition into something like a traditional nation. Alternatively and perhaps more logically, the state might split apart to form two new units in which the Shona and the Ndebele would form the respective national units. The point is that if the currently constituted state is to endure within the Westphalian order, the sense of nationhood must supersede the older tribal rivalries.

Similarly, where sovereignty is the goal, nationhood (or its appearance) is the prerequisite. One may argue that as recently as fifty years ago, there was no such thing as a Palestinian nation as judged by objective criteria and definitions. Yet as Palestinians have increased their struggle to achieve statehood, they also have turned themselves into a nation, and one perceived as such by much of the rest of the world, thereby legitimizing their claim. The only acceptable status for participation in a Westphalian world is that of the sovereign state, and since nationhood appears to be a precondition, or at least a concomitant, of statehood, it is characteristic of our time not only that sovereign states or states-in-waiting should wish to appear as nations, but also that over time they will very likely become nations.

THE DYNAMICS OF SOVEREIGN EQUALITY

As we have seen, the chief characteristic of power capabilities in the modern world system is their fragmentation, their dispersal among many centers of authority. Westphalia's greatest genius lies in its having made the best of that situation by creating a system of order that derives from fragmented capabilities rather than trying to overcome them through centralization. In other words, Westphalia is a blueprint for order based upon a factual situation of considerable anarchy. In theory, it needs no central authority, no governmental institutions, to maintain acceptable social order among the component units. Before we consider the kinds of problems arising from that conception of world order, particularly in the current period, we should be clear about its logical implications for state behavior if it is to be an acceptable arrangement for social order.

Among the most basic implications are the mutually supportive ones of self-help and nonintervention. The first describes the directive to the sovereign whose own values are threatened, and the second is meant to prevent the sovereign from threatening the values of others. Together they serve to sustain the decentralization of power and authority and the essential impermeability of the territorial state. Neither precept would receive nearly as prominent a place in the social code of any domestic order, which is characterized by a much greater degree of centralized authority than exists in the Westphalian world. In domestic systems, individuals are strongly discouraged from relying on self-help to redress their grievances. Instead, they are expected to turn to the authorities for such action. By the same token, though individuals are not expected to intervene willy-nilly in the affairs of their neighbors—a precept that generally goes under the heading of respecting the rights of others—they nonetheless are expected to intervene to help stop a crime and to prevent, or at least report, any other violation of the society's laws. What is unacceptable behavior toward fellow citizens within one's own state is truly moral for the state authority acting in relation to other sovereigns.

The logic of Westphalia is that it is a positive good to keep the various subjects apart from each other, insofar as possible, and with the general understanding that their apartness itself can be maintained only if they all agree upon its mutual value for each. Two interrelated examples among the characteristic normative developments of the Westphalian period are the emergence of a doctrine of neutrality for states in time of war between other sovereigns and the gradual abandonment of earlier, pre-Westphalian doctrines that attempted to ascertain the justness of one's cause in war. If nonintervention in the affairs of others is a fundamental directive of the normative order, then these two developments helped maintain it.

A sovereign declaring its neutrality manifests its unwillingness to intervene in someone else's quarrel. In doing so, the logic of sovereign equality is supported (support of neutrality suggests that no sovereign has the right to judge the motivations of fellow sovereigns, including whatever factors have led them into war), and the logic of the system's ordering rationale is maintained (some violence between sovereigns may be unavoidable, but it can be kept within narrow bounds if disinterested sovereigns avoid entering the conflict). Neutrality supports a kind of quarantining of interstate violence so that it does not infect all parts of the system. Similarly, the decline of just war doctrine in the modern world reflects the view that the attempt to determine justice in a conflict is incompatible with a system of decentralized authority. If various sovereigns perceive the justness of a particular conflict variously, the result would be the inevitable widening of the war if they intervened to support their favored belligerent, rather than refused to judge in the matter and remained aloof.[11] Contrary as it may seem to our own experience within domestic systems of order, the absence of centralized authority in the international system requires that each local authority largely ignore the rights and wrongs of other sovereigns' grievances. The outcome may not be just in any advanced understanding of that term, but it is meant to secure the more basic value, that of the general security of the whole.

The important thing to note is that these behavioral imperatives do not indicate the absence of all social order; rather, they help clarify a different kind of ordering arrangement than we are accustomed to seeing at work in our daily lives. Already some of the implications of these normative precepts for international political behavior should be apparent. Reliance upon self-help explains why nation-states typically arm themselves and seldom hesitate to use military force if that appears to be the only means left for achieving their objectives. The fact that most states have such a military capability may also help reinforce the general disavowal of intervention in each other's affairs. And support of neutrality can lead in extreme cases to a general policy of isolationism in which the state carries the effort to keep itself largely apart from its fellows to its farthest possible conclusion. There are, of course, a great many other implications, but this sketch of some basic doctrines of the Westphalian order suggests both that it is a true system of law and order and that it bears little resemblance to the hierarchical ordering with which we are all most familiar domestically.

Still another reason for the success of the Westphalian mode, although a lesser one, has been the very simplicity of its ordering logic and of the conditions required for full participation. Once the prerequisites for sovereignty are met—traditionally a government's effective control over a discrete population and territory—recognition by other sovereigns is virtually assured. With that, the new sovereign actor can instantly participate within the normative system on an equal footing with all others. Each is ostensibly bound by the same rights and duties, and each, regardless of its relative power, is likely to have a dominant interest in supporting and maintaining them. For the weak, that interest is particularly apparent because the common legal system affords them whatever protections they have against the strong.[12] But the strong have an interest in maintaining the system as well; first, it is *their* system in the sense that it supports a status quo in which they prosper, giving them certain freedoms within both the power and the normative dimensions of their lives that are not available to the weak—most notably in the realm of conflict regulation and in their greater ability to extend their own values and interests beyond their territorial boundaries. Second, however, by providing regularity and predictability in terms of the rules of participation, it thereby ensures the kind of minimum order necessary for the achievement of many of their own goals.

The triumph of the organizing logic of Westphalia became evident by the mid-twentieth century. Then for the first time, the European normative system became truly a world system as non-European actors in great numbers achieved statehood. In fact, this globalization of the European order has certainly created new and unprecedented strains within it, so that it is anything but clear that the Westphalian order in any meaningful, traditional sense has triumphed. But the fact that its ground rules for participation have now been so widely accepted is at least a demonstration of their economy and appeal.

LAISSEZ-FAIRE IN WORLD POLITICS

The Westphalian system must be counted as one of history's success stories in very important respects. Its endurance over more than three hundred years attests to that. The factors that account for that endurance relate significantly to Westphalia's relevance to the real social and physical world this normative system has sought to order. In general terms, Westphalia's success is a function of its utility, its helpfulness at least to dominant political elites, in ordering the realm of power capabilities. Perhaps it is most helpful to our understanding of Westphalia's success if we consider its guiding principles as supporting an international arrangement of considerable laissez-faire.[13]

In its broadest implication, the concept of laissez-faire (literally "allow to do") supposes that the common good is best served by giving the largest measure of freedom possible to individual actors within society to serve their own interests. Such an outlook is most frequently applied in matters of economics, particularly in association with the work of Adam Smith and other proponents of economic capitalism. Here, laissez-faire theory assumes that the less governmental regulation of the economic marketplace, the better, because the market itself will act to encourage the profit motive, from which will come investment, growth, and a competition among producers that will assure the consumer of the availability of goods at the lowest possible cost. Underlying these claims is the view that the market is self-regulating when left alone and that governmental intervention simply interferes with and distorts the natural tendency for a free market to provide the greatest economic good to the greatest number within the society.

One might also advocate a political system of considerable laissez-faire if one believed that individuals might best achieve their most important values when left largely alone by governments. The English philosopher John Locke did almost exactly that by arguing that individuals should be freed from the heavy hand of governmental interference beyond what was minimally necessary to maintain basic social order.[14] Locke assumed that such an arrangement would release the creative energies of liberated individuals to generate wealth, culture, and enlightenment—all products that would contribute to the health of the society at large. The modern liberal democratic state owes much of its existence to Locke in the same way that modern capitalism counts Smith as its founding father.

The Westphalian international system is also best characterized as a laissez-faire system, inasmuch as it too proceeds on the assumption that unrestrained and coequal actors (here nation-states rather than individual persons) should be allowed to help themselves, to a great extent, to the values of their choice and thereby assist the achievement of the general welfare of all members of the society. The man known as the father of modern international law, Hugo Grotius, stands in relation to the world order system of Westphalia much as Locke does to limited constitutional government and Smith to free enterprise in economics. Each writer emphasized the good that would come to the whole of the respective domain he studied from an absence of strong centralized control and thus a relatively great amount of freedom for the individual actors within the system. Each was an advocate of laissez-faire.

Where the laissez-faire quality of the Westphalian order is concerned, its strength and persistence can be partially explained in the fact that it has served the interests of those who have created, maintained, and been subjected to it—the sovereign states themselves. Again, to analogize to the Lockean civil state, which legitimized the rule and values of an ever more powerful middle class, Westphalia created an environment conducive to the free development and growth of sovereign states. There is even a certain similarity in the nature of the law within the two systems: Both regard a primary function of the law to be restraining other actors—including, most obviously in Locke's civil state, community or central institutions—from dominating or coercing the individual actor. The law provides a set of negative constraints against the would-be dominant forces so that individual actors may develop freely. In this respect, the U.S. Bill of Rights, with its emphasis upon what the federal government may *not* do to the individual citizen, is philosophically akin to the Grotian doctrine of freedom of the seas. Both of these prescriptions are meant to prevent the growth of central regulatory power into areas where private realization of values is regarded as preferable for the individual and, as a result, indirectly the whole society.

Much has been said to criticize the laissez-faire outlook in economics and in the political systems of nation-states. Much that follows in this book will amount to a critique of laissez-faire as an organizing principle for the world's normative order. But to start, we should be clear about the basic context needed to make any doctrine of laissez-faire, political or economic, appealing and successful. It can best be described as a context of great and perhaps nearly unlimited potential abundance.[15]

Consider the following allegory: Each of two couples has three children, but the first family is poor and the second is extremely wealthy. The first set of parents want their children to have toys but have money to buy only one, not three, playthings. The second set of parents feel virtually no limitations at all on the amount of money they may spend for toys for their children. Now the first set of parents, seeking justice and order among their children in their condition of scarcity, will surely buy a toy that all three children can enjoy, and to ensure that end, may lay down certain rules as to which child is to play with it at what times. A certain amount of authoritarian rule from on high is essential to produce fundamental fairness in this situation of scarcity. Yet the second set of parents may reasonably send each child into the toy store with the happy instruction to buy whatever he or she desires. Leaving aside all questions about the long-term effects such indulgent behavior may have upon the children, we may suppose that they will emerge happy with their purchases and without having undergone any conflict among them, for we must suppose that the store has stocked duplicates of toys to avoid the hair pulling that might result if more than one child wished for the same plaything. Laissez-faire in this case has produced mutually satisfactory rewards. All the parents were required to do was to supply the context of abundance.

Underlying Locke's view of what civil society ought to be like is his not always unspoken assumption that the world is a place of nearly unlimited abundance, able to provide sustenance and even riches for all. And if forced to admit that late seventeenth-century England did not always look like such a place, his usual response was to argue that one should then go to America, which for him was almost a metaphor of the boundlessly rich natural state, needing only entrepreneurship to bring forth its bounty.[16]

Similarly, the Grotian view that the seas of the world should be open to all on the basis of reciprocity supposed that the seas themselves were almost endlessly vast and bountiful. No actor could gain a permanent advantage by trying to close off a portion of the sea to others; the sea was too huge for that, the costs entailed not worth the effort. But all sovereigns could benefit mutually through their commerce on the seas, provided all were allowed equal access. If certain states had a natural advantage in the resulting competition for trade, so did certain members of Lockean society within their universe, for in neither instance was it supposed that equal rights necessarily produced equal results for individual actors.

The technology and population density of the seventeenth century were such that both Locke's and Grotius's expectations of great abundance were quite sensible. Neither could have imagined exploitation of the earth's resources on a scale that would have threatened their very continuation by an exploding population that would fill virtually all the land space of the earth. Potential abundance was the reality of the time that nurtured both notions of laissez-faire. Just as the unrestrained individual might, through his unrestricted labor, prosper within domestic societies, so too could the unhampered sovereign turn most of its energies inward when no longer checked by external authority, thereby concentrating on the state's development economically, politically, and socially. At both domestic and international levels of society, the enshrinement of laissez-faire gave free rein to the potential growth of the individual unit acting more or less in isolation from its fellows.

SHARED VALUES AND THE DOUBLE STANDARD

The Lockean and the Grotian world views were also alike in their optimism that those given freedom to act without serious restraints would not themselves make life intolerable for others, including those over whom they exercised power. Although Locke was the apologist for the rising middle class, he can be read as having supposed that the creative potential of the unfettered individual could eliminate class lines, opening successful entrepreneurship to everyone. That at least is the favorite reading of Locke by Americans who find themselves unable to see class divisions in their own, strongly Lockean society.

For Grotius, the issue is somewhat more complex but nonetheless analogous. Grotians had to approach the issue from a reverse path from that of Lockeans: Whereas Locke sought to justify greater limitations upon the central authority, Grotius had to consider what kind of justice was possible within a system that had lost its central authority.[17] He and his followers had essentially two sorts of responses. First, they supported the view that even in the absence of centralized institutions in Europe, a large measure of common values presumably still guided sovereigns. Those common values made the new normative system possible, after all. Therefore, by encouraging actors to recognize their common obligations and responsibilities to each other, those values presumably could be protected. Limitations on the depredations one sovereign actor might do to others would have to flow from the greater pull of recognized shared values.

Second, Grotians recognized and encouraged the growth of the liberal state in civil society. If tyranny and the arbitrary uses of power domestically could truly be ended thereby, then the protection of individual rights could safely be left to the new limited governments themselves, rather than seeking the ephemeral intervention of some higher, but by definition, weaker, body. In keeping with this view, by the nineteenth century strict positivists had found general acceptance of their theory that international law acted only upon sovereigns directly and upon individuals only to the extent that the law was incorporated into civil law. That view, in turn, was acceptable only because the underlying community of values upon which it was built still stood. The bourgeois state of that period was indeed one of more or less limited government, but the state itself was remarkably free of normative restraints from above it (through the reduced authority of the natural legal tradition most evidently) to regulate its conduct toward those within its jurisdiction.

Both of these sets of expectations proved realistic enough over the two hundred years and more after Grotius wrote to allow Westphalian laissez-faire to function and even to thrive. There were periodic dislocations, of course, as when Napoleon seized upon a pre-Westphalian, imperial vision of European order with himself at the apex of authority, but what is notable is that Napoleon did not succeed. When the Congress of Vienna cleaned up after the Napoleonic wars in 1815, its participants were careful to restore the pre-Napoleonic map of Europe so that the game of nation-state coexistence in accordance with laissez-faire rules could be played again. The French empire in Europe was dismantled, but France the nation-state was restored to its place as coequal actor. Later in the nineteenth century, the unification of Germany produced several military conflicts among European powers, the most damaging of which was between the emergent German state and France. Yet whatever the long-term injury to French interests, the result was essentially and most importantly the creation of simply one more major nation-state capable of participating in the Westphalian order in a way its predecessor principalities and other small sovereigns could not.

For the Europe-centered Westphalia of the early modern period, the context of abundance was the rest of the world, the technique for exploiting its resources, imperialism. No doubt the availability of the larger world did much to reinforce standards of nonintervention and mutual respect within the European framework, for these principal state actors never assumed that such standards should apply in their treatment of peoples and territories outside Europe. Their paramount diplomatic concern in this age of extra-European imperialism was the effects of their colonizing and trading activities abroad on their relations with fellow sovereigns, i.e., fellow European actors. Once a European power secured its claim to a colonized territory overseas, that region became, in effect, a part of the sovereign's own state from the standpoint of international law and was subject to the same standards of noninterference and nonintervention that applied to the metropolitan territory and population. Seen in this light, the European imperial powers did not even need to recognize that they were operating on a double standard, for that would have assumed that colonized peoples had been sovereign, or at least were potentially sovereign, in the absence of European imperialism, whereas it was much neater and less troubling to make no such assumptions about those living beyond the bounds of Europe. The rest of the world lived simply in the state of nature, to use the Lockean conception of human existence prior to the formation of society, from which the European order could continue to form itself.

Needless to say, the economic and political conceptions of laissez-faire often coalesced in the history of European imperialism. That is, the process of acquiring colonies abroad was often much less the result of conscious policy at the seat of the European government than it was the result of the entrepreneurial activity of its private or semiprivate citizens. The role of the British East India Company during the eighteenth century in India is an obvious case in point. It became the duty of the state to extend the protection of the flag where the entrepreneurial activity of its citizens demanded it so long, of course, as such claims were not attempted within the spheres already demarcated to other European sovereigns.

This conception of the operative international rules of the game was flexible enough to permit the occasional and usually gradual addition of new sovereign actors over time. Late in the eighteenth century, English colonists in North America grew weary of being treated as second-class subjects (they objected to the double standard mentality as it applied to themselves), and after a fight, emerged as a new sovereign within the Westphalian system. More than a century later, Japan was added as a sovereign actor, but not until its government had demonstrated its willingness and ability to play by the rules of the game imposed by Westphalia, a demonstration no doubt made all the more persuasive by the Japanese penchant for adopting many Western styles of behavior in addition to those characteristic of the conduct of diplomacy. Throughout much of this period, Ottoman Turkey, which was neither Christian nor wholly within Europe, played a somewhat anomalous role on the fringes of the system, but gradually it assumed a recognized place within the international order as an imperial power. Finally, by the end of World War I, the logic of Westphalia had triumphed in that region too, creating several new nation-states out of the ashes of the traditional empire.

The place of much of Latin America in this system after its independence from Spanish and Portuguese rule early in the nineteenth century reveals Westphalia's ability to accommodate new actors and its inherent tendency (which would become more apparent in the second half of the twentieth century) actually to foster the proliferation of sovereign states. The success of the liberationist struggle could be tested with considerable objectivity in European capitals, for it entailed, as elsewhere, evidence of effective control by independence-minded political elites in Latin America over populations and territories. Then, however, European recognition of the new nations helped ensure that formal political change in the new world would not also bring radical shifts in the capabilities and influence of core European actors behaving as imperialists there. If Spanish rule had been replaced by, say, French dominion in South America, the general equilibrium of European great powers might well have been shattered. Instead, recognition of the new states clearly supported the maintenance of the European balance by formalizing the hands-off relationship toward them that is fundamental to Westphalian rules.[18]

BALANCING POWER IN A DECENTRALIZED WORLD

This example suggests that the tendency toward balancing power may be characteristic of any highly decentralized social system whose actors have diverse interests. What is entailed in the balancing process is a search for allies, that is, other individuals who are perceived to share at least some of the same interests, with whom one can counteract opposing interests from other members of the group. If some approximation of true balance is the result, no one's unwanted values will crowd out the others, which then can be maintained within the group without being imposed upon unwilling members. The solution is not a true resolution of the conflict of the values in question but a perpetuation and a reinforcement of the various actors' freedom to pursue their own interests as long as they do not infringe upon the right of others to do the same.[19]

Clearly, for some such outcome to work, there must be prior agreement among the contestants upon the underlying rules of the game, upon the fundamental importance of maintaining the system so that the game may continue to be played. In short, those game-playing values must be shared so that other, diverse interests may be contested in the game itself. That in turn requires that the players, and especially the most important players, remain convinced that they have more to lose by abandoning the game and engaging in a free-for-all than they do by staying within the established rules. For that to happen, they must be reasonably content with their lot already, more willing to defend it than to risk it all in the chance of winning more.

The history of the modern state system makes clear that its stability demands that most of the most important actors maintain foreign policies essentially oriented toward maintaining the international status quo. That generalization is an important one, as can be seen by anyone who tests it in studying the diplomatic history of the European states in the modern period. It does not mean, of course, that satisfied states will never go to war, but rather that they will only (or at least usually) resort to violence as a means of preventing radical shifts in the capabilities of other actors, and as a result, in their own position in the world. In this sense, Westphalia permits the resort to force by states as the ultimate available police power when nonviolent forms of coercion fail. And since force is the ultimate instrument of coercion, its employment by status quo great powers corresponds to their perception of a threat to the stability of the system itself, an effort to overthrow the rules of the game.

The difficulty with these propositions, which have long been generally understood by the leading diplomats of Europe, is not their lack of clarity or logic in principle, but the possibilities for their subjective and therefore varying application in practice—a matter of some consequence in a world of numerous sovereign authorities, all equally entitled to make their own subjective applications of the principles. To take an important example, we may suppose that from the viewpoint of the Prussian Chancellor Bismarck in the 1860s, his policies directed toward the unification of the north German states under the centralized leadership of Prussia were not challenges to the rules of the game. Rather, they were entirely within the logic of the nation-state conception that had long prevailed elsewhere in Europe and were intended merely to bring a unified Germany into line, albeit by enhancing Prussian leadership in that process, with the established arrangement of sovereign actors. However, from the point of view of Napoleon III's government, the prospect of enhanced German capabilities unacceptably threatened the French status quo, with the ultimate result that France felt compelled to go to war to prevent such a development. In the end, the victory of a united Germany did not destroy the system, although we can say with the vision of a century's hindsight that the nearly complete collapse of the French military effort no doubt resulted in a settlement that in turn changed France from a status quo to revisionist power, with long-term destabilizing consequences for France, Germany, and the entire world order system of the first half of the twentieth century.[20]

As suggested above, the balance of power game traditionally has been played principally, if not exclusively, by the greatest powers within the Westphalian world. That has been so, first, because their greater capabilities permitted them to engage in more assertive foreign policy than that of smaller powers (not coincidentally, traditional neutral states in the modern period, e.g., Sweden and Switzerland, have been small powers), and no doubt led their statesmen to define the national interest in active, more than in passive, terms. To say this much is little more than tautological, for great power status has always supposed such a state's willingness to play a leading role—that is, a dynamic, far ranging, and multifaceted one—in international diplomacy. The second reason for great power interest in balancing power is more precise; *because* they are great powers, leading states typically have the greatest stake in maintaining the established order from which they have clearly profited. Their capabilities combine with their interests to make them the effective managers of the world's political system.[21]

GREAT POWER CONCERTS

As a result of that special role, great powers sometimes have been able to take a clearer, more highly rationalized, position of leadership than the uncertainties of balancing power alone permit. On such occasions, they have consciously formed themselves into a directorate for conflict control, transforming competing alliances into a joint condominium. The classic example was the nineteenth-century Concert of Europe, a somewhat flexible grouping of the greatest powers on the continent and in the world. The Concert had its origins in the Congress of Vienna, which met in 1815 in the aftermath of Napoleon's defeat to restore the map of Europe to its pre-Napoleonic configuration. The earlier success of Napoleon's imperialism, after all, had marked the failure of traditional balance of power diplomacy to check his ambitions; now he had been brought down by the concerted action of those with a vested interest in restoring the pre-Napoleonic status quo. Therefore, the creation of the Concert marked the determination of those conservative states not to allow a new imperialist to arise. Its work during the remainder of the century amounted to periodic meetings of its statesmen to find consensus on how to treat international political developments that threatened, in the absence of great power agreement, to disrupt the system.

A sense of the Concert of Europe's successes, and therefore of its importance as a kind of police force for the European system, is apparent in the following comment by Inis L. Claude, Jr.:

> The Concert decided on the admission of new members to "Europe," as when it accepted Greece and Belgium as independent states in 1830, and declared that non-Christian Turkey was entitled to full status in the European system in 1856. It undertook . . . "to maintain the equilibrium of Europe," and in pursuance of this aim, intervened in such matters as the Russo-Turkish conflicts of the 1850's with a view to preventing the disruption of the balance of power upon which European order was deemed to depend. It assumed the responsibility of formulating certain standards of European public policy, as when it insisted at the Congress of Berlin in 1878 that Serbia could "enter the European family" only if it recognized the religious liberty of its subjects, described as one of "the principles which are the basis of social organization in all States of Europe."[22]

In a very general sense, the Westphalian order had managed to survive its first two centuries because from the beginning it had embodied a rudimentary community of interest among the states of Europe, which alone had kept conflicts within acceptable bounds and perpetuated the basic arrangement of sovereignty. But the creation of the Concert of Europe in the nineteenth century was a clear advance toward greater order within the system, although at the expense of the opposite of order: freedom for the individual units to go their own way. The Concert was made possible only because the great powers of the period perceived themselves as sharing a considerable pool of common interests in their foreign policies, not the least of which was their mutual desire to maintain their own exalted positions within the international arena.

Yet even when the Concert was at its height, the separate pulls of sovereignty generally guaranteed enough simultaneous distrust among the great powers to prevent them from becoming dictators in all aspects of the lives of lesser or excluded nations. A complex range of interests and capabilities, some competing, some in harmony, converged to create an acceptable middle ground between rigid, centralized control and disintegrative freedom for Europe and the rest of the noncolonized world. The twentieth-century world has seldom succeeded in replicating this situation, certainly not with the success or the longevity of that in the nineteenth century. Whatever the injustices of international politics that accompanied the reign of the Concert—and there were many—it was, when measured in terms of the comparatively low levels of interstate violence in the period, the most successful ordering arrangement yet devised by the Westphalian world.

NOTES

1. For a discussion of Westphalia's importance, see Leo Gross, "The Peace of Westphalia, 1648–1948," *American Journal of International Law* 42 (1948):20–41. A lucid account of the different normative system of medieval Europe is contained in Ernest Barker, "Introductory: Mediaeval Political Thought," in *The Social and Political Ideas of Some Great Mediaeval Thinkers*, ed. F.J.C. Hearnshaw (New York: Barnes and Noble, 1923), pp. 9–33.

2. Ernest Barker reminded us that "when we speak of Church and State in any consideration of the Middle Ages, we must remember that we are not speaking of two societies, but rather of the two governments of a single society. . . . It was a single *Respublica Christiana*, in which churchmanship was coextensive with citizenship. You could not be a member of a political society unless you were a baptized Christian; and if you were excommunicated by the Church you lost all legal and political rights" (ibid., p. 14).

3. The Holy Roman Empire is a classic example of a political arrangement that long outlived the values that gave rise to it, so much so that by the eighteenth century its by then anachronistic quality prompted Voltaire's famous quip: The Holy Roman Empire, he said, was neither holy, nor Roman, nor an empire.

4. In Barker's words, "there was no organized State to confront the clergy. It has often been said that in the Middle Ages there was no State; and at any rate we may say that . . . there were only feudal communities, dissipated in fiefs and communes, with no regular officials or organized methods of action" ("Introductory: Mediaeval Political Thought," p. 16). For a more recent analysis of the origin and meaning of feudal anarchy, see Gianfranco Poggi, *The Development of the Modern State* (Stanford, Calif.: Stanford University Press, 1978), p. 31.

5. Bodin's writings, *Six Books of the Republic*, are summarized in George H. Sabine, *A History of Political Theory*, 4th ed., rev. Thomas Landon Thorson (Hinsdale, Ill.: Dryden Press, 1973), Chapter 21.

6. Modern colonialism, i.e., that which was widely engaged in by the great European powers until very recently, of course, coexisted with sovereign equality in the international legal system for centuries. The jurisprudential argument was that colonial holdings, which by definition were not sovereign,

had their interests represented by the imperial (and sovereign) metropoles. It could not very well be argued that colonial peoples were treated by their own sovereigns on an equal basis with citizens of the metropole, but not until late in the colonial period did such an observation develop an irresistible moral force. In purely legalistic terms, there are no difficulties in rationalizing the double standard as stemming from the separate facts of sovereign equality for the international actors on the one hand and inequality within domestic, imperial structures on the other.

7. For an excellent discussion of the way in which the great German philosopher of the early modern period, Baron von Leibniz, defined *sovereignty* as dependent upon the essential impermeability of the territorial state, see John H. Herz, *International Politics in the Atomic Age* (New York: Columbia University Press, 1959; Columbia Paperback Edition, 1962), pp. 49–61, 1962 ed. In this context, impermeability means the ability of the territorial ruler (the sovereign) to constrain his subjects while not being so constrainable by superior power. By the time Leibniz wrote, whatever loyalty the emperor still commanded from his princes had become largely a matter of personal fealty. He generally could no longer constrain them into doing his will.

8. The European wars of religion had been motivated by the mutual desire of Protestants and Catholics to suppress—even eliminate, for the most zealous among them—the other, which would have required dominant or hierarchical control. The great ideological achievement of Westphalia was to secularize Europe's international politics thereafter through adoption of the principle *cuius regio eius religio* (whose the region, his the religion), which paved the way for genuine religious toleration in political affairs. That achievement was in an important sense the result of the perceived destructive cost of religious warfare and was supported by Westphalia's more general principle of non-hierarchical organization.

9. A classic work on this subject remains Carlton H. J. Hayes, *The Historical Evolution of Modern Nationalism* (New York: Macmillan, 1931).

10. However, the recent rapid growth in the Soviet Union's non-European and largely Muslim populations has led some observers to suppose that non-Russian nationalism of various minority groups is likely to become an increasing problem for Soviet leaders in the near future.

11. For a brief analysis of the emergence of a just war doctrine in the early modern period and of its subsequent demise in international law, see Lynn H. Miller, "The Contemporary Significance of the Doctrine of Just War," *World Politics* 16 (January 1964):254–286. For a more detailed analysis of the continuing importance of the doctrine and its new relevance today, see Michael Walzer, *Just and Unjust Wars* (New York: Basic Books, 1977).

12. As much a truism for states as for individual human beings are the words of a member of the French National Assembly in 1848, "entre le fort et le faible c'est le pouvoir qui opprime et la loi qui affranchit" ([in relations] between the strong and the weak, power oppresses and law sets free).

13. Richard A. Falk has frequently made use of the term *laissez-faire* to describe the basic organizational principle of Westphalia, and I am indebted to him for its explanatory value in this context. See, for example, Falk's *This Endangered Planet* (New York: Random House, 1971).

14. John Locke, *Of Civil Government: Second Essay* (Chicago: Gateway Editions, 1955), especially Chapters 9–13, 15, 18, and 19.

15. In the words of Richard A. Falk, "any laissez-faire system of organization presupposes the absence of scarcity as a basic condition. Scarcity calls for

allocation; excess capacity in a system of automatic checks is consistent with unrestricted use" ("Toward Equilibrium in the World Order System," *American Journal of International Law* 54, 4 [September 1970]:217–224).

16. Locke, *Of Civil Government,* Chapter 5 ("Of Property"), pp. 25, 29–30. I am indebted to Peter Bachrach for calling my attention to Locke's metaphorical references to America in this regard.

17. This issue is explored in Cornelius J. Murphy, "The Grotian Vision of World Order," *American Journal of International Law* 76, 3 (July 1982):477–498.

18. As always in my effort to elucidate basic rules of the game for sovereign actors, this account deliberately ignores the incentives for actors to disregard them in their maneuvering for increased capabilities. The diplomatic history of this period makes clear that certain European great powers did attempt to extend neoimperial influence into Latin America after its general independence and that for the most part the efforts of the Holy Alliance in these directions were opposed by Great Britain and the United States, a policy the latter country articulated in its Monroe Doctrine. There is no reason to argue that the British and U.S. policy was any more high minded or motivated by devotion to the rules of the game than that of the continental European powers; their own interests, they determined, could be best supported by opposing radical shifts in the international power balance of the kind that might have resulted from ignoring Holy Alliance power plays in Latin America. The historical record merely supports the generalization that the Westphalian mode of organizing world politics strongly encourages the balancing of power relationships.

19. Students of U.S. politics will note the similarity between the operations of the balance of power internationally and the theory of pluralism as an explanation for how democracy operates within the United States. The authors of *The Federalist* were the classic pluralists in the American tradition; but see also contemporary writings that take a similar point of view, for example, Edward C. Banfield, *Political Influence* (New York: Free Press, 1961); Robert A. Dahl, *Pluralist Democracy in the United States* (Chicago: Rand McNally, 1967); and E. E. Schattschneider, *The Semi-Sovereign People* (New York: Holt, Rinehart and Winston, 1960).

20. France's humiliating defeat included the proclamation of the new German empire, not in Berlin, but in Paris and, more substantively, Germany's annexation of the French provinces of Alsace and Lorraine. Thereafter, France and Germany became long-term enemies, a condition that naturally prevented them from becoming even temporary allies as they sometimes should have been in keeping with balance of power requirements over the next seventy years. On this point, see Morton A. Kaplan and Nicholas deB. Katzenbach, *The Political Foundations of International Law* (New York: John Wiley and Sons, 1969), pp. 36ff.

21. Harold Nicolson, *The Evolution of Diplomacy* (New York: Collier Books, 1962), pp. 99–105.

22. Inis L. Claude, Jr., *Swords into Plowshares,* 4th ed. rev. (New York: Random House, 1971), p. 26.

3
The Twentieth-Century Challenge to Westphalian Order

> The record of Sumerian, Hellenic, Chinese, and medieval Italian history demonstrates that a set of local sovereign states can be no more than a transitory political configuration.
> —Arnold Toynbee, *Mankind and Mother Earth*

We have seen how a group of treaties negotiated more than three hundred years ago in Western Europe became the constitutional basis for the conduct of all states in their relations with each other down to the present day. Although that is a true depiction of the ongoing international order in fundamental respects, now we must explore the extent to which it may no longer be the whole truth. Over the past seventy or eighty years, there clearly have been many striking changes in the way we live, in the issues that find their way to the top of the international agenda, and therefore in the values that have helped to shape the content of international relations. Are these changes evidence that the traditional international order has been undermined, or should we suppose that the altered agenda of international politics (which still shares something with that of the past) has little bearing on the underlying constitutional system of states, that issues come and go while the basic mode for dealing with them stays essentially the same?

One of the major problems we have in assessing the continuing power of the Westphalian order stems from the limitations of our own perspective as creatures of our time. We are so much a part of the twentieth century that we cannot be certain whether, for instance, any of the important multilateral treaties of our era, such as the United Nations Charter, will one day be regarded as we now regard the Peace of Westphalia, as altering in fundamental ways the rules of the game for international society and even of the nature and relationships of the actors within the world system. Many intelligent observers have insisted that no such fundamental change has taken place. They caution us not to be misled by wishful thinking into supposing that basic changes have actually taken place if state behavior has changed little regardless of some apparent novelties in formal commitments. To pursue the example of the United Nations, they might point out that even though the Charter grants the Security Council the authority to act to maintain international peace on behalf of all UN members—a novelty in Westphalian terms—the record makes clear that the Council seldom has been able to reach agreement on important peace-threatening matters, let alone enforce its decision.

That kind of skepticism regarding the formal commitments of states without attention to their behavior is perfectly justified, and any analysis of the real world of international politics that ignores it is doomed to failure. At the same time, the possibility also always exists that our timeboundedness may present us with the perennial problem of not being able to see the forest for the trees. When considering important social change throughout the planet, one can be far less sure of the significance of what is happening in one's own lifetime than in the more distant past. The Anglo-American world has long given homage to Magna Charta, for example, as the first great constitutional restraint on arbitrary government in our common history. Yet if we imagine ourselves in the place of, say, a yeoman farmer of England in the year 1220 or 1250 or even later, we may doubt that he had any reason to celebrate the signing of that document at Runnymede, assuming he even knew of the event. It would be many centuries before the descendants of that farmer would feel the impact of Magna Charta on their lives.

Even though it may be a very long time before future generations are able to find with assurance comparable benchmarks in our century, we can start to assess their presence by examining the major historical developments in international politics in recent decades as they appear to us today.

WORLD WAR I AND THE COLLAPSE OF THE BALANCE OF POWER

Much of the evidence now available suggests that World War I should be regarded as one of the most important conflicts in human history, a rare watershed event that ended an era in international politics and ushered in a new one. It was the first general European war in more than two-and-a-half centuries, more like the Thirty Years' War in that respect than like any of the other conflicts separating those two great events. As such, it marked both the triumph and the collapse of the balance of power policies that had been developed to so high a degree during the nineteenth century. The balance of power triumphed in the fact that the alliance commitments of various European powers were honored: Russia supported Serbia, as it had pledged to do, in the face of an ultimatum against the little Balkan republic by Austro-Hungary; Germany thereby honored its commitment in the Dual Alliance by supporting Austria; France and ultimately Britain joined Russia, their ally in the Triple Entente, in the fight against the central powers, and World War I was underway.[1]

Yet that is not at all the way balance of power politics were intended to work, and thus the general outbreak of war also signaled the failure of those policies. An ominous prelude had been sounded in 1907 when British statesmen felt compelled to abandon their traditional aloofness in the political rivalries of the Continent—a posture that had permitted them to play the role of balancer and peacekeeper throughout the nineteenth century—by aligning themselves with France and Russia in opposition to the growing militarism of Kaiser Wilhelm II. As a result, when the conflict started it quickly spread. In the absence of an effective balancer, the logic of counterbalancing power with power had become perverse. The coalitions were *too* evenly matched now, and neither could be intimidated into foresaking the battlefield by the threat of overwhelming opposing force. The honoring of commitments ineluctably closed off other avenues of choice, and states played out their roles as if caught up in a Greek tragedy.[2]

So it appeared to many as the war ground on, among whom the most articulate critic of the failure of the balance of power became U.S. President Woodrow Wilson. Once the United States finally entered the war, thus ensuring, as we know in retrospect, the defeat of the Central Powers, Wilson repeatedly called attention to the need to prevent such a catastrophe from happening again. He insisted that once peace was restored, what the world needed was "not a balance of power, but a community of power, not organized rivalries, but an organized common peace."[3] The logic of his position was based upon a shrewder assessment of the balance of power politics long practiced by major European states than his later critics sometimes credited him with. He noted in effect that the balance of power was a double-edged sword and one whose destructive power more than offset whatever ability it once had had to keep the peace. When such policies worked, as undeniably they had in the past, they did so only by threatening war, a paradox that no doubt troubled Wilson at least in part on moral grounds: How humane was it, he might have asked himself, to maintain order through the threat of unacceptable disorder, to try to build peace on policies that emphasized states' differences rather than their common ground?

But certainly Wilson's most telling critique of the balance of power was unarguably realistic. As with any system of order built upon deterrence, it lost all credibility once it failed, for in its failure it produced conflicts vastly wider and more devastating than could be expected by unprincipled behavior alone. If one can imagine a pre–World War I Europe in which *no* alliances existed and, further, where no major actor was willing to offer the slightest assistance to any state threatened by a fellow sovereign, then one can also picture a situation in which the assassination of the Archduke Ferdinand at Sarajevo would have produced, perhaps, the crushing of Serbia's independence by an outraged Austro-Hungary—and nothing more! We may regret such a hypothetical outcome for the Serbians, but in a world where one must always attempt to pursue the lesser and avoid the greater evil, it is difficult to argue that such a fate would not have been preferable for the larger human society than the actual outcome.

As we know, Wilson did not argue that such an outcome would have been preferable.[4] He called instead for the nations of the world to make not just a different, but an opposite, commitment from that of turning their backs on their neighbors. They should form themselves into a worldwide community pledged to assist each other mutually in restraining any would-be violator of the peace. They should transform their rival alliances, whose results were so disastrous when they failed to deter, into a single, overarching global alliance whose deterrent capabilities would be unquestioned because of the evident overwhelming force available to it. They should, in short, create a collective security system to replace the vagaries, the uncertainties, and the dangers of balance of power politics.

The Wilsonian vision was not, in fact, particularly original to Woodrow Wilson. From the earliest days of the Westphalian order, a number of thinkers had advanced similar views of a collective security alternative to what they saw as the dangerous every-state-for-itself permissiveness of the European normative system.[5] None of these earlier proposals had ever received serious attention by sovereign decision makers, so it is easy to dismiss them as unrealistic within the context of their times.[6] In the cataclysm of World War I, however, many people, including many leaders of sovereign states, apparently were persuaded that a new commitment to the peace of the whole community was needed as the only discernible way to protect the rights and interests of the individual units. Self-help strategies had brought disaster; now was the time to create a League of Nations that would embody the historic turn away from self-help toward a worldwide commitment to mobilize whatever power was necessary to keep or restore the peace.

COLLECTIVE SECURITY: THE HUNTERS AND THE STAG

Rousseau's well-known parable of the hunters and the stag seems particularly relevant to the experiences of the League of Nations, a creation Rousseau could only have imagined. A group of hunters, armed with primitive weapons, agree that the only way they can catch a stag is to form a circle around the spot where it is grazing and then slowly close in on it for the kill, after which they will share the spoils. They proceed as planned until one of the hunters sees a hare dart before his path and, calculating quickly that it would provide sufficient food for his immediate wants, breaks from the circle to capture it. When he does so, the stag is able to escape through the breach and the other hunters go hungry. The collective effort has been thwarted by the selfish act of one.

The parable demonstrates a critical truth about the concept of collective security. If it is to succeed, the element of free choice to opt out must be virtually eliminated once the commitment to the common good has been made. How such a state of affairs is dependably produced is an issue that goes to the very heart of community building at any level. Clearly, there is no single, simple technique of the sort a chemist may use to produce compounds of the elements in a laboratory. But just as clearly, the creation of such a social contract is not impossible, for if it were, no human communities would have been formed throughout our history. Within such communities, typically nation-states in the modern period, we take it for granted that the freedom of individuals to opt out at times and places of their own choosing is severely restricted. We can predict that most citizens will pay their taxes or serve in their nation's armed forces when compelled to do so, to take as examples two of what many consider to be the more distasteful restrictions on their absolute freedom.

The Covenant of the League of Nations, at whose heart lay the collective security commitment, was in form and in theory a social contract among the states that ratified it (covenant = contract). We know through hindsight that it was a failed contract, which left those who had committed themselves to it like the hungry hunters in Rousseau's parable. In the final analysis, the deeply ingrained compulsion for self-help, for going it, if not alone, then with particular friends of one's own choosing, won out over the more abstract commitment to support the established peace and thereby the long-range interests of all the members. Where do we look for the reasons for this failure?

First, we look to what were no doubt serious flaws in the Covenant itself, flaws that reflected the initial reluctance of those states that created it to subordinate very many of their traditional freedoms to the common good. If universal collective security is to work, the threat of stringent sanctions must be credible to a would-be warring nation in much the same way that the government of any viable state can threaten arrest and prison terms to would-be criminals. Yet the Covenant was somewhat vague on the point of whether collective military action might be needed against an aggressor, nowhere specifying what procedures League members should follow in that case, and was specific only in its depiction of nonmilitary sanctions—diplomatic and economic—that could be invoked against the outlaw state.[7] In the most well-known and fatally unsuccessful collective action undertaken by the League, that of economic sanctions invoked against Mussolini's Italy for its invasion of Ethiopia in 1935, the rueful conclusion of many was that the League lacked "teeth"; the League's action failed because it became troublingly clear that it was not having the desired effect. Mussolini was not coerced into obeying the law but instead got away with his illegal action. Therefore it seemed clea. enough with hindsight that stronger police powers should have been prescribed in the Covenant, although when the Covenant was written, few participants would have found it realistic, that is, acceptable to their own governments, to commit themselves more fully to support a police power for the world.

The League's constitutional document also contained the rather murky provision that "nothing in this Covenant shall be deemed to affect the validity of . . . regional understandings like the Monroe doctrine, for securing the maintenance of peace."[8] These innocent-sounding words reflected a hard-fought battle at the Versailles conference won by those who frankly did not trust the logic of Wilson's universal collective security commitment, preferring instead to maintain the principle that more traditional, partial alliances of states could continue to maintain the peace as they had attempted to do in the past. The result was a bit like trying to square the circle: The Covenant sought to obligate states under the principle that world peace was indivisible, that every violation of the peace anywhere in the world was everybody's business, but at the same time it suggested that some states would naturally maintain their own priorities—no doubt determined largely by geographical considerations—in deciding which peace-threatening issues would demand more determined responses than others.[9] Carried to its logical conclusion, this concession to regional ordering techniques invited the reestablishment of balance of power policies within a framework that would have no chance of maintaining peace if such policies were not forbidden.

These comments on some important weaknesses and inconsistencies in the Covenant in fact are comments on the unwillingness of those who created the League to abandon altogether traditional Westphalian modes of behavior even while they supposedly were committing themselves to a radically new concept. Ironically, even this somewhat timid departure from traditional international patterns proved too radical for Woodrow Wilson's own United States. That country's refusal to become a member of the League struck a serious blow, at least symbolically, to the future practicability of collective security itself. When important actors refuse to be bound by the collective will of the larger community, others are likely to find the temptation overwhelming to follow suit. In fact, out of the total membership of sixty-three states in the League, seventeen, or more than one quarter, withdrew before the organization collapsed. The hunters' circle developed holes in so many places it was little wonder the League's major effort at universal sanctions in the Italian case was doomed to failure.

The League did, of course, have some record of success, although in general the successes lay outside the realm of collective security action in the strictest sense. On more than one occasion, League involvement in an international dispute as an objective third party, whose role included the investigation of issues, efforts at mediation and the like, helped produce a peaceful settlement.[10] Obviously, such techniques, including the extension of good offices and similar offers of help by neutral parties to assist in the settlement of disputes, long predated the creation of the League and are probably as old as diplomacy itself. In this respect, the novel place of the League as an instrument of order within a traditional system may have enhanced its role as peacemaker, but it was evidently not a role reflective of a transformed system. A friend may act as go-between when a marriage appears headed for the rocks and assist at a reconciliation, but not because she can coerce the unhappy couple into a rapprochement that neither wants. That is because the relationships among such parties are those of sovereign equals, capable perhaps of persuading, but not of commanding each other. Only a judge has the authority in such a situation to command the couple, and the League never effectively and consistently carried out a judge's role.

Are we then simply to conclude that the Covenant of the League amounted to a false social contract, one that misguidedly purported to reflect the creation of a true world community where none in fact existed? This has been the thrust of much of the realist criticism of both Wilson and the League when its failure became evident.[11] As a sweeping generalization, it is no doubt an accurate conclusion although, as with all such generalizations, countertruths may lie hidden beneath it. What is much more difficult to determine because far less susceptible to generalization is the extent to which the League experiment may have nibbled away at some of the characteristic self-help expectations of the traditional Westphalian system, even without demolishing them. Such a possibility no doubt would not have teased our minds for long in, say, 1939 or 1940, for at that time we would have been justified in concluding that the noble experiment had failed and that Hitler's *Realpolitik* appeared to be a more vicious variant for the future of the game of politics characteristic of the past. But now we know that after World War II, a new version of the League was created in the United Nations, and although we may suspect that it too has failed to make the collective security commitment a predictably obligatory force in the contemporary world, we can at least not be so certain that it has been discarded as useless.

For the moment, there appear to be two lessons to keep in mind, their contradictory assertions serving as healthy correctives to each other: First, formal social contracts do not in themselves make a community if the underlying behavioral patterns supporting such an arrangement are not in place. Second, such a contract, even when it fails, may constitute a kind of chart for searching out and strengthening those patterns of behavior that support a developing community ideal.

INTERWAR CHALLENGES TO THE ESTABLISHED ORDER

We can also see with hindsight what could not have been clear at the time the League of Nations was created: The twenty-year period between the world wars was one of unusual and nearly unprecedented challenges to Westphalian rules of the game by various state actors and of extensive ferment on the part of peoples that hitherto had been largely ignored by the Westphalian order. In the aftermath of the Treaty of Versailles, economic and social upheaval in Germany transformed that country into a humiliated, dissatisfied power, the long-term result of which brought the rise of one of the most maniacally aggressive governmental leaders the world had ever known. Meanwhile, tsarist Russia had undergone a sweeping social revolution during the course of World War I, which brought to power a Communist party of a type long feared by political elites in the West, so much so that the new Soviet state was widely regarded as a rogue, not to be trusted or included within international political councils.[12] Italy also produced a dictator who espoused an extremely virulent strain of nationalism with increasingly revisionist demands to make upon his neighbors, and in the Far East, the rise of Japanese militarism led that country down a similar path.

The elites of all these states now gave evidence of their unwillingness to accept the general status quo, commitment to which by such great powers had always been critical to the stability of the Westphalian order,[13] just as that status quo orientation remained an essential assumption on which collective security in the League was built. Of the traditional great power keepers of the order, only Great Britain and France continued to play these roles; Austria-Hungary and the Ottoman Empire both had been dismembered in the war, whereas a prospective new great power with a considerable stake in the established order, the United States, refused to have that kind of greatness thrust upon it until after the interwar period had ended.

The result could not have been more unfortunate for developing a strong collective security system within the League, for that principle could work only if most of the great powers that had bound themselves to the Covenant were essentially satisfied powers willing to defend with their like-minded fellows against threats to violent disruptions of the territorial status quo as the cost that must be paid for the peace from which they above all profited. Nowhere was the presumed satisfaction with the status quo more clearly expressed than in the Covenant's Article 10, by which members undertook "to respect and preserve as against external aggression the territorial integrity and existing political independence of all Members of the League." Once revisionists came to power in Germany, Italy, and Japan, they found their policies in conflict with that provision of the Covenant whereupon, one by one, they simply renounced their countries' earlier commitment and left the organization. Only Stalin, in his cynicism, apparently thought that a by then moribund League would look the other way for his violation of Article 10, only to find his government expelled.

The interwar period also marked the first chapter in an extended process of opening up the system to new sovereign actors. That phenomenon has produced continuing conflict over the proper goals of world order down to the present; in its immediate post–World War I phase, it complicated the task of responding effectively and with justice to the demands of revisionist great powers. Under the name of self-determination, the World War I peace settlements granted independence to a number of national groups long under the imperial domination of the Austrian Hapsburgs or the Ottoman Turks. Furthermore, the League's mandates system embodied the enlightened view for its time that the colonial dependencies of the defeated great powers (those "not yet able to stand by themselves under the strenuous conditions of the modern world") should not simply be annexed by the victors, but should be administered by League members in a kind of public trust, with the eventual goal of self-determination.[14]

The statesmen who struggled with the peace treaties at Paris, as well as their successors down to the present day, discovered that self-determination is a formidable weapon for challenging the established order. National groups, particularly in Eastern Europe, did not always live within cohesive territorial regions, particularly not after centuries of alien imperial rule. As a result, statesmen of the 1920s and 1930s had to wrestle with the attempt to reconcile the new sovereignties they had created with the injustices felt by many at the destruction of the traditional map of Europe. Of the revisionist leaders, Hitler was particularly adept at manipulating the self-determination ethic to support the Nazis' aggressive nationalism. He could point to the situation of the Sudeten Germans within the borders of Czechoslovakia to justify the annexation of large chunks of that country's territory, and when the British, French, and Italian leaders all agreed to his claims at Munich in 1938, they not only sealed Czechoslovakia's fate, but also emboldened Hitler to make good on his irredentist claims to Memel and the Polish Corridor. Within a year came the German attack on Poland and the fateful start of the second world war in the twentieth century.

A somewhat different light is cast on this interwar struggle between self-determination and imperialism when we consider the following:

At the end of World War I, Great Britain laid claim to the loyalty of some 500 million people, about one fourth of the earth's population, and a quarter of its territory. The French Empire was only about one-third that size, but nonetheless encompassed more than 100 million people. In contrast, Germany, Italy, and Japan held total populations about one-third larger than the total home populations of Britain and France, although without any of their overseas imperial territories. What were to become the three Axis powers ruled over a combined territory of less than 1.5 million square miles, as opposed to the British-French control over nearly twelve times that amount of territory. Those facts alone give a sense of the strength of the Axis impulse to acquire empires of their own in this period, especially because—and this is no doubt the most forceful engine of that impulse—the Western democracies obviously had not yet faced up to their own hypocritical postures on this subject. They had given their support to self-determination for national groups within the empires of defeated powers; self-determination for their own colonized peoples was quite another matter.[15]

Seen in this light, the interwar period is one of a global struggle between the two opposing forces, empire building and empire maintenance on one side and national self-determination on the other. World War II may have been above all an ultimately successful struggle to prevent the revisionist states from advancing their new imperial claims, claims which, subsequent history shows us, were truly reactionary, for the outcome of World War II was, ironically, to produce the beginning of the end of British and French imperialism as well. Here we have another of the truly momentous global changes of the twentieth century. After two world wars and several decades of contesting change, the double standard of the traditional order, which had justified inequality between European and non-European peoples, finally was overthrown, although not without one of the most prolonged and often violent struggles of the age.

WESTPHALIA AS A GLOBAL SYSTEM

It is tempting today to see the almost complete demise of formal imperialism as historically predestined, but whether or not we take such a view—as, for example, a Leninist interpretation of history requires—we should at least remember that imperialism in various forms has been a recurring phenomenon throughout human history, that therefore announcements of its death may well be premature. What we can say is that within our lifetimes imperialism has lost virtually all the sense of legitimacy it once had, even for those nations that were very recently the major imperialist powers. It is not simply coincidental that the system of international order devised by a handful of European statesmen more than three hundred years ago has proved to be so congenial to non-Europeans struggling to assert their equal rights as international actors. The concept of sovereign equality has proved to be as powerful an idea for abolishing twentieth-century imperialism as it was for ending the legitimacy of European feudalism in the seventeenth century.

We should draw two conclusions from this experience to guide our thinking about the Westphalian order's likely future. First, any legal order that claims rights for some cannot resist indefinitely the logical conclusion that they must be granted to all like actors if it is to maintain a claim to any semblance of being a system of justice. As the history of Westphalia shows, those served by the system can deny the logic of such an idea for a very long time simply by defining unequal participants as not truly like themselves and therefore not entitled to participate on an equal footing. Nonetheless, the very idea of equality—whether of sovereigns or of individual citizens within a domestic order—has proved to be an extremely dangerous idea to let loose upon a hierarchical society, for as larger numbers of actors meet whatever requirements are demanded to be treated like equals, the tendency is irresistible to qualify still other members of the society as well.

The second conclusion, which reinforces the first where global ordering arrangements are concerned, is that the concept of sovereign equality, with its comparatively simple and concrete tests to qualify as such an actor, remains the only alternative the modern world has been able to devise in opposition to hierarchical governmental principles. The result has not been an unmixed blessing from the standpoint of effective control over social disorder, but it undoubtedly has guaranteed greater freedom for more groups of people than any other kind of legal order known in history.

One paradoxical result today is that spreading the legal order to make it truly global may have stretched it beyond its capacity to do its work, that of maintaining acceptable order. The more actors who must agree before any plan or policy can be implemented, the more cumbersome and difficult is the process of achieving consensus. During the nineteenth century, no more than half a dozen governments in Europe determined the destinies of several hundred million people in Africa and Asia, and to do so their representatives had to meet face to face only on a very occasional basis. In contrast, when by the 1970s it became necessary to try to regulate the exploitation of the ocean's resources, the representatives of 157 states had to meet over the course of some ten years, during ninety-three weeks of which the delegates were actually in session, before a treaty could be completed.

But it is not just that widespread participation is more cumbersome. Democratization has brought new issues and priorities to the agenda of international politics. This fact may not in itself threaten the way in which the business of international politics is conducted, but it is often impossible until long after the event to separate the actual impact of a policy goal from the way in which it is perceived by other, especially hostile, actors. The dominant Western view of Soviet policy goals throughout its history, or of the People's Republic of China in the 1950s and 1960s, was of dangerously revisionist elites bent on destabilizing the international order wherever possible to further their ultimate aim of world revolution and conquest. Yet an objective reading of the foreign policy record of either of these powers is at best ambiguous proof of such motivations, nor is it particularly difficult to read much of those records as evidence of comparatively restrained and even conservative foreign policies in keeping with traditional Westphalian values.[16] The question of the revolutionary or status quo orientation of important Communist governments *is* debatable, as the entire history of the cold war era makes clear, and those who are inclined to accept the first rather than the second characterization will make very different assessments about the extent of their threat to traditional Westphalian values.

A converse case was that posed by the rise of Hitler and Mussolini. Had not so many of their irredentist claims appeared to the elites of other major actors at the time as examples of somewhat extreme but nonetheless traditional, and therefore acceptable, goals of major actors, they probably would have been more strongly opposed at an earlier stage, with the result that World War II might have been averted. Clearly, perceptions of the goals of other sovereigns may matter even more than their actual goals—if such matters ever exist in an objective vacuum—in determining the course of international politics.

Now that the Westphalian system has been opened to embrace the world, one of the inherent difficulties confronting, especially, traditional Western actors is that not only of judging the revolutionary or nonrevolutionary character of the demands for change made by the newer states but, even more important, assessing their likely world order impact if they are implemented. For example, a basic interpretation of the interwar period is to characterize the revisionist Axis powers as "have-not" states who sought the kinds of overseas empires that the Western democracies had long since acquired. We have some sense of the kinds of injustices to large numbers of peoples that would have resulted had they succeeded.[17] Today the continuing contest between much of the industrialized North and the formerly colonized, underdeveloped South is again one between haves and have-nots. Not surprisingly, the economically dominant Northern states are extremely resistant to demands for the kind of structural change in the world's economic system that would undermine their privileged position. But there the parallels between the interwar and the contemporary situations end, for whatever the consequences if today's international economic order were to be radically reordered along the lines proposed by the Group of 77, it is difficult to suppose that the imposition of a rabid imperialism would be among them.[18]

The East-West split and the North-South conflict—together they are labels for the perception of many that the homogeneity of the Westphalian system, visible to and visibly encouraged by Grotius, has vanished as that ordering arrangement has been stretched to fit the needs of the twentieth century. Our own forest-and-trees dilemma lies in trying to assess whether that outcome is producing a true revolution in the nature and structure of the international order. A case against the revolutionary view is readily apparent in the formal operation of the system, for there Westphalia remains triumphant through whatever social change the century has brought. The smallest of the new states has all the formal trappings of its older European counterparts; the rules surrounding diplomatic intercourse today look much as they did to eighteenth-century statesmen; the mode of operation of, say, the UN General Assembly is Westphalian in its purest form.

But on the other hand, we know that underneath the formal continuity with the traditional mode, social changes may be transforming a system that, at a symbolic level, looks much as it always has. In Britain the queen still "commands" her subjects, even though for centuries the British Parliament has ruled in any meaningful sense of the term. The continuity of form in British government during nearly a thousand years does not hide the fact that both the government and the values that support it are radically different today than in the times of either William the Conqueror or Henry VIII. Will future historians discern a transformed international system in our time, perhaps in social change that we are blind to as we focus instead on the traditional trappings of international interaction?

THE EMERGENCE OF BIPOLARITY

For some purposes, it is useful to view the world wars of this century as bracketing an intense period of upheaval initiated by the death of the traditional balance of power structure and ending in the novelty of a bipolar configuration in the post–World War II period. In these terms, the three decades from 1914 to 1945 were characterized by vast reordering change whose most immediately apparent outcome was the emergence of two new world actors, the United States and the Soviet Union, and the precipitate decline of the traditional great powers: Great Britain, France, Austro-Hungary, Germany, Italy, and the old Russia. A new term, superpower, had to be coined to label the two new world actors, for their capabilities and influence in the post–World War II period left them alone at the center of the world stage.[19]

This development was accompanied by the onset of cold war with all that it implied regarding a vast global conflict for world leadership between two opposing forces. In its crudest terms, and especially in its earliest phases, the cold war was marked by the general attitude in each of the power centers that all who were not publicly committed to its own cause were at best suspect and at worst implacably hostile, a situation that made the prospect of balancing power across ideological lines a clear impossibility.[20] We search in vain throughout the Westphalian period for any parallel condition at the international level.

Only when we examine the European wars of religion of the sixteenth and seventeenth centuries do we begin to see some ominous similarities with our own time. Then, as now, the most zealous ideologues, whether Protestant or Catholic, regarded their opposite number as implacably hostile foes, to be eliminated if they could not be converted. Then as now, emotive labels for the enemy—*papist, heretic, Communist,* or *capitalist imperialist*—were used as reminders of the impassable gulf that separated one's own community from that of the enemy, even of the other side's lack of common humanity. Then as now, some regarded any war as just that could be inflicted upon the enemy camp, to the point that the perceived righteousness of the conflict itself could overwhelm considerations of restraint and humane treatment of the enemy once war had broken out. We may find it repugnant that in the earlier conflict those identified as not of the true faith were drawn and quartered or burned at the stake; yet the cold war also has been characterized by its devil myth; the almost infinitely cunning enemy, the devil, is capable of brainwashing our innocent victims, and no doubt of worse, and therefore we feel justified, as some of us did during the war in Vietnam, in dropping them from helicopters or murdering their civilians because presumably none of "them" is innocent.

These similarities of course do not describe the whole picture of bipolarity in the contemporary period. A major difference is that we have not yet actually seen the Eastern and Western camps plunge into battle, except somewhat indirectly, as did Protestants and Catholics in the Thirty Years' War. Yet, to carry the parallel one step further, we know that the Thirty Years' War, more than any other upheaval, transformed medieval into Westphalian Europe. Do we not also suppose that were the superpowers ever to engage in direct conflict, particularly with nuclear explosives, the modern system of world order would be left in the rubble? It is far less clear that such a conflict could be restrained enough even to leave exhausted societies with the ability to maintain some semblance of civilization, let alone transform it into a more orderly arrangement, but we should be blind indeed to suppose that the basic system of sovereign states free to wreak such mutual destruction would survive.

The tendency of the cold war to take on the coloration of religious warfare has long been apparent and frightening to many. Much of the justification for the growth of nonalignment as an appropriate political stance *between* the interests and demands of the superpower camps must stem from the perceived dangers of an ideologically polarized world. Any such refusal to join irrevocably either of those parties who claim ideological supremacy becomes a force that works against both claims. Thus we can see in contemporary nonalignment another point of comparison to the early Westphalian age. In the early modern period, the role of the neutral became a respectable, conflict-limiting position in conjunction with the decline in ideological politics. Skepticism as to who is right and wrong in political disputes does not support just wars. Neutralism and nonalignment are the marks of actors who refuse to regard others, or the enemies of others, as devilish, even when they may not agree with them.

Perhaps the development of such skepticism and detachment in any social system marks at least a decline in dangerous polarization within the society and, further, the rise of a sense of toleration that can lead ultimately to a new, if heterogeneous or pluralistic, sense of community built upon new dominant values that need not so much defeat as supersede the old ones. In this way, neither Protestants nor Catholics have been driven out of modern European society; rather, the two groups have learned to live together in dependable peace as other, shared values have been allowed to develop. If there is a reliable analogy in the growth of nonalignment in the contemporary bipolar period, it also seems that we are still very far from having evolved a post–cold war world of dependably nonideological politics, shared basic values, and from them, a sense of limited and negotiable competing interests.

If we consider the relationship of nonalignment to bipolarity in a slightly different way, however, we acquire an ominous sense of a fundamental structural difference that remains between nineteenth-century balance of power politics and our current situation. No nonaligned state today—indeed, not even the whole numerous group of the nonaligned—can play the role of balancer, as Great Britain typically did in the earlier period, for a very simple and obvious reason: They do not have the capability to threaten a major would-be violator of the peace with effective counterforce. Such threats can come credibly only from one of the two cold war camps—ultimately, from the threat of the superpowers to use nuclear weapons. That threat may succeed as a deterrent; it may even succeed as well over a long period as the great power balancing act of the nineteenth century succeeded in its time, but with one subtle yet fundamentally different effect. The bipolar nuclear deterrent depends for its effectiveness upon maintaining the perception of a world split socially into two enemy communities, each willing to risk its own annihilation rather than succumb to any of the devil's demands. To the extent that the enemy comes to be perceived as similarly human and not devilish, the credibility of that threat is eroded.

In contrast, the nineteenth-century balancer's role supported the perception of a common interest in general peace, and thus of the mutual stake in preserving minimum order, as overriding the competing interests for particular changes in the status quo. Moreover, since nuclear weapons had not yet been invented, the threat by competing great powers to use force to achieve their goals did not amount to a pledge of mutual suicide, as it does today. Since no one supposed the actual engagement of armies would annihilate their societies, the threat to go to war could be made credible against a lesser opponent than the devil, perhaps even one with whom one shared some values in common.

Now we see more clearly what is unique, and uniquely dangerous, for modern times about the religious war mentality of the cold war outlook. Even though similar polarization has divided various local communities in our time—Muslims and Hindus in India, Protestants and Catholics in Northern Ireland, for example—in those cases the mutual destruction of enemy zealots has been contained within particular regions or actors without infecting the entire international structure. In the case of the cold war, in contrast, the holy war has been made global and feeds upon its own mentality to maintain equilibrium not through accommodation but by threatening global terror. No doubt *any* bipolar situation is most unfortunate, in human terms, in its tendency to deepen divisions between groups rather than to encourage recognition of common interests. It is a tendency, now embedded in the dynamics of world order, that can only add to our sense of helplessness and fright when the antagonists attempt to build their shaky standoff on arsenals of mass destruction.

A REVIVAL OF THE BALANCE OF POWER?

Some statesmen have responded to the dangers of this situation by seeking to resurrect the balance of power model of the past. In the 1970s, the policies of U.S. Secretary of State Henry Kissinger were a clear example. The reestablishment of normal relations with China marked one Nixon-Kissinger effort to counterbalance Soviet influence by supporting the enemy's enemy even though that required brushing aside the kind of rhetoric and attitudes that had prevented a U.S. accommodation with China during the previous twenty-five years.[21] At the same time, Kissinger sought détente with the Soviet Union because he regarded U.S.-Soviet interests as so deeply, even permanently, in conflict as to require constant efforts at amelioration if they were not to lead to disastrous, all-out war. The main thrust of that effort at détente was to support the mutual U.S.-Soviet interest in maintaining their dominant roles as great powers in the traditional sense. The newer states' demands for a greater sharing of economic power in particular were for the most part firmly opposed while, at the same time, U.S. policy encouraged the growth of Western Europe and Japan as traditional, capitalist economic centers with an increased U.S.-style interest in resisting revolutionary change.[22]

It is no coincidence that Kissinger strongly admired the policies of the early nineteenth-century Austrian statesman, Metternich, who was the principal architect of the Congress of Vienna in 1815 that ushered in the long period of great power management of a status quo that preserved their dominant positions in Europe and around the world.[23] Both statesmen held profoundly conservative world order views in the sense that they sought to encourage the dominance of the most conservative or satisfied state actors within the international system, who could be counted upon to work to maintain the basic status quo. Metternich's policies encouraged just such conservative tendencies in post-Napoleonic France at a time when it surely would have been tempting to treat defeated France as a kind of outlaw state for its excesses under Napoleon's rule, punishing it unmercifully and no doubt thereby sowing the seeds for further revisionist demands by France toward the rest of Europe. But by treating France as a member of the great power club instead, he helped transform that country from a revisionist to a status quo power in support of the conservative order.

Careful analysis of Kissinger's policies toward the Soviet Union reveals a similar motivation, although it is difficult from our current perspective to see that he met with anything like Metternich's success. In the years since Kissinger left office, détente has been dropped from the vocabulary of U.S. statesmen, presumably because of its unpopularity in some quarters, and under both the Carter and, more dramatically, the Reagan administrations, the cold war has been resumed in terms that give a sense of *déjà vu* to those who lived through the 1950s. This development may simply be proof of our earlier conclusion that the balance of terror depends upon a perception within each camp that the other side is unrelentingly hostile to its interests. Bipolarity tends to perpetuate itself as long as the nuclear deterrent works or seems to work, for we can never know with certainty what nation's would-be expansionism has or has not been deterred by the threat of others to use nuclear weapons in that event. We assume that "they" may be so constrained if our nuclear deterrent is credible, yet we do not like to admit that when our country does not behave aggressively abroad in situations in which it clearly has the military power to do so, we are deterred by anything other than the greater goodness of our leaders.

Certainly it remains clear in the world of the 1980s that if we consider nuclear capabilities alone, bipolarity remains strongly in place. Only the superpowers have more or less evenly matched nuclear arsenals; only they are capable of producing doomsday prospects for the world. It is conceivable, but not very likely, that this situation could change in the near future. The enormous technological and financial requirements of these weapons systems and the overwhelming lead of the superpowers suggests that other actors are not likely to catch up with them even though new members may be added to the nuclear club. To think otherwise is somewhat like the fallacy in supposing that nonaligned nations, even as a whole, can act as balancer in any traditional sense to one or the other of the superpowers.

To take a plausible example of a nonsuperpower nuclear actor, we might imagine a situation in which China developed some foreign policy goal of such overriding interest to itself that it would threaten to bring its nuclear capability into play, but we cannot imagine that China could succeed in that threat in the face of the determined opposition of one or both superpowers. Should the Soviets support the Chinese in this imagined scenario, the result would be the traditional cold war confrontation. Should the United States support China in opposition to the Soviets, we would witness a new twist to bipolarity with a once-committed actor (China) now clearly on the other side; yet the outcome would be every bit as bipolar as in the first case. Should both superpowers oppose the Chinese nuclear threat with a joint threat of their own the result would be not bipolar but hegemonic or condominium action by the world's two greatest status quo powers. That kind of action is always a possibility inherent in the structure of bipolarity, although its extreme rarity in recent decades suggests how much stronger are the forces that typically divide, rather than unite, the superpowers. We may suppose that only a threat to the established order of the magnitude posited here typically would frighten both Washington and Moscow into at least momentary unity. But the essential point for the moment is that not even this kind of hegemonic action would return the world to a balance of power ordering arrangement. It would, if anything, move even further away from it.

Forces may be at work in the world today other than these strictly military—or more precisely, nuclear—ones that are supporting the reestablishment of a more traditional balance of power system of several major actors. If so, these forces must run counter to the nuclear factor alone. Also, nuclear capabilities present complex and even paradoxical challenges to the political analyst's traditional equation of a nation-state's status with its armed might. All these considerations will be explored more fully in Chapter 5. For the moment, however, we must remain skeptical of the likelihood that bipolarity is giving way at fundamental levels to a reborn balance of power system.

Before leaving this brief look at efforts to restore a balance of power, it should be emphasized that when considered as the conscious policy of statesmen like Henry Kissinger, it expresses the value preferences of a strongly statist, or traditionally Westphalian, outlook. Nation-states are seldom questioned to be the immutably important actors of international politics, particularly not when they happen also to be great powers, and these are perceived to have interests that change little over time and are in conflict with those of other states with whom temporary accommodations may nonetheless be possible. Such accommodations are in fact required by respect for the basic rules of the game, but they are never perceived as transforming or eradicating basic interests or traditional state-based values. This vision is probably very widely, if inchoately, shared by the world's public for the simple reason that it is the least imaginative way to address the world. Certainly it accords with many of the fundamental realities of the past three centuries and therefore may be supposed by those without a view of history that predates the modern period to apply to the present and the future as well.

GLOBAL ISSUES CONFRONT WESTPHALIA

We cannot possibly account for all the factors that may be producing or resisting global change, because the normative system we live in is the complex and often unplanned product of human development, evolving continually. What follows is little more than a listing of the most salient social and political concerns on today's international agenda. Each of these issues will be explored for its world order implications in succeeding chapters.

First, the security problem for the globe's citizens today is multi-faceted and in at least some of its aspects seems to be inadequately treated by the Westphalian system. We should recall the intimate connection Leibniz pointed to at the beginning of the modern age between the ability to provide protection throughout a largely impermeable state and the growth of sovereignty.[24] That connection between security and sovereignty is still evident in many of the international conflicts that have occurred in recent years. In those cases, the Westphalian mode may be said to remain adequate. But we are equally aware that novel security challenges seem less susceptible to adequate resolution through Westphalian means.

This seems most dramatically true of the still largely kinetic change in international conflict through the growth of nuclear and other weapons of mass destruction. The basic security issue here is not simply the power of these weapons, which is itself of an order to challenge Westphalia's traditional tolerance of much international conflict, but their basic indefensibility. Given their pinpoint accuracy on targets halfway around the world, their nearly instantaneous delivery time, and their ability to penetrate deeply into enemy territory without a prior assault on the enemy's borders, they seem to have made the territory of the sovereign state permeable in a way never before encountered in human history.[25]

These weapons have not yet been used on the scale imagined here; rather, the great nuclear powers have built their foreign policies on the threat to use them in the event of certain kinds of behavior by their opponents. As long as they are not used and their use is merely threatened, one evidently cannot argue that the basis of sovereignty actually has been destroyed. Indeed, deterrence theory may be viewed as the embodiment of the Westphalian approach to order stretched to its logical conclusion, for it says something like "I will leave you to your sovereign freedom so long as you do the same toward me, but should you, in your freedom, take some action unacceptable to me (as I define it), then I shall see to it that we are both destroyed, as well as the global system of order itself."

Although such reasoning may be the logical end result of the Westphalian approach, it cannot also be said to be the logical result of what we generally mean by the art of politics. That refers to the process of advancing and protecting certain social values among conflicting ones, and it is ordinarily practiced through competing, bargaining, and using one's capabilities to achieve desired ends. Traditionally, politics has included at the international level, though far less acceptably at the level of domestic society, the use of force to achieve policies that cannot be had by peaceful means. Warfare has not traditionally guaranteed that one's own values would be advanced and one's opponent's overthrown, but it has provided at least the gamble that such might be the outcome. But, as antinuclear arguments have noted for several decades now, it is difficult if not impossible to imagine what kinds of social values would survive, let alone be protected or advanced, in an all-out nuclear exchange. For this reason we need to explore the likelihood that deterrence politics, at least as currently practiced by the superpowers, may be profoundly antipolitical, whatever their logic in Westphalian terms.

But not only the nuclear issue strains Westphalian security assumptions today in novel ways. In contemporary insurgency and revolution, we see the challenge to the sovereign from within. When the aim of such movements is simply the replacement of one set of spokesmen for the sovereign with another, the traditional normative system is generally well equipped to deal with the matter. International law provides a fair measure of restraints against intervention by outside actors, seeking to isolate the action until it is resolved, and is designed to ensure that the winning side will be able to act in a sovereign capacity as soon as possible.

But a second kind of insurgency has emerged in the twentieth century that is less easily addressed by the traditional body of law. It unites, or appears to unite, a revolutionary group with an external agent, creating what has variously been seen as a fifth column, an international communist conspiracy, neoimperialistic counterrevolution, and the like. The common denominator is the clouding of the line between the domestic and the international conflict. What the Westphalian order once succeeded in sealing off and containing outside the scope of international conflict has tended to grow inexorably from a local to an international eruption of widespread violence.

A third type of insurgency is that of the secessionist group. What may be novel here for our time is the extent of such movements. Clearly, Westphalia is able to meet secessions to the extent that they are merely the attempted creation of new sovereign actors, but the sociological implications of at least some of these efforts seem an attack upon the nature of the large, multi-ethnic sovereign state as it has developed in the past.

Within this century, too, the laissez-faire underpinnings of Westphalia have begun to look increasingly inadequate as the basis for addressing other important issues. The developments that help to define these center about the increasing crowding of the planet with the closing of the world frontier and more or less simultaneously the growing interdependence of states.[26] The limitless potential abundance presupposed by both Locke and Grotius is now all too evidently limited and finite, a condition exacerbated by the enormous pressures on the biosphere created by the modern industrial state. Industrialization itself has closed the frontier beyond which, in the past, there always seemed to be abundant resources for all. The industrial process has entailed such an enormous increase in the use of fossil fuels that the once seemingly limitless supply of some is now being rapidly exhausted. We are forced to come to terms, for the first time in human history, with the finiteness of the earth's resources.

Moreover, industrialization has ravaged the environment in the form of pollution of the air and water, a phenomenon that has begun to make clear, also for the first time, humanity's awesome ability to have an impact on the life chain in devastating ways. From any kind of Olympian view of the earth over the past century, one can see that the laissez-faire approach to social organization has allowed enormous energies of individual actors to be unleashed, but that their activities have been largely heedless of each other and of the inevitable relationship they have to the nonhuman components of the earth.

Awareness of these kinds of issues generally came within advanced industrial states earlier than it did among them. Since early in this century, most such civil societies began enacting legislation designed to curb some of the worst depredations of unrestrained entrepreneurship. As a result, most governments of modern industrial states now intervene much more powerfully in the private sector than they once did, to establish standards and enforce them—all as the result of the reaction against an untrammeled laissez-faire. At the international level, such a reaction has not proceeded nearly so far, if it has any more than begun. At present the most serious problems raised by the workings of an international system of laissez-faire seem not to have been addressed by effective global centers of regulation and control.

We also have begun to see new, international dimensions to the problems of human rights and human welfare. What is new here is the perception that many of these issues now ought to be dealt with by the international normative order even though traditionally they have been excluded from it. They ought to be included, according to this reasoning, for the very simple reason that only by addressing them with effective power and authority at a global level will they be alleviated. Sovereigns, after all, have proved to be the principal violators of the rights of individuals; if such practice is to stop, then it is sovereigns who must be restrained, and from beyond the state if forces within it cannot do the job.

No doubt many factors have contributed to this perception, but among the most important are the unparalleled (at least in modern times) atrocities governments have engaged in during this century, a fact made possible by the more ruthless, totalitarian control of populations today than in the past; those facts, combined with the speed and global reach of modern communication, have meant that it is becoming possible to mobilize effective action against such behavior from abroad in ways that were not possible much before this century. By the mid-nineteenth century, legal positivism had developed to the point that the dualism of international and national legal systems was generally accepted as adequate to social order. Individuals could be viewed as subject solely to state sovereigns when authoritative structures beyond the state were not developed to a point that international control over sovereign treatment of their subjects could be effective. However risky, that condition could be tolerated so long as sovereigns generally could be counted upon to grant a measure of respect to those they ruled. The normative acceptability, in other words, of much sovereign treatment of the individual may have inhibited the growth of universally enforceable standards to which sovereigns were subject.

But by the 1940s, important actors in the international system asserted for the first time the need to bring egregious sovereign violators of human rights within the purview of community standards. The Nuremberg and Tokyo tribunals were the first, dramatic steps in that process, which continues to the present day. That development has necessarily confronted legal positivism with the ancient tradition of natural law, a confrontation that has not in itself confounded the Westphalian approach to order—Grotius and other international lawyers since his time have drawn upon the natural law tradition—although it has raised questions about the Westphalian approach that may or may not prove to be fundamental.

These developments, in turn, have helped foster the contemporary global concern with distributive justice. Not until recent decades have many of the poorest segments of the globe's population been enfranchised as their states have achieved sovereignty; hence, their values and demands against an international economic system that appears to them unjust have come to be expressed within the Westphalian framework. The growth of industrialization and economic interdependence has focused attention, as a result, on the problems of economic inequality whereas the Westphalian approach itself has, in general, not proved capable of addressing those problems effectively. Laissez-faire, whether for individuals or sovereigns, must rely on conscience rather than coercion if those who have most of the wealth are to prove willing to share it with those who have little. In this respect, the current debate between the haves and the have-nots over a new international economic order may be viewed as the opening salvo at the global level to create an international welfare state or society.

Intertwined with several of these growing contradictions of our time is the issue of the shifting locus of political loyalty in the contemporary world. Perhaps as much or more congruity is really present today than ever before between group loyalty and self-government across the globe; yet there appear to be at least two characteristic features about the nature of disaffection and opposition to political authority at present, and these are so pronounced that they constitute a novel kind of challenge to the state system itself.

The first flows from the revolutionary nature of the concept of self-determination. Since the Paris peace settlement after World War I, self-determination has risen in an irresistible tide, sweeping empires away as nation after nation has achieved sovereign statehood. The force of nationalism has seemed an almost infinitely fragmenting process as a result, energizing secessionist movements in many parts of the non-European world, and from them, violence and repression on the part of challenged governments. Nor has Europe itself, the birthplace of the nation-state, proved immune from this process, as is attested to by renewed violence in Northern Ireland, in the Basque regions of Spain, in Quebec separatism, even in incipient black nationalism within the United States (the latter two regions being "European" in everything but geography). Such movements are evidently strengthened by elements that would not have been available to them in the past, namely, the widely shared value favoring self-determination itself, which makes it difficult especially for governments regarded as democratic to resist the claims of their own minorities; the ease of access to the information media available to the leadership of such groups; the resulting ability to enlist support, including financial support, from sympathizers around the world;[27] and the availability in our time of "terroristic" methods for advancing the cause of such groups.

The second characteristic feature of minority dissidence today is in some respects almost antinationalistic, at least in the traditional sense, and stems from the kind of cosmopolitanism and class consciousness that has accompanied the enormous acceleration in communication. It is still too amorphous a phenomenon to allow precise definition, but it is to be seen in a variety of examples: black separatism in North America, which is fueled not merely by black pride (which

owes a debt to the independence movement in Africa) but by iden-
tification with poor nonwhite populations throughout the third world;
French separatism in Canada, which arises with the awareness of many
Quebecois of their inferior cultural status within their own country;
the disaffection of usually well-educated and affluent members of
advanced industrial societies from the acquisitive and militaristic values
that characterize the role of those societies in the world; the re-
emergence of at least feeble signs of incipient pluralism through
antigovernmental dissent and organization within some of the most
highly centralized and authoritarian societies in the world. And no
doubt all of these developments have been encouraged by the perceived
emergence in this century of a world class political elite that has been
largely Europeanized, is basically conservative, and is more fascinated
with maintaining and expanding its own powers than with achieving
social justice. A common thread through most of these phenomena
is that they do not appear to seek something so simple (in Westphalian
terms) as secession and the creation of new sovereign states. Rather,
their dissent results from what are seen as certain negative features
of the state or of the very state system. Are these only ephemeral
developments or important ones? Can they be expected to run their
course without serious impact on the Westphalian system or will they
alter it in fundamental ways?

Perhaps the phenomenon just described can be most sensibly related
to an additional development that is characteristic of our time and
important in its own right, that of the growth of both private and
public international organizations. Whether we refer to the creation
and development of international government organizations (IGOs),
international nongovernmental organizations (INGOs), or transnational corporations (TNCs), to use the usual terminology, the increase
in the numbers and activities of such organizations in recent decades
has been dramatic.[28] That alone does not of course tell us much about
the real impact of international organization on the world today; nor
should it be read as proof of the weakening of the Westphalian system,
particularly not when many, although not all, such organizations are
clearly the product of the Westphalian mode.

Yet some of the developments in this area look as if they would
or could transform the system. That may seem to be most obviously
true of those intergovernmental arrangements whose overt purpose
is to integrate certain governmental functions at a suprastate level,
as, for example, in the European communities. Nonetheless, it is still
an open question whether or not such regional integrative movements
will count themselves successful once they have created a single
superstate where several states once existed. If so, then Westphalia
itself will not have been transformed but merely rearranged with
regard to a few of its component actors, the superstates now major
powers, perhaps, in a revived version of a balance of power system.

The activities of multinational enterprises also may seem evidence of the growing inability today for the sovereign state to control and regulate effectively economic activities within the private sector. If that is so, then one of the traditional rationales for modern sovereignty is undermined. Moreover, we may find on closer examination that even those intergovernmental organizations that look to be the hand-maidens of the Westphalian system, in the sense that they seem the clear instruments of sovereign states, may be having a more complex impact than that on the contemporary normative order.

The novel security challenges and the need to control more effectively the uses of violence, efforts to ameliorate economic disparities at the global level, the promotion of human rights, the threats to the very biosphere in which we live through the practices of modern industrial society—all these are problems that in our time need to be addressed by world order values if we are to survive and flourish.[29] Do we have the social resources at our command, the imagination and the will to make the better possibilities prevail over the worst?

NOTES

1. See, for example, Luigi Albertini, *The Origins of the War of 1914*, trans. and ed. Isabella M. Massey (London: Oxford University Press, 1952); Sidney Bradshaw Fay, *The Origins of the World War*, 2d ed. rev. (New York: Free Press, 1966); D. F. Fleming, *The Origins and Legacies of World War I* (Garden City, N.Y.: Doubleday, 1968); Richard Langhorne, *The Collapse of the Concert of Europe* (London: Macmillan, 1981).

2. Conservative estimates are that 10 million died and an additional 20 million were wounded in the war, although this figure does not include the large number of civilian deaths in the immediate postwar period from epidemics and starvation.

3. From Wilson's address to the U.S. Senate on January 22, 1917. *The Papers of Woodrow Wilson*, ed. Arthur S. Link (Princeton, N.J.: Princeton University Press, 1982), vol. 40, p. 536.

4. Nor do I want to suggest that an international normative system based rigidly on self-help would have been in any way a realistic alternative by the twentieth century, but wish to demonstrate merely that, in principle, it might have produced less violence than the mixed system, containing some elements of self-help and some of community obligation, that prevailed in 1914. An extreme self-help system assumes the absence of *any* of the features and characteristics of an organized society, and as such, is difficult to imagine in any concatenation of interacting units. No doubt it is the only plausible strategy for the lone individual marooned on a desert island or for larger social groups completely isolated from any other, but for most of recorded history, such situations have been rare. Thus it is little wonder that serious theorists of social order are always inclined to discover both practical and moral limitations on the unrestricted practice of self-help.

5. Included among these were Maximilien de Béthune, Duc de Sully (1559–1641); Emeric Crucé (1590–1648); William Penn (1644–1718); and Charles Irénée Castel, Abbé de Saint-Pierre (1658–1743). Harold K. Jacobson

has described the communal alternatives posited by these and other writers in a way that makes clear their commonality in what today we should describe as the collective security principle: "They all would have forbade organization members to use military force, at least in Europe, except when authorized by the common institution. . . . [M]ilitary force should be employed to ensure compliance with at least some common decisions, particularly those relating to disputes. . . . Most of the plans relied on military units under the control of organization members, but some . . . provided that the organization would have military units assigned to it" (*Networks of Interdependence* [New York: Alfred A. Knopf, 1979], pp. 28–29). For a fuller discussion of these and other plans for collective maintenance of the peace, see Sylvester John Hemleben, *Plans for World Peace Through Six Centuries* (Chicago: University of Chicago Press, 1943).

6. The adjective *unrealistic* is simply a label for an idea that has not notably influenced relevant behavior; it provides no reasons for that failure. In broadest terms, we can say that the reasons why these peace plans had so little success in earlier centuries lay in the fact that the only actors in international society capable of bringing them into being, the sovereign states, remained unpersuaded that they had a greater interest in subordinating their own freedom of choice, i.e., their sovereignty, to the common good than they did in continuing to go largely their own way, cooperating with fellow sovereigns when that seemed appropriate and fighting with them when that seemed the most likely way to advance their own interests. Underlying that stance was the sovereigns' general conclusion that the costs of going it alone—principally the risks in ending up a loser in a war—were far outweighed by the benefits of freedom from control by some distant authority.

7. League of Nations Covenant, Article 16.

8. Ibid., Article 21. For a discussion of the political context at Versailles that underlay the drafting of this and other provisions of the Covenant, see Stephen S. Goodspeed, *The Nature and Function of International Organization*, 2d. ed. (New York: Oxford University Press, 1967), pp. 31–33.

9. For a fuller explanation of the pulls of regionalism within the framework of the League's collective security system, see Lynn H. Miller, *Organizing Mankind* (Boston: Holbrook Press, 1972), Chapter 2.

10. Among the most notable of these were the resolution of a Turkish-Iraqi border dispute in the years 1924–1926, conflicts between Greece and Bulgaria in 1925–1917, and between Poland and Lithuania in 1927. For a full account, see F. P. Walters, *A History of the League of Nations* (Oxford: Oxford University Press, 1964), pp. 305–315, 398–400; and E. H. Carr, *International Relations Since the Peace Treaties* (London: Macmillan, 1937), pp. 103–108.

11. See, for example, Nicholas J. Spykman, *The Geography of the Peace* (New York: Harcourt, Brace, 1944); E. H. Carr, *The Twenty Years' Crisis, 1919–1939* (London: Macmillan, 1946); and Frederick L. Schuman, "International Ideals and the National Interest," *Annals of the American Academy of Political and Social Science* 280 (March 1952):27–36.

12. Ironically, virtually the last act of a disintegrating League of Nations was to expel the Soviet Union, on December 14, 1939, from membership—the only state ever so treated—for its attack on Finland. That action was a symbolic reflection of the wariness with which the Western democracies, in particular, had regarded the USSR since its inception. Britain, France, and the United States all had violated nonintervention standards when they

introduced troops into Russian territory in 1918–1920 to try to prevent the success of the Soviet revolution. See George F. Kennan, *Russia and the West Under Lenin and Stalin* (Boston: Little, Brown, 1961). Some have viewed this deep-seated mutual distrust by traditional powers and Russian Communists as, in effect, an international civil war, beginning in the Soviet revolution in 1917 and continuing to the present day. See, for example, Arno J. Mayer, *Politics and Diplomacy of Peacemaking* (New York: Alfred A. Knopf, 1967).

13. In the case of the Soviet Union, the elite's revisionist demands on the international order probably were more apparent to traditional governments than real in Soviet eyes, a fact explained by a somewhat irrational fear of the "Red menace" in the West and by extrapolation from the clearly revisionist intentions of the Soviets regarding the construction of Russian society. Needless to say, the question of the extent of the Soviet Union's revisionist goals for the non-Soviet world is still hotly debated some sixty-five years after the revolution in Russia, defining, as it does, the dimensions of the cold war, making it probably the greatest controversy in the international political arena of the twentieth century.

14. The quotation is from Article 22, paragraph 1 of the Covenant. The entire article spells out the concept of the mandates system and is particularly expressive of the Europe-centered attitudes and values regarding colonialism of its time. The reader who reflects on the evident quaintness of its tone today will have noted an example of how dominant world order values indeed do change over time.

15. Parts of the British Empire already had become independent sovereign states within the British Commonwealth of Nations, which was created in the Statute of Westminster in 1931. Many other British colonies would take this route in the post–World War II period, which makes clear in retrospect that a model already existed in the interwar period, whether British officials then saw it consistently as such or not, that showed the way to the dismemberment of empire and the creation of new sovereignties without totally severing the links that had developed through the colonial period. This orderly effort at creating sovereign states from British colonies can be traced to the British North America Act of 1867, which became the constitution of the independent "Dominion" of Canada.

16. This is the frequent contention of the revisionist school of cold war historians in the West, who tend to reverse the orthodox U.S. interpretation that views this country as peaceful and satisfied, acting only in the international sphere to counter an unacceptable expansionism on the part of the Soviet Union or China. Revisionists generally see the United States as the initiator of action in this period, and their Communist enemies as behaving more defensively. See, for example, Gabriel Kolko, *The Politics of War* (New York: Random House, 1968), and *The Roots of American Foreign Policy* (Boston: Beacon Press, 1969); William Appleman Williams, *The Tragedy of American Diplomacy* (New York: Delta Books, 1962); and Gar Alperovitz, *Atomic Diplomacy: Hiroshima and Potsdam* (New York: Simon and Schuster, 1965).

17. One need only recall the Nazis' "final solution" to the "Jewish problem" in territories they occupied for the most horrifying suggestion.

18. The Group of 77 is the name still used by the non-European and for the most part formerly colonized nations whose number today has risen to about 120, that first caucused as an economic bloc at the first UN Conference on Trade and Development (UNCTAD) in 1964. They have maintained a

fair measure of unity and, since 1973, have called for the establishment of a New International Economic Order (NIEO).

19. This transformation in the status of important state actors has been manifest to most students of international politics in recent decades, although the writings of Morton A. Kaplan pioneered in abstracting and clarifying the basic behavioral and normative requirements of the shift from a balance of power to a loosely bipolar world. For one depiction of those models (as well as other, hypothetical model sytems) see his "Constitutional Structures and Processes in the International Arena," in *The Future of the International Legal Order*, ed. Richard A. Falk and Cyril E. Black, vol. 1, *Trends and Patterns* (Princeton, N.J.: Princeton University Press, 1969), pp. 155–182.

20. Such views generally were tempered later in the cold war period as nonalignment grew, and as the early perception of monolithic loyalties within East-West power blocs was seen to be a myth, particularly after the People's Republic of China parted company from the Soviet Union. Even so, the Reagan reaction in the United States largely embodied a return to cold war primitivism, two decades and more after the early virulence of the cold war had been dissipating fairly steadily. See, for evidence, President Reagan's reference to the Soviets as "the embodiment of evil."

21. Henry Kissinger, *White House Years* (Boston: Little, Brown, 1979). For an incisive review of this first volume of Kissinger's memoirs and an analysis of his foreign policy, see Stanley Hoffmann, "The Case of Dr. Kissinger," *New York Review of Books* 27, 19 (December 6, 1979):14–29. The second volume of the Kissinger memoirs is entitled *Years of Upheaval* (Boston: Little, Brown, 1982).

22. Kissinger's lack of interest in international economic matters is apparent in the comparatively miniscule attention he devotes to them in the two volumes of his memoirs.

23. Kissinger's dissertation on Metternich was published under the title *A World Restored: Metternich, Castlereagh and the Problem of Peace, 1812-22* (Boston: Houghton Mifflin, 1957).

24. See Chapter 2, especially note 7.

25. See John Herz, *International Politics in the Atomic Age* (New York: Columbia University Press, Columbia Paperback Edition, 1962), especially Chapters 2–3, 7–8.

26. This development reminds us of the much-debated significance of the closing of the American frontier at the end of the nineteenth century, a debate stimulated by Frederick Jackson Turner's famous essay, "The Significance of the Frontier in American History." Reprinted, with commentary, in *The Turner Thesis*, in the series, *Problems in American Civilization* (Boston: D.C. Heath, 1956). Turner ascribed many of the characteristic ideas and values of the American democratic experience over several centuries to the influence of the Westward-moving frontier, an historical condition that had just ended when he wrote, with, he presumed, far-reaching consequences for future American development. See Chapter 8 of this book.

27. For example, certain groups among the Irish community in the United States have given strong backing to the anti-British cause in Northern Ireland in recent years.

28. On the eve of World War I, there were about 50 intergovernmental organizations; by the outbreak of World War II, about 80; by the 1970s, between 250 and 300. Nongovernmental organizations began to appear in

the nineteenth century. By World War I, there were approxin
World War II more than double that number, and by the 197(
Not until the 1960s did it become common, because of the grea.
in corporate activity worldwide, to use the newly coined terms *transnan.*
or *multinational* corporations to refer to the actors involved in that phenomenon.
See Jacobson, *Networks of Interdependence*, pp. 10–11.

29. These are essentially the same problem areas that the World Order
Models Project of the Institute for World Order, Inc., has placed at the top
of its agenda demanding greater worldwide normative attention. See the
editor's introduction to Saul H. Mendlovitz, ed., *On the Creation of a Just World
Order* (New York: Free Press, 1975).

4
Power and Values
in World Society

No change of system or machinery can . . . secure that men live
up to their principles. What it can do is to establish their social
order upon principles to which, if they please, they can live up
and not live down. It cannot control their actions. It can offer
them an end on which to fix their minds. And, as their minds
are, so in the long run and with exceptions, their practical activity
will be.

—R. H. Tawney, *The Acquisitive Society*

Our task is to explore some of the possible directions in which
the world may be heading in the near future, as well as the ways in
which its course may be directed by intelligent human action. We
cannot usefully begin, however, without first clarifying two fundamental
aspects of the human condition in all times and places, both of which
are implied in the previous sentence. These can be given a variety
of labels, such as those that make distinctions in ethics between the
is and the *ought;* in philosophy between the *real* world of the physical
universe and the *ideal* realm of human thought; in religion between
the *material* and the *spiritual* sides of our existence, and so on. In the
study of world politics, it is often useful to describe this dialectical
distinction in terms of *power* as opposed to *normative* considerations
of the issues.

This linking of apparent opposites is in fact a basic and recurrent
theme in the whole history of human thought simply because these
dichotomies arise from the very stuff of every human life. We are
indeed physical, material creatures, part of a substantial universe that
we can experience, however limitedly, through our senses. Our basic
needs are physical, and these must be satisfied if we are to live. But
we also possess minds that let us know, or try to know, the cosmos

through our ideas and imaginations, minds that help us link the disparate, chaotic experiences of our senses into coherent patterns that "explain" them in ways that are more or less satisfactory to us. Without ideas, the physical universe would be largely formless, for ideas, and ideas alone, bring us a sense of order out of chaos. Ideas permit us to master, to the extent we can, the material universe, and so the link between the ideal and the real is critical to our knowledge.

POLITICS: POWER AND NORMATIVE ORIENTATIONS

Nowhere is this more apparent than in the political dimension of our lives. Politics is "about" the exercise of power and control over human societies to further specific social values or ideals. Our lives assume a political dimension only with the wedding of capability (power) and value (normative) factors relevant to human society. The articulation of any social value is the attempt to legitimize the quest for power; conversely, the will to power must be accompanied by the articulation of a social value, or set of values, if it is to assume a political quality. When we say that certain political ideals are powerful, we mean that they have succeeded in mobilizing substantial numbers of people to seek to advance them by achieving the means to implement them in society.

The burglar who survives by robbing people's homes undoubtedly wields a kind of power over the physical universe—as long as he is not caught—but his power is outside the political process since he has not articulated any social purpose for his actions. Conversely, the ascetic hermit who withdraws to a cave may live in considerable harmony with his own ideals by making the choice not to interact with the material world, including other human beings, around him. Yet his withdrawal also removes him from the political process because he has left the dimension of power over others behind him. However, as soon as either of these individuals incorporates the missing dimension in his life, he begins to move into the political realm. So we may imagine that the burglar justifies his theft on grounds that, say, the political institutions of his society are unjust to men like himself, forcing him to steal. To the extent he can persuade others to follow his own example, he may become part of a political force in which his idea is tested ever more widely within the society. The hermit, on the other hand, may persuade so many others to follow his ideals, whether intentionally or not, about how people ought to live, that eventually the world must take notice of them and respond in some way to the values they articulate.

So even though the distinction between the power and the normative dimensions is a clear one, they always coexist within the realm of politics. They are dichotomous features of human life, yet are inextricably linked, molding and directing each other. All political activity must encompass both dimensions, as must all political analysis. The interesting questions in the interpretation of international political phenomena always revolve about what is thought to be the correct mix of power and normative orientations.

A need exists today for analysis with a stronger sensitivity to normative factors than is typical in the study of international politics. This is so in a basic sense because ideas permit us to generalize and theorize about real-world phenomena, and therefore more attention to normative factors should deepen our understanding of the possibilities inherent in world political behavior today. But more particularly, the need exists to correct the dominance of power-oriented analysis in much of the literature of international politics in recent decades, a dominance that may have biased our understanding of the important trends and possibilities that are removed from a grasp of immediate, empirical reality.

REALISM VERSUS IDEALISM IN INTERNATIONAL POLITICS

In U.S. academic circles, a great debate began at about the time of World War II among students of international politics between so-called realists and those they labeled as utopians or idealists. By the 1950s, the realist critique had clearly triumphed; its victory proved so large that it dominated most of the analysis of international politics down to the present day.

Realists first got a hearing through their criticism of what was seen to be an overemphasis in much of the interwar period upon the kinds of ideas that ought to govern international relationships, most notably the Wilsonian vision of a League of Nations that would keep the peace through collective security. Realist criticism of Wilsonian thinking began by noting its strong emphasis on moral solutions to the world's problems that failed, according to this view, to take sufficient account of some unchanging realities about international politics, particularly the unwillingness of states, regardless of their formal commitments, to abdicate their time-honored ability to act freely and independently of one another as sovereigns. In simplest terms, the realist critique viewed the commitment to the new international normative standard as ephemeral, perhaps even insincere, given the unwillingness of states to forego the exercise of accustomed power. Adherence to the League Covenant amounted to little more than lip service to an ideal that did not move fundamentally important behavior in the same direction as the new standard.[1]

What was especially dangerous about this, according to the realists, was that the acceptance of these normative commitments at face value had amounted to wishful thinking and the triumph of an illusion, for it had lulled many into supposing solutions had been found to world problems through the stroke of a pen, when in fact the problems and the nation-states' responses to them had remained much the same as in the past. Throughout the League's existence, states had continued to be driven by the quest for power, which ensured continuing competition among them to advance their diverse interests, and that would sometimes result in the future, as in the past, in war.

The realists typically urged us to note that all states sought security for themselves, first and foremost, and that their most durable interests (a favorite term of realist analysis) therefore were those most closely tied to the facts of their physical place in the world. To take one characteristic example, a realist analysis of Soviet foreign policy in the aftermath of World War II was likely to argue that Russian geography long had induced its leaders to search for secure warm water ports, particularly in Eastern Europe and the Middle East, as a way of improving its strategic position in a world in which it had such limited access to the sea.[2] In this respect, the actions of the Soviet government were little different from what the tsars had long attempted; traditional Russian interests were what mattered regardless of who controlled the Russian state. Analysis of those interests had more explanatory power than, as an idealist interpretation might have assumed, such matters as the revisionist ideology of the Soviets, their presumed revolutionary fervor, or their suspicions of the motives of bourgeois states.

Undoubtedly, the realist critique was a healthy corrective to some of the more naive and optimistic expectations held by many people in the Western democracies, and perhaps especially in the United States,[3] in the earlier decades of this century. Realist interpretations triumphed when they did because they fell upon fertile ground: The leaders of the major revisionist powers between the wars appear to have been about as cynical in the pursuit of power and as devoid of socially acceptable values in that search as any in modern times. For them, the mix of power and normative considerations in their own careers contained overwhelmingly more of the former than the latter.

Even in a world whose leaders behaved more morally, we should be well advised to keep in mind the realists' most important lessons, among which are the following: (1) the leaders of any nation-state have a primary responsibility to provide it with security; it follows, therefore, that (2) they will perceive a duty to try to maintain or, if possible, enhance their own state's position vis-à-vis others through competition, diplomacy, and, when all else fails, the use of force; (3) all such sovereign leaders, whether their interests are revisionist or status quo in orientation, are certain to be conservative in the basic sense that they have a mutual interest in maintaining their individual states and collectively the state system; finally (4) state leaders are bound to advance value systems peculiar to their positions in the world, values that place extraordinary emphasis upon self-interest, and comparatively little upon obligations to those beyond the nation-state, or even to those within the state who do not share their statist outlook. Unquestionably these are important lessons precisely because they embody insights that explain many important facts about the continuing nature of international politics in our time. Any consideration of how to make a better world that ignores those lessons does so at its peril.

Yet it is just as important to recognize that the realist analysis does not provide absolute truths about the nature of international politics. There are no absolutes in this realm because of the fundamentally divergent nature of politics themselves. Sound political analysis must search for the correct mix of realist and idealist considerations, and the rightness of the mix will always be determined within a particular historical context and even then will vary with the analyst's own biases and purposes.

STATISM: THE REALIST BIAS

One of the clear biases of the realists is their (usually unstated) assumption that the traditional interests of states are also their unchanging interests and that the determination of what those interests are also changes little if at all over time. If neutrality for, say, France and Great Britain was a sensible policy for them in the Russo-Japanese War of 1904–1905 (even though France was an ally of Russia and Britain of Japan at the time), then neutrality presumably would remain in their interest in a comparable conflict in the future, regardless of any other normative considerations that might have arisen in the meantime.

An example used by one of the most influential writers of the realist school, Hans J. Morgenthau, illustrates the point. He cited the Soviet attack upon Finland in 1939 as presenting France and Great Britain with two issues, one he calls legal (and I term normative) and the other political, i.e., power (Morgenthau often *equates* the power factor with what he calls the political, as he does here, thereby relegating normative considerations to a kind of nonpolitical limbo). In his terms, the legal issue was whether or not the attack violated the Covenant of the League of Nations, which was easily answered in the affirmative, "for obviously the Soviet Union had done what was prohibited by the Covenant." The political issue entailed assessing the attack upon the interests of the two Western democracies, including what it would mean for "the future distribution of power" in Europe.

According to Morgenthau, Britain and France muddled the legal with the political considerations when they not only saw to it that the Soviet Union was expelled from the League (the appropriate legal response, evidently), but also planned to join Finland in the war against the Soviets, an action that was thwarted by Sweden's refusal to allow their troops to pass through Swedish territory on the way to Finland. Morgenthau concluded: "The policy of France and Great Britain was a classic example of legalism in that they allowed the answer to the legal question, legitimate within its sphere, to determine their political action. Instead of asking both questions, that of law and that of power, they asked only the question of law; and the answer they received could have no bearing on the issue that their very existence might have depended upon."[4]

It is assumed in this assessment that had the two countries asked the right political or power question, they would have known it was contrary to their interests to enter a war with the Soviet Union at the same time they were fighting Germany. That assumption seems to mean they would have seen that they could not win both contests and hence should not have entered the second one. But Morgenthau's conclusion tacitly ensures that what he calls the legal issue shall forever remain a trivial consideration in the world of international politics, for he has separated it from political considerations and thereby decreed its impotence. He seems to argue that it was acceptable for Britain and France to work to expel the Soviet Union from the League but that it was unacceptable for them to attempt the kinds of sanctions (i.e., the use of their power) called for by the Covenant to make the collective security system an effective police agent.

By the time of the Soviet attack on Finland, the reversion to traditional power politics through the use of military force may already have proceeded too far for the Western democracies reasonably to expect to succeed in supporting League principles. Yet their willingness even at that late date to try to take collective security action can be read as resulting from their own realistic assessment that their national interests now lay in opposing aggression, collectively, if possible. One of the interests their leaders may have come to see, however belatedly, was the creation of an effective security system; however, such a system could not have been regarded as a traditional interest, for traditionally the logic of Westphalia encouraged noninvolvement in other sovereigns' quarrels. It became a possibility only with the creation of the League. Had these two countries consistently used their capabilities to support collective security during the 1920s and 1930s, the legal issue would have been far less separable from that of power calculations in European capitals by 1939. A new normative factor would have mobilized effective power in a novel, useful way. Had that occurred, no rational Soviet leader would have been nearly so sanguine about the use of force against its small neighbor as was Stalin. The point is that nothing was preordained in nature to prevent that occurrence, although Morgenthau's interpretation comes very close to implying that something was.

STATIST VERSUS WORLD ORDER PERSPECTIVES

Morgenthau's analysis of the Finnish case is typical of the realist point of view. Implicit in his critique of the British-French decision is the assumption that one and only one standard exists for the evaluation of action in the international arena: that of whether or not it serves the interests of the particular nation-states under scrutiny. Leaving aside the question of the ambiguity involved in determining just what such an interest truly is, the realist approach always proceeds from the point of view of state actors, never from the standpoint that would regard states as subordinate units within the single, larger international community. What results is the inevitable bias of a particular level of analysis or point of view.[5]

Analysis that proceeds from a global perspective will produce different biases of its own, as my own critique of Morgenthau should show. The world outlook is essentially that of the space traveler who looks back upon the earth from a great distance. From such a viewpoint many detailed features of the globe's topography are invisible or blurred, the boundaries between states are nonexistent, and the main impression is that the various parts of the earth's surface form a harmonious whole. The foreign policy analyst in contrast is fixed firmly within the territory of a particular state, whose importance naturally looms largest for him. The more distant points on the globe's surface assume less importance for him than those close at hand. Unable to see the whole sphere, he will naturally see his own domain as central to the world.

It follows that those who take the world view are more open to the charge of idealism than are those who start from the foreign policy outlook of particular states. This results because the statist view is so much more strongly rooted in the concrete reality of our everyday experience, so much more attuned to physical nuance and detail than is the world view. Throughout human history, experience with one world has been minimal in the social sense; most of us live and die within a particular locality and only have occasion to grasp the larger whole imaginatively, if at all. Conversely, it is no accident that the world's greatest ethical and religious systems are strongly universalistic in their metaphysics, which is exactly what has stimulated the human imagination about what might or ought to be when we find ourselves living in an imperfect material world.

We need only consider for a moment the way in which the student of international affairs typically receives information about these matters to sense the ways in which realist perspectives far overbalance idealist or normative considerations. Virtually all that information comes through the news media. Characteristically, these media report the immediate, the particular, and the concrete events of international politics; they select as newsworthy those daily happenings that bring political groups into conflict rather than harmony (surely nothing is more newsworthy than the outbreak of a war, nothing less so than another day of peace between Manitobans and North Dakotans); and, regardless of their efforts at objectivity, their reports reflect the values of the society that produces them, almost always reinforcing the parochial at the expense of the global outlook. As a result, it is little wonder that most of us, including those who are well informed in the usual sense about world events, are inclined to regard the international arena as nothing but a jungle and therefore are discouraged from turning our minds toward the effort to improve it.

POWER AND LAW IN WORLD SOCIETY

In sum, a sensible regard for what is possible and preferable in the way of international conduct must always seek not the divorce, but the marriage, of some form of the ideal with the real or practical. We are quite accustomed to this kind of joining in the politics of vigorous and viable domestic societies; in fact, it is the relative success of that joining of the normative with the power dimension that makes them viable and vigorous. When the United States, for example, enacted far-reaching civil rights legislation during the 1960s, no intelligent observer supposed either that the laws were meaningless, in the sense that they would have no effect on real behavior of Americans or that they would make all behavior instantly conform to the new standard. What they correctly expected was that the power of the federal government would now be marshaled at least to nudge behavior into the directions specified in the legislation, changing attitudes in the process.

It may be argued that this example, drawn from a domestic rather than the international social order, is misleading. After all, the existence of a stronger normative cohesion is what chiefly separates a domestic polity from world society. True enough, but the difference is one of degree and not kind. Just as not all political behavior within a domestic society is controlled by the normative order, neither is all international behavior devoid of normative concerns. It is useful to think of all activity within both spheres, domestic and worldwide, as falling somewhere along a continuum that runs from the most extreme form of the exercise of raw power we can imagine at one pole to the most rigid kind of normative control at the other. Even though neither of these extremes actually exists in the world of human experience, certain thinkers have found it useful to imagine them for what they can teach us about the world we actually inhabit. The following two polar visions happen to have had profound effects on Western thought, although they are by no means the only such models that might have been selected from the intellectual storehouse of our inheritance.

Seventeenth-century English writer Thomas Hobbes imagined a time before humans formed civil societies, in which each individual was motivated by the mechanistic impulse to gain such power over nature as was necessary to survive. In that "state of nature," each person was necessarily at constant war with all other individuals in the battle for life, a condition so terrible that it made the lives of all "nasty, brutish, and short."[6] No evidence exists to suggest that Hobbes's state of nature is a true picture of any actual historical condition known to members of the species. It is even difficult to imagine it as a literal description of the condition of our prehuman ancestors, who must have cooperated with each other for their own survival, however primitive or instinctual such cooperation might appear to us today. It demonstrates, however, by painting the intolerable quality of such a state of things, why humans do *not* live in the power dimension alone. In their mutual relationships they must advance the kinds of values that permit them to live together in a more or less orderly way if they are to survive, not just randomly as individuals, but as a species.

The opposite extreme of total social order, entirely freed from considerations of power advantages, is at least vaguely known to Christians in the image of the Kingdom of Heaven. The first great Christian theologian, St. Augustine, related that vision to the temporal world in his work *The City of God*, in which he took the view that God was preparing through history two mystical cities, one of God and one of the devil. The duty of the Christian was to try to live so that he or she would enter the City of God—the perfect, ideal kingdom—and that meant avoidance of the corruption, the "unreality" of the imperfect physical world, that of the devil. While on earth, Christians could not expect the perfection of the City of God, but they could, through their devotion, try however imperfectly to emulate it.[7] From this great work, and from the Platonic idealism that had so influenced Augustine, grew the Western tradition of natural law. That tradition assumes the existence of ideal laws in nature that govern, or ought to govern, human relations on earth, it being our duty to discover those laws—principally through the use of our ability to reason—and try to live by them.

Today when we view global society as a whole, we naturally see that in terms of our continuum it seems much closer to the Hobbesian or power pole than it does to the Augustinian or normative pole. It displays more exercise of power politics than evidence of dependable legal order. This perception is no doubt accurate regardless of any criticisms we might have of realist analysis, in which the self-interest of the individual state can be seen as analogous to that of the individual man in Hobbes' state of nature. If we have not attained the City of God in our domestic societies, how much farther are we from that ideal state at the world level! Nonetheless, we are only *relatively* closer to the Hobbesian pole internationally than domestically, for international behavior is guided by normative concerns that remove it from the absolute state of nature, as our overview of Westphalian principles demonstrated, even though these are often less commanding and less obvious to the untrained eye than their domestic counterparts.

FORMAL GOVERNMENTAL AND INTERNATIONAL INSTITUTIONS

What can easily mislead the untrained eye is the apparent absence of governmental structures at the world level, when governments apparently go hand in hand with legal order inside every sovereign state. Governments are the channels through which flow social power and values, there to be stirred into a legitimate mix before flowing back as the dominant current over society. States have created such institutions as congresses, parliaments, supreme soviets, and the like and given them clear and accepted responsibilities for declaring what is the law of the particular society; they have created judges and other tribunals to assist in definitive rulings as to what constitutes the law in the face of conflicting claims by its subjects; and they have given executives and other heads of state the responsibility and the right to enforce it. Governments are the product of a legal system as well as its maker. They are what shape and sustain the legal order. They embody the sovereign's ability to command the members of society.[8]

We look about the international arena and see nothing comparable in the way of governmental structures. There are, it is true, in our day a number of international institutions that look a bit like the governmental structures of our domestic societies. For Americans, it is not hard to see a resemblance between the UN Security Council and General Assembly and the two houses of Congress. Perhaps we note too that the UN Secretary-General looks like the organization's chief executive, and the International Court of Justice sitting in The Hague a bit like a world supreme court.

But we rightly suspect that these comparisons are misleading. These international institutions do not seem truly governmental in the sense that they can command individuals to obey their orders. They do not simply represent the sovereign states of the world; they evidently embody the conflicting interests of those states, institutionalizing their traditional freedom to disagree with each other. They evidently have little more authority over states than each sovereign seems to submit to voluntarily. The World Court, for example, has no power of compulsory jurisdiction, but only hears cases that state governments volunteer to bring before it. And once the court decides such cases, it cannot turn to a world executive with a monopoly of police powers to enforce its decision. This, at least, is our conclusion when we, first, equate legal authority with a social process of subordination, in which the authority commands the subject to obey its decree, and second, identify such an arrangement as possible only where institutional structures exist to mark the hierarchical authority.

Yet this conclusion has taken us too far. We have forgotten that the pole of power and the pole of order are joined in the continuum of politics, internationally as well as domestically. We have fallen into the common error of supposing that the usual features of a domestic legal order are the necessary prerequisites for *any* legal order.[9] Few international institutions today have the power to command that is generally characteristic of domestic governments, but it does not follow that they are without any ability to persuade international actors, that they have no impact on the articulation and advancement of particular social values relevant to ordered international behavior. The extent of their ability to shape the international order varies with the situation. It is tested by the extent to which nation-states and other international actors act upon the directives expressed through the international institutions, directives to which the states themselves have contributed, of course.

Examples relating to three different international institutions help illustrate this point. For a number of years, the UN Security Council refused to recognize the unilateral independence of the white minority government of Rhodesia, which prevented universal suffrage in that formerly British colony and with it the inevitable coming to power of a black majority. On May 29, 1968, a unanimous Security Council called for mandatory economic sanctions against the white minority regime. Even though the United States was among those voting in favor of sanctions, the U.S. Congress in 1971 adopted the Byrd Amendment to permit the importation of Rhodesian chromium into the United States in clear violation of the UN sanctions. Other members of the United Nations repeatedly objected to this U.S. breach of sanctions and publicly condemned it, but they had no effective means at their disposal to coerce the United States into obeying the directive. What had looked like an authoritative action by the Security Council evidently was not truly governmental in its effect, for one important subject was able to ignore it with impunity.

That is the clearest point at which to leave the story for one bent on demonstrating that the Security Council does not have, in spite of some UN Charter provisions that suggest otherwise, truly governmental capability. But the picture gets somewhat muddled when we note that the Byrd Amendment was strongly opposed by some U.S. political groups, and a new president, Jimmy Carter, succeeded in getting Congress to repeal it. As a result, by March 1977, the U.S. law was once again in compliance with the Security Council directive. And did the Security Council's action succeed in its real purpose of bringing an end to Rhodesia's white minority rule? Certainly not in and of itself. In fact, a cynically realistic analysis would argue that black rule eventually came to Rhodesia (now Zimbabwe) because of the force of arms of the Patriotic Front, thereby proving once again the commanding role of force in such cases. A more normatively ordered interpretation might insist that the use of force in this instance should be seen in its relation to the legal directive of the Security Council; from this viewpoint, the Rhodesian Patriotic Front exercised a quasi-police power on behalf of the international community. The realist view is too simplistic—although easier to grasp because it is— whereas the normative analysis points toward the complex and often ambiguous interrelationship of forces in the world order process. If it cannot show that the Security Council behaved like a government in the usual sense, it at least suggests that it was not devoid of any governmental quality whatever in moving the situation toward its preferred outcome.

Some analysts have looked to the roles of what they call functional international organizations in our time for evidence of how quasi-governmental functions can develop at the world level when compliance is not likely to demand the kind of coercive force evident in the Rhodesian case.[10] A good example is one of the oldest of these, the Universal Postal Union, which for more than a hundred years has assured us that when a citizen of Japan sends a letter to a friend in Peru, the Peruvian post office will honor the Japanese stamp and deliver it to the correct address. That may not seem a very dramatic example of a governmental capability at the world level, although its importance becomes apparent when we think about the consequences if such a system were not in place today. Significantly, the Universal Postal Union was created once nineteenth-century communication increased to the point that a widely shared value favoring a dependable global arrangement had developed. Governments keep it operating because of the social need it serves.

The Universal Postal Union is by no means a unique example of a functional inter-governmental organization exercising truly governmental powers over societies, even if those powers are limited to particular areas of human life. Within the last few years, smallpox, that dread disease responsible for many of the plagues of earlier periods, has been eradicated throughout the globe, thanks mainly to the governmental power of the World Health Organization (WHO). That power consisted in an ability to monitor the locale and progress of the disease worldwide, to assist nation-states in providing necessary health and sanitation measures to control it, and so on—all on a scale beyond the reach of particular state governments. It was clearly in the interest of us all to see smallpox ended, and that interest became the basis for WHO's power to act.[11]

These examples from the UN Security Council, the Universal Postal Union, and the World Health Organization all suggest that governmental capability does not always and everywhere rest only with the formal governments of sovereign states. They should remind us too that the governmental process is more complex than we generally suppose, difficult to trace and hard to describe when we cannot fall back on the customary references to parliaments or presidents, which are only labels for the formal institutions of government, explaining nothing about its meaning or how it functions. How and where should we expect to find it, particularly in its informal guise? What is its place in the contemporary world order system?

GOVERNMENT AND THE SUPPORT OF SOCIAL ORDER

Consider the following: We are all accustomed to the place and function of traffic lights in modern cities. They are meant to serve social order by commanding cars to stop and go in patterns that ensure the safety of all, which is our common interest when we drive. Traffic lights may be seen as symbolic or institutional representations of the city government's formal power to command us in the common good. They stand for government in the sense that they represent a kind of socially legitimate power, one that we accept as useful. But what happens when, because of a malfunction of some kind, the traffic lights at a busy intersection suddenly fail? The symbol of government ceases to operate; yet we would not expect every semblance of social order there to break down as a result. The drivers of the cars approaching that intersection still have a mutual interest in their own safety. As a result, they almost certainly will begin to create an ordering, or quasi-governmental, system of their own, perhaps even without any verbal communication. We should expect such drivers at least to slow down when they see the traffic lights not functioning, and then proceed only when they deem it safe. Logically, each will defer to the driver who arrives at the intersection next before him, for if all drivers do that, none will be more than minimally inconvenienced, and a dependable stop-and-go system, clear to all, will be in place.

We should not regard such a system as ideal, partly because we might fear that some drivers will fail to abide by the etiquette or norm tacitly agreed to by most, and will, as if they have reverted to a state of nature, take advantage of some car's slowing to speed on through the intersection at risk to themselves and others. Yet common sense (i.e., perception of the mutual self-interest) will make the system work well enough at least as a temporary measure for everyone's safety.

The situation at a busy intersection is a clear example in which the self-interest of the individual (or person, tribe, nation-state, or other unit) coincides with the interests of the community as a whole. It is like the individual and common human interest in seeing smallpox eradicated. When this kind of clear and evident harmony exists between the self and the social interest, a functional governmental system is likely to develop. It need not be a formal system, though formalization no doubt helps to clarify it, and it need not rest upon an evident police power at the top; each subject's common sense recognition of its own self-interest induces its compliance.

Yet we have guessed that in the absence of an effective police power, symbolized by functioning traffic lights, some brash driver may bull his way through the intersection in disregard of the rights of others. It may not be very farfetched to see such a person as resembling the government of the United States when it violated the Rhodesian sanctions with regard to chromium. If we picture the type of driver most likely to behave antisocially at the intersection, we should probably expect our culprit to be, not a timid, grandmotherly type, but a virile young male, one that a psychologist might describe as unusually aggressive. To pursue the analogy (perhaps too far), we probably would not expect a small country whose traditional policy has been based upon the effort to get along well with its larger neighbors— say Finland or Burma—to violate a Security Council resolution of this kind. That role would far more likely fall to a great power with a habit of supposing it could generally call the shots in the world arena, particularly when it also doubted if the so-called community interest necessarily coincided with what some formal organization of the community claimed it to be. For such an individual or state the appearance of the policeman with a nightstick may be needed to compel obedience; short of that, should he decide to defer to the community standard, he will no doubt convince himself that he did so voluntarily and not because anyone else made him. Such are the ambiguities surrounding free choice and deference to the standards of the group in all aspects of our lives.

These analogies should remind us that we generally find it easier to obey the policeman's signal than to figure out our own interest in conforming to a tacit ordering arrangement when the formal symbol of government is absent. The policeman's presence eliminates the need for us to engage in analysis of our own interest compared to that of others; that analysis has, in effect, already been done, and we know the answer, as well as the consequences to ourselves if we fail to accept it. That is one reason why formalized, tangible governments are useful things. In the world order system, that kind of evidence of government almost never is present, and when it is, sovereign actors find that its bark is worse than its bite, for it can often be thwarted. The policeman (e.g., the Security Council of the United Nations) has no nightstick and no gun in his holster to enforce compliance. He must persuade us that we should adhere to the general social consensus of interest, and only to the extent that he is successful in shaping and directing recognizable patterns of social order will he assume a greater sense of legitimacy as an authoritative figure within the legal order. Until that happens, however, we will probably regard him as ineffectual and assume our compliance is freely given.

Wherever social values command behavior over time, government emerges, perhaps gradually and with enough behavioral variations to be invisible for a long initial period. Eventually, however, if the patterns persist, the likely end product will be defined and visible institutions: *governments* in the everyday sense of the word. A government is formed when the power available to those whose political values dominate a society is joined to authority, which is the formal grant of competence to wield that power in specified ways and for certain ends. This is nothing more than a particularized version of that continual duality within the social world of the power-oriented and the normative, and of the necessity of joining them to form the political—here the governmental—process.

THE CONGRUENCE OF POWER AND AUTHORITY

The greater the measure of congruence between political power and authority, the more we are inclined to regard the resulting government as legitimate. To the extent that one dimension dominates the other, governmental capability is weakened to the point that, as we approach either extreme, we eventually must regard the case as not governmental at all. Some familiar examples will illustrate these imbalances.

The Kellogg-Briand Pact of 1928, formally known as the Pact of Paris, condemned "recourse to war for the solution of international controversies." Although it was ratified by sixty-two nations, it stands as a classic example in international law of the creation of a specific authority (declaring the resort to war to be illegal) left essentially unattached to relevant power, for it provided no enforcement measures. As a result, its authority grew hollow and failed to shape behavior. Little more than ten years after its signing, most of the signatories were themselves embroiled in World War II. It assuredly did not govern international relations in any effective way. At the power end of the spectrum, when the United States intervened in the war in Vietnam in the 1960s, it did so without authorization by any formal institution of the international community and, as a result, could scarcely be regarded, from this perspective, as acting governmentally. Yet the United States clearly had the power to have a considerable impact on the political situation in Southeast Asia. In the one instance, authority without effective power and, in the other, effective power without authority both produced nongovernmental behavior within the world's legal system.

But preoccupation with extreme cases can make us forever blind to the quasi-governmental implications of much international activity that lies between them. In fact, even the above examples can be read as having implications that place them in the ambiguous middle ground between the extremes of power unrelated to authority and the reverse. When the Nazi war criminals were tried at Nuremberg at the end of World War II, one of the charges against them was that they had planned and initiated a war in violation of the international norm set forth in Kellogg-Briand.[12] The Nuremberg tribunal was patently in a position to enforce this interpretation of Nazi criminality, which is to say it began to align relevant power with the authority expressed in the 1928 treaty. Our sense of justice tells us that the creation of governmental capability should at least be evident to all who must submit to it. Therefore, we may argue that the relevant power should have been clearly in place when the authoritative standard was first expressed. We think that we are unfairly treated when a policeman appears at our neighborhood recreation center to arrest us for playing poker on Sunday, since we thought the old blue law that permitted him to do so had not been operative for years. Yet, like it or not, the slow and painful development of government in any emerging social system seems always to be asymmetrical and uneven and to deprive some people of the sense of fairness advanced legal systems attempt to honor.

In the Vietnam case, the official position of the United States justifying its intervention was that some actor with the capability had the right and responsibility to assist South Vietnam in its effort to repel aggression from beyond its borders. This view saw the Vietcong as having committed the illegal act that demanded the sanction of forcible resistance from some other sovereign if the collectivity of sovereigns embodied in the United Nations could not agree to do so. No doubt there were serious flaws in this argument—South Vietnam was not a sovereign and could be viewed as engaged in a civil war with its northern half, a condition that demanded nonintervention by outside powers according to agreed-upon normative standards— but U.S. spokesmen were at pains to articulate the normative implications of their behavior for world order.[13]

As both these cases illustrate, one of the frustrations in trying to understand the contemporary international legal order stems from the absence of those formal governmental authorities at the world level capable of telling us definitively whose interpretation of normative standards and behavior is right and whose is wrong. We must usually make that determination for ourselves, just as the spokesmen for sovereign states do. The situation in Vietnam in the 1960s was like that of two parties to a suit before a local court. We hear the attorneys' arguments for the plaintiff and the defendant, arguments that make very different yet plausible cases from the same set of facts. Then we find that after arguments are heard, no judge is present to make an authoritative decision. We spectators in the courtroom must decide the case, although we are hardly in a position to make our decision stick. Perhaps the moral authority of our collective voice will influence compliance, if we can find a collective voice, but there is also a strong possibility, in the absence of the judge and the coercive power of the state, that the guilty party will refuse to abide by our decision. In that case, a new mix of power and normative factors will flow out into the larger world to be assessed by any actors finding themselves in comparable situations in the future.

DEPENDABLE EXPECTATIONS OF PEACEFUL CHANGE

Individuals and groups are by no means perpetually in conflict with each other within the larger social order, for in many situations the perceived self-interest of the one coincides with that of others to the point that a common interest in identical or comparable behavior is clear to all. In such cases, it is possible to eliminate the threat of smallpox or to deliver the mail without notable coercion from a formal governmental authority. Such activities are in fact so noncontroversial, so evidently right and proper in all our minds, that we rightly regard them as nonpolitical matters even though some intergovernmental direction, through a World Health Organization or a Universal Postal Union, may be necessary to implement our common value.

We have little difficulty, on the other hand, in listing the kinds of issues that are likely to be highly charged politically, as least susceptible to this kind of functional international management. Our list would no doubt be headed by the military provocations across international boundaries that lead to war, since issues of war and peace are at the very heart of international politics. The problems of governing such war-threatening issues before they lead to dreadful costs in human lives are clearly much greater. Our experience in the twentieth century suggests that to be successful the effort to control large-scale outbreaks of violence internationally requires at least the following: first, agreement by virtually all actors in the international system on standards of conduct required by all; second, clear articulation of those standards, so that would-be violators and those who judge them will at least be clear about the normative implications of their actions; third, agreement on the kind and scale of sanctions appropriate to impose for various unlawful actions; and fourth, a demonstrable willingness to enforce adherence to the standards through the exercise of a police power.

The importance of these measures in the abstract is not particularly difficult to understand since in effect they summarize the requirements underlying effective police power at any level of society. Yet our experience with the League of Nations and the United Nations seems conclusive proof that as a world society we have only begun to grapple with the implications of an effective monopoly of authoritative force at some central level, that we dimly perceive the logic of the police power imperative, but are not yet prepared—thanks to the habitual thinking and values of centuries—to act effectively upon it. We have read Hobbes's description of the state of nature but either think that it is too grim a depiction of our place in the world or, more likely, are at a loss to know how to create a world order that will not do unacceptable violence to our treasured, pluralistic freedom of choice.

These problems are critically important for our future as a species, but even while we continue the effort to construct dependable police power to serve the international community, we need to recognize and look for support outside the realm of such formal activity as writing treaties, amending charters, or defining aggression. We need to try to understand how social groups come to develop peaceful interrelationships even where no formal agreements or institutions bind them.

For example, many, even neighboring, states have coexisted over long periods of time in relationships so peaceful that we have not the slightest realistic expectation that they might fall into war.[14] The situation of the United States and Canada is a good example, separated as they are by the world's longest undefended border. The relationship between the two was not always peaceful, and a fundamental difference in political allegiance has divided them from the beginning of their separate histories. Nor are their political and economic relations without conflict today, but no one seriously expects them to settle differences by the force of arms. A pioneering study of the process of social integration across national lines called this a model of a "pluralistic security-community," integrated to the point that there existed between the units "dependable expectations of peaceful change."[15]

By distinguishing such pluralistic communities from "amalgamated" ones, such as the fifty states of the United States, the authors helped us see that this fundamentally important characteristic of an integrated society—that its members coexist in peace—is not necessarily dependent upon union under a single, formal government. What is most important about the pluralistic community is that it has somehow produced effective informal government to ensure peaceful change without subordinating all the differences in values, culture, and the like that make the separate units distinctively free and independent. The most fundamental problem of international politics has been resolved without the hierarchical domination and control of the powerful over the weak.

The world unquestionably would be a better place in which to live if all the states that now exist could become a single, pluralistic security community. That would, by definition, eliminate the large-scale violence we know as war. Utopian? No doubt, for what we know of this process of community formation tells us that it is enormously complex and deeply rooted in a sense of shared historical experience, with all the possibilities for the development of similar values that implies. It cannot be duplicated in the laboratory or manipulated in the short run by a handful of people of good will. Still, many lessons are to be learned from the formation of particular security-communities that have application to the larger world.

PLURALISTIC INTEGRATION IN WESTERN EUROPE

One other such case is worth our attention, if only because of its dramatic move toward peaceful change and away from frequent armed conflict in a comparatively short time. Western Europe has been the site of numerous wars over the course of centuries, none more devastating or with greater reverberations globally than the two world wars of this century. At the root of each of these great conflicts lay Franco-German enmity, which itself had been fed by their war in 1870–1871 that led to the triumph of the German Empire and France's humiliating defeat. After World War I, a number of leaders began talking of the need for European unity, yet the traditional suspicions and fears dividing France and Germany continued to grow and deepen. Unity seemed an impossible dream. The best efforts of the visionaries were punily inadequate to stave off another general European war.

Amazingly, however, within a scant twenty or twenty-five years after the end of World War II, France and Germany had become the core of a recognizable security-community, so firmly in place that today no one seriously supposes that they or their neighbors within the European Community will again resort to arms to settle their differences. How did such a fundamental transformation take place within so short a time? The general answer is simply that "the time was ripe" for it, in the sense that huge numbers of Western Europeans, weary of the killing and the destruction, passionately desired an alternative to the war system and so were susceptible to novel ideas and policies designed to lead toward a preferable alternative. The widespread social upheaval produced by general war can have revolutionary effects by calling into question the traditional prejudices and values that have led to the general misery.

That still does not say much about the ways in which European integration came about and even less about its implications for the rest of the world. Among the factors that help explain this development, the following seem particularly important: First, the process of building today's European Community began with a very specific, functional agreement to create an integrated coal and steel industry for the core countries. Among the war-threatening issues dividing France and Germany, and threatening the Low Countries as well, were their competing interests for control of the important coal-producing regions of the Saar (now in Germany) and the iron ore of French Lorraine. It was not hard to see that if mining and processing operations could take place without regard for political boundaries, a more economical steel industry should result. Therefore, a West European coal and steel authority was created in a 1951 treaty for just that purpose.[16] The result was the almost immediate economic gain of all concerned within the industry, benefits that flowed throughout the industrial economies of the region, simultaneous with the effective elimination of a traditional source of political conflict among the powers in the region. That "pocketbook" success no doubt encouraged a habit of cooperation that seemed increasingly sensible from a strict self-interest point of view to growing numbers of French, Germans, Belgians, and their partners. As a result, within a decade a far more ambitious plan for the general integration of the economies of the participating states was created, the so-called Common Market.[17]

Second, the creation of the European Coal and Steel Community was itself made possible because the social disruption of the war brought to power in Germany and Italy elites that clearly rejected the imperialist, militarist values of those recently defeated. For the first time in living memory, all the states of the region were governed by parties that were committed to parliamentary democracy, to the goals of building societies at least moderately committed to social welfare, to reinvigorating their economies through considerable encouragement of private enterprise, and so on. They could "talk the same language" and seek out their common interests in ways their predecessors could not. Even so, they had to learn by trial and error that the functional route to integration was the least threatening to traditional attitudes, and therefore the pathway to success. In 1954, after a very emotional debate, the French National Assembly rejected a proposed treaty whose purpose was to create an integrated European Defense Community; so radical a change in traditional security arrangements raised fears in French minds of their army's domination by the Germans. This issue of high politics was too highly charged to find acceptance at the time.[18] In contrast, the integration of a basic industry could proceed without confronting traditional dogmas of national military power.

Third, the new elites had come to power because of the final defeat of the imperialist ethos in World War II. The virulent imperialism of the defeated powers had been eliminated, but just as important, it soon became increasingly clear to the victorious powers—among whom France, Britain, and the Netherlands still held sizable empires—that these traditional sources of their wealth and power could not be sustained indefinitely. They had to find alternatives for their continued economic growth, and the most plausible one was the creation of a common market that would thrive by eliminating all the barriers to trade and economic exchange that had separated their economies in the past.[19] Sweeping new economic and political imperatives served to encourage this break and, once the European Economic Community (EEC) was created, it helped advance the new economic imperatives that otherwise would have remained nothing more than visions.

Fourth, at every major step the integration of Western Europe proceeded at a formal level through treatymaking that served to clarify and advance agreement on the governmental capabilities acceptable to all. That is, integration has been a gradualist process, proceeding from the particular and the simplest to the most complex. It has also been a rational process, in the sense that participants have known basically what they were doing, submitting voluntarily to the new authority that they themselves progressively created. It has also been a process based upon the faith that not all problems had to be solved at once. Problems that looked intractable yesterday may be far less serious by tomorrow, if only because between yesterday and tomorrow a social process of cooperation has continued that may well change the context in which tomorrow's problems must be tackled. The process in short has been a model of the importance of attending to the normative dimension as a counter to the raw coercive power of integration through conquest. The widespread consent to creation of the European Community reflects the articulation of its goals within a pluralistic setting, with all that suggests regarding the diverse social values that have had to be accommodated.

Fifth, the pluralism of this enterprise is such that political differences of importance remain, and no doubt will continue, within member societies. Not every group within the area is happy, especially with the economic thrust of integration. Some, and particularly some socialist parties, oppose what they see as its discouragement of greater economic equality within their own populations and of its tendency to create neoimperial economic relationships with third world countries. In 1983, the British Labour Party pledged to take Britain out of the Community if it came to power, so there is no assurance that the Community's successes in marshaling and acting upon the general integrationist consensus will proceed unchallenged indefinitely into the future. But that possibility also reminds us of the worth of pluralism: If the consensus that makes unity possible erodes away, it is because important social values are being denied fulfillment. If a pluralistic community cannot accommodate diverse interests, it is no longer what it claims to be.

Finally, a security-community has been created in Western Europe without any overt effort to amalgamate its separate institutions of government. A majority of the members remain constitutional monarchies (and one, Luxembourg, is a grand duchy) while the rest are republics. Virtually all the traditional symbols of those varied systems remain in place, and the fact that they remain so visible does little more than hide from casual observation that in important, specified areas of social interest, not they, but the Community's central Authority has become sovereign. A Community institution, the European Parliament, is now in place and exemplifies the care and caution with which member states have moved to begin to build a centralized institution that may some day, but does not yet, have true legislative powers. The Parliament began life with its delegates all appointed by member governments, to meet at Strasbourg periodically to exchange views and arrive at recommendations they could make to their various legislative bodies. Since 1978, representatives have been popularly elected within their respective countries, although their powers remain largely recommendatory to date. By proceeding in this way, no time-honored threats to separate sovereignties can raise their heads, even though direct election of parliamentary delegates now clearly marks an effort to raise the consciousness of electorates as to what is taking place in Strasbourg, and to get them in the habit of viewing a Community-wide institution of this kind as right and natural.

Implied in several of these factors that have led to Western Europe's integration is the European impulse to form a more competitive unit, both economically and politically, in a world dominated by the super-powers. In such a world, the European self-interest in integration naturally became increasingly apparent. Yet it is important not to read this impulse as having produced, or as likely to produce, an Orwellian superstate of the traditional Westphalian sort, but grown immense and unaccountable. Integration has proceeded by protecting first the democratic pluralism of the region, which in itself is the most effective barrier one can imagine to the growth of a highly centralized and authoritarian superstate. But just as important, European integration is taking place, not in isolation from the rest of the world but with considerable openness. As North Americans in particular must be aware, their ties to Western Europe are no doubt greater and more complex at many levels today than at any time in the past, so much so that the peoples of both continents are now plausibly integrated in a pluralistic security-community, even though North America is not included in the Treaty of Rome.

In spite of periodic, ongoing conflicts over pocketbook issues, we must conclude that Europe's integration appears to be producing a set of political and social relationships that are largely unexplainable in Westphalian terms, something truly new under the sun.[20]

It would be naive to expect the West European model to apply fully to countries elsewhere in the world. For instance, its success may largely reflect the imperatives of advanced industrial capitalism; certainly, it is built upon two thousand years of a common European culture. But, whatever the criticisms of the Community's thrust or the problems that it still must face, it shows us at the very least that one of the most conflict-ridden regions of the world, long a source of infection in global international politics, can with vision, careful planning, and great sensitivity to the values of different groups be transformed into an area of peace. Not coincidentally, it has shown us in the process that our Westphalian views of sovereignty and separateness are becoming badly out of date.

NOTES

1. Much of the tone for the realist-idealist debate was set in an important book by E. H. Carr, *The Twenty-Years Crisis, 1919–1939* (London: Macmillan,

1939), which lucidly explored the implications of the idealist versus the materialist bent in a variety of human types and social settings relevant to international politics.

2. See ibid., Chapter 5, for a general realist critique. See also George F. Kennan, *Russia and the West Under Lenin and Stalin* (Boston: Little, Brown, 1960).

3. George F. Kennan criticized what he termed the "legalism-moralism" of U.S. foreign policy in an influential set of lectures published as *American Diplomacy, 1900–1950* (Chicago: University of Chicago Press, 1951). The theme of an ongoing, naive idealism in U.S. diplomacy is also the object of criticism in the writings of Stanley Hoffmann. See, for example, his *Gulliver's Troubles* (New York: McGraw-Hill, 1968) and *Primacy or World Order* (New York: McGraw-Hill, 1978).

4. Hans J. Morgenthau, *Politics Among Nations*, 4th ed. rev. (New York: Alfred A. Knopf, 1967), p. 12.

5. The importance of and intellectual considerations inherent in the level of analysis undertaken in international politics is explored in J. David Singer, "The Level-of-Analysis Problem in International Relations," in *The International System: Theoretical Essays*, ed. Klaus Knorr and Sidney Verba (Princeton, N.J.: Princeton University Press, 1969), pp. 77–92.

6. Thomas Hobbes, *Leviathan*, edited with an introduction by C. B. Macpherson (Harmondsworth: Penguin, 1968).

7. St. Augustine, *The City of God*, ed. Vernon J. Bourke (Garden City, N.Y.: Image Books, 1958). See especially the foreword by Etienne Gilson.

8. The assertion that "law is the command of the sovereign" is that of the leading English Positivist writer on the law of the nineteenth century, John Austin. His strong emphasis on law as a system of subordination greatly influenced his contemporaries and many other writers down to the present day. The Austinian outlook tends to denigrate international patterns of order, which so seldom conform to the conception of law acting upon subordinate subjects. Positivism is the jurisprudential philosophy that downplays or negates the place of natural law and thereby corresponds to the realist or materialist vision of politics more generally. For a brief discussion of Austin's work, see Charles G. Fenwick, *International Law*, 4th ed. (New York: Appleton-Century-Crofts, 1965), pp. 44–45.

9. See Richard A. Falk, "International Jurisdiction: Horizontal and Vertical Conceptions of Legal Order," *Temple Law Quarterly* 32, 3 (Spring 1959):295–320.

10. Functionalism constitutes one of the important theoretical explanations of how separate sovereigns become integrated over time. See David A. Mitrany, *The Progress of International Government* (New Haven, Conn.: Yale University Press, 1933), and *A Working Peace System* (Chicago: Quadrangle Books, 1966). For a clear interpretation of the functional approach, see Inis L. Claude, Jr., *Swords into Plowshares*, 4th ed. rev. (New York: Random House, 1971), Chapter 17.

11. Two perceptive analyses, written early in this century, of the potentialities for this kind of functional growth of government outside the traditional institutions of government still are instructive today: Paul S. Reinsch, *Public International Unions* (Boston: Ginn, 1911); and J. A. Salter, *Allied Shipping Control* (Oxford: Clarendon Press, 1921).

12. For a discussion of this and other issues at Nuremberg, see Quincy Wright, "The Law of the Nuremberg Trial," *American Journal of International Law* 41 (1947):38–72.

13. See, for example, John Norton Moore, *Law and the Indo-China War* (Princeton, N.J.: Princeton University Press, 1972), and Richard A. Falk, ed., *The Vietnam War and International Law* (Princeton, N.J.: Princeton University Press, 1968).

14. Neighboring states have the greatest potential capability for military conflict simply because of their proximity, as well as the greater likelihood that they may hold competing claims to the same territory and resources. Traditionally, most states widely separated from each other (except for great powers) have interacted so little that the fact that their relations have been peaceful has meant little to the student of peaceful change on the part of socially interacting units.

15. Karl W. Deutsch et al., *Political Community and the North Atlantic Area* (Princeton, N.J.: Princeton University Press, 1957).

16. The founding members of the European Coal and Steel Community (ECSC) were Belgium, the Federal Republic of Germany, France, Italy, Luxembourg, and the Netherlands. For a brief summary of the development, organization, and powers of the European Community from its beginnings in ECSC, see "The European Community," *The European Community and the Third World*, November 1977, Directorate-General for Information, Commission of the European Communities, Brussels, Belgium. Also see James Barber and Bruce Reed, eds., *European Community: Vision and Reality* (London: Croom Helm, 1973).

17. The Common Market (European Economic Community) was created by the Treaty of Rome, March 25, 1957. Among the most readable of the numerous studies of the integration process in Europe and its implications for the world is George Lichtheim, *The New Europe—Today and Tomorrow* (New York: Frederick A. Praeger, 1963).

18. For a brief discussion of the origins and purposes of the EDC proposal and the reasons for its failure, see Robert E. Osgood, *NATO: The Entangling Alliance* (Chicago: University of Chicago Press, 1962), pp. 35–36, 91–96.

19. Great Britain was the last of these imperialist powers to be persuaded of the new economic imperatives, and it refused to become an original member of the Common Market's Treaty of Rome in 1957 because of its special economic relationships with members of the Commonwealth. Eventually, those economic ties to its one-time colonies proved less compelling than the prospective gains from joining Europe. There followed a period in which British applications to the EEC were vetoed by France, and then finally, after DeGaulle left office, its application was accepted. The United Kingdom entered the EEC along with Denmark and Ireland in January 1973.

20. Throughout 1983 and much of 1984, the heads of member governments were unable to agree on relative budgetary payments from each for Community operations, a conflict that centered upon the expensive subsidization of Community farmers. The British government claimed that payment for the agricultural subsidy was inequitable, since most of those protected were continental farmers, and refused to pay its predetermined budgetary share.

5
Minimizing the Resort to Violence

The underpinnings of logic [which] served historically to justify resort to war as the lesser of several evils have shifted or . . . quite disappeared. Victory has been deprived of its historical meaning.

—C. Vann Woodward
Address to the American Historical Association, 1959

On June 12, 1982, one of the largest political rallies ever assembled took place in New York at the start of the United Nations Second Special Session on Disarmament. Some three quarters of a million people marched from UN headquarters on the East River to Central Park to express their opposition to the ever-increasing threat of nuclear weapons stockpiles and strategies. For hours they stood under pleasant skies listening to speakers describing the horrifying effects of nuclear blast on cities and the dangers of the nuclear policies adhered to by the superpowers. In spite of the nearly unimaginable grimness of the verbal pictures painted, an air of festivity pervaded the huge throng as demonstrators exulted in their zest for continuing life and their apparent sense that they could begin to change the world. Still, when the UN disarmament session ended several weeks later, it was generally described as disappointing at best, since none of the governmental delegations that mattered most had moved toward acceptance of arms control proposals that could begin to rid us of the nuclear threat. Once the hoopla of the disarmament rally had faded, nuclear arsenals and nuclear rhetoric continued to dot the landscape.

Intelligent political observers could explain why this outcome of the UN session was hardly unexpected and why we continue to see our governments proceed with business as usual in the development and deployment of nuclear weapons and delivery systems, even though these same observers must also know, as did those who demonstrated in New York, that the continuation of such policies leads us deeper and deeper into the most profound conundrum of global political life that humanity has ever had to face. The policies and the capabilities of a handful of governments confront those of us alive today with the prospect of our own extinction and what is unimaginably worse, with the possible end to all human life on earth. How have we arrived at a state in which we clearly face our own mass deaths as the result of actions designed to promote the exact opposite, our security? Why can we not cut through the mad illogic of our presumed security preparations even when we recognize that they have led us perilously close to the precipice?

NUCLEAR WEAPONS AND THE PERMEABLE STATE

The answers are to be found in the collision course that states are riding in the Westphalian international system as they have taken to themselves the unique and virtually limitless destructive power of nuclear technology. The atomic genie was first let out of the bottle in response to the Westphalian urge to win a particular military victory in World War II, although many of those best informed about its destructive potentialities from the beginning knew that it could not for long serve the traditional security interests of states. Rather, it undermined those interests by loosing a destructive force against which there never has been and almost surely never will be an adequate defense. The irony of the situation, particularly for Americans, is underlined in the plain words of a retired admiral of the U.S. Navy, Noel Gayler: "When we invented the atomic bomb, we invented the one thing that could place the United States at risk."[1] Even more poignant is the reported comment of Albert Einstein, whose great theoretical advances in physics made it possible to unlock the hidden power of the atom, to fellow scientist Linus Pauling not long before Einstein's death. The greatest mistake of his life, he told Pauling, was signing the letter to President Roosevelt that urged him to establish the Manhattan Project that led to the first atomic bomb.

To say that we are on a collision course is simply one way of calling attention to the nearly incredible paradox we have produced in behaving as if thermonuclear instruments of destruction were simply the most advanced instruments of our security available to the governments of nation-states. In fact, they cannot rationally be regarded as instruments of *protection* in any meaningful sense of the term, even though the structure and the ingrained modes of thought inherent in the West-phalian system have deluded millions of people and a number of governments into supposing that they did enhance our security, at least as long—and here was the incredible condition—as they were never used.

In Chapter 2 we saw that the rise of the Westphalian system more than three hundred years ago could be explained largely in terms of then novel developments that permitted the defense of large territorial units through the military technologies of the day more successfully than had been possible for the preceding millennium in Europe. The Middle Ages had been characterized by their walled towns and citadels, with little effective control outside them; the modern era produced nation-states whose sovereigns achieved that status principally through their ability to provide security—and thus enhance basic values—for large groups of people who gave them in return loyalty and fought to keep their homeland impermeable from without. Warfare retained a prominent place in that system simply because it remained the possible means of last resort for advancing or protecting socially important values of the community. In spite of the misery and the destruction warfare produced, it was regarded as an occasionally necessary undertaking for fundamentally political purposes, its socially disruptive consequences outweighed by its political necessity. In particular, it could justifiably be used to maintain the overall Westphalian arrangement so that it would function in the future more or less as it had in the past. Since, in theory at least, it joined the military power of the state to its important security values, warfare was, in Clausewitz's classic definition, truly the continuation of politics by other means.[2]

Yet when we examine the uses to which the nuclear arsenals of the superpowers might be put, we are at a loss to imagine how they could enhance or even protect the important political values of either society. The end result of even a brief nuclear exchange almost certainly would produce such damage, so many millions of deaths in both societies, as to make largely irrelevant the original reason for releasing those weapons. Each society would probably be so seriously dislocated that far more basic concerns than domination by a foreign power would immediately become all-important for the survivors. Both would have lost control over so many of the higher values whose enhancement is the sovereign's chief raison d'être as probably to render meaningless our prenuclear preoccupations with such notions as sovereignty, independence, and freedom. Instead, the living in both countries would face massive problems: how to dispose of the millions of dead human and animal bodies; what, if anything, could be done to assist the millions more suffering from radiation burns; how they themselves would long survive in an environment whose food and water supplies either had been poisoned or were now inaccessible, since much of the transportation and communication systems of both countries would have been destroyed.

A great many sober and realistic assessments have been made of the concrete impact of a general nuclear conflict on civilian populations and the continuation of social life generally.[3] All are chilling in their portrayal of human disaster on a scale no previous generation of humanity has ever had to imagine. All of them should be read, not simply for their scare value, but with the question in mind whether any conceivable political defeat by nonnuclear means in the hands of one's adversary could possibly be as repugnant as the defeat of human life, social order, and civilized values that would result from a major nuclear exchange.[4]

The fundamental fact of our nuclear technology is that such instruments of destruction cannot be defended against. In the language used by John Herz nearly twenty-five years ago, thermonuclear weapons put an end to the impermeability of the territorial state.[5] Since then, expansions of and refinements in the nuclear arsenals of the world have proceeded at an astounding pace, but the basic thrust of those developments has been to place their possessors at ever greater risk of intolerable destruction from their opponents than was the case several decades ago. In the 1950s, cities deep in the interior of North America or Siberia would have had some six or eight hours' warning time in the event of a nuclear attack from the other side. That forewarning would scarcely have left time for their defense, although some limited evacuation might have been possible. But since the advent of intercontinental ballistic missiles, that time has been cut to about fifteen minutes, making virtually any realistic security measures impossible. The nuclear arsenals of the superpowers remain what they have always been: instruments that, if used, most likely will result in the mutual suicide of those who wield them.

As we have understood ever since Leibniz defined sovereignty at the beginning of the modern period, a state that cannot provide its people and territory with a reasonable assurance of security from without scarcely deserves to be called sovereign. Perhaps the crowning irony of the nuclear issue is that those who possess the largest stockpiles of these mightiest of "weapons" are those who are most threatened by their use. The most powerful are also the most insecure and thus, in a fundamental sense, the weakest. That situation is so paradoxical that it undermines our traditional conception of military power.

Nor are the new questions of sovereign incapacity to protect confined to the nuclear actors themselves, for the destructive power of nuclear weapons is so great that it threatens nonnuclear sovereigns as well. A major nuclear exchange would be most devastating for those who engaged in it directly; yet the damage would not be confined to them. Radioactive fallout would poison vast areas of the globe whose governments had not participated at all in the decision to unleash the weapons, and that is a threat no sovereign in history ever had to face before the nuclear age. Even a low-level, or battlefield, use of nuclear weapons in Europe would render pointless the effort of several small European powers—Austria, Finland, Sweden, and Switzerland—to retain their sovereign capability through neutralism. Their locations would make some or all of them hapless victims of decisions over which they had no control.

In short, no matter where we turn to examine the implications of nuclear weapons, we see that, although they are the products of Westphalian approaches to security, they provide insecurity instead, and not "just" for people, but for the foundations upon which the international system itself is built.

Surely, some will argue, this view of our nuclear situation is too extreme. Even though we all may grant that a prolonged, or strategic, nuclear exchange could prove devastating if it occurred tomorrow, are there not alternatives, both to defend against a massive nuclear attack and to prevent an outbreak of hostilities at a tactical nuclear level from expanding into such a cataclysm? Adherents of both views clearly have their proponents, particularly within the governmental establishments of the nuclear powers, where they are in a position to convince millions of the truth of their visions. Their insistence upon viewing nuclear weapons not as profoundly inimical to the interests of their states, but merely as the most advanced, if troubling, instruments of statecraft, perpetuates when it does not accelerate the nuclear arms race. Can they be so wrong in their appraisals when their appraisals have commanded relevant governments since the dawn of the nuclear age?

Indeed they are, although it is the apparent "rightness" of their technical solutions (that is, their believability, given what all of us know, or think we know, about technology), combined with the "correctness" from the traditional, statist orientation of the premises that still imprison them, that has kept most of us blind to the tragic wrongness of their conclusions for the political welfare of the earth. Let us consider first the matter of the possibilities of defense against nuclear weapons.

STAR WARS TECHNOLOGY AND VALUE CHOICES

In the 1960s, both Soviet and U.S. planners stepped up research and development in antiballistic missile (ABM) systems, whose purpose was to create defensive capabilities for the nuclear powers for the first time. The concept was clear enough: ABMs would be able to destroy incoming enemy missiles either in space or after they had re-entered the earth's atmosphere, and thus protect the attacked territory from nuclear destruction. The nuclear state would once again be rendered impermeable; nuclear technology would have assumed its clear place within the Westphalian approach to military security.

Yet, in the words of one distinguished British scientist, "the whole thing was a mirage,"[6] because no ABM systems could be devised that could provide an adequate defense of the state. With the kind of megatonnage anticipated in an all-out nuclear attack, no political leader would be satisfied with an ABM capability that might destroy half, or two-thirds, or even seven eighths of the enemy's incoming missiles. The easiest response to an ever-more-accurate ABM defense was for the enemy simply to deploy ever greater numbers of offensive missiles. Moreover, decoys could be devised to fool the ABMs into striking at them while lethal missiles slipped through to their targets. By the end of the decade it was clear even to the governments of the United States and the USSR that further ABM development would not and could not transform nuclear arsenals into usable instruments of warfare; rather, it would be ever more costly, add an enormous impetus to the arms race by encouraging the development of weapons systems that would render ABMs ineffective, and, most seriously, actually increase the threat of a first or preemptive nuclear strike by adding to the fear on each side that the other would soon achieve an unacceptable advantage and therefore must be "taken out" before that happened. This realization led directly to the Nixon-Brezhnev treaty of 1972 to limit ABM production on both sides, although, thanks to the deeply entrenched habit of the technological imperative (perhaps our most vivid example of the convergent fallacy), research and development in these matters continued.

The convergent fallacy regarding an effective nuclear defense raised its head again most prominently on March 23, 1983, when President Reagan projected his vision of a laser-weapon defensive system that he hoped the United States could build by the end of the century. Clearly enchanted by recent technological developments that might overcome some of the deficiencies of ground-based radar guidance systems of existing ABMs, the president imagined a perfect defensive capability that presumably could make the United States and its allies invulnerable to any threat of nuclear attack for all time.

As usual when one is seduced by the vision of what high technology might do, the president conveniently forgot, first, that technology's very nature is such as to preclude the possibility of final solutions— there is every reason to expect that as new defensive systems are perfected, so will be new offensive weapons to nullify their full effectiveness—and, second, that his dream of an absolutely perfect defensive system is an impossibility thanks to the very laws of physics. There should be no argument on the need for perfection here: Such a system would have to be perfect in its reliability if it were to lead to Reagan's vision of an invulnerable United States. In the words of a prominent MIT scientist, "even a system of 95 percent effectiveness (a technological impossibility) wouldn't prevent 450 of the 9,000 strategic Soviet nuclear weapons from exploding in the United States— many more than would be needed to extinguish this country as a modern society."[7] Meanwhile, all the politically destabilizing implications of the effort to create and deploy space-based defenses remain exactly akin to those for the earlier ABM technology.

So the convergent fallacy remains the false solution it has always been for solving the nuclear dilemma, even though it remains very much alive. Its allure is fed by the centuries-old assumption that an instrument of destruction in the hands of a government by rights ought to be a usable instrument of warfare. If it demonstrably is not so now, this thinking goes, then if we follow the way of technology far enough, surely we can make it so.

But let us assume for the purposes of this argument that President Reagan's "star wars" scenario is more plausible than the best informed of our scientists think it is. Let us suppose that even if it cannot provide us with a perfect defense against nuclear weapons, it might at least provide so small a measure of risk to the population as to be perceived as politically acceptable. Even then, does an ethically informed nation prefer to choose so unimaginably expensive a means of searching for its security while leaving unaddressed the political conflicts and the tensions that have seemed to require it? There are far cheaper and ultimately more ethical means of achieving what should be a much greater measure of security for the people of the world, that could release vast amounts of the ever-rising expenditures that go into the creation of these engines of potential genocide and use them for socially desirable ends, improving the quality of all our lives. Since every dollar ever spent on military might is wasteful from the standpoint that it robs support of constructive human values, it should always be the goal of statesmanship to provide security through the cheapest available material means.

TACTICAL NUCLEAR WEAPONS

If the idea of creating a perfect nuclear defense has been fueled by the technological imperative and the convergent fallacy, then the development of tactical or theater nuclear weapons has responded to the desire to limit the destructive power of nuclear explosives so as to make them usable instruments in warfare in the true Clausewitzian sense. In simplest terms, as the megatonnage of thermonuclear weapons began to grow at a fantastic rate, a recognition grew with it, particularly in the United States, that they were becoming too powerful to be used or even to have their use threatened, for such threats of mutual suicide would not be credible for any but the most far-reaching international conflicts imaginable. The issue was compounded by the fact that in the early years of the cold war, the United States had a commanding lead in the number of nuclear weapons at its disposal whereas the NATO countries generally did not have as many conventional forces deployed in Europe as did the Warsaw Pact countries on the other side of the iron curtain. One way, it was argued, to redress this imbalance and at the same time make the Western nuclear arsenal more believable as a deterrent force was to create and deploy in Europe smaller-yield nuclear weapons of various types, so that they could be used in the event of a general war there, much as artillery traditionally had been.

As a result, since the early 1960s a huge armory of tactical nuclear weapons has been deployed within the NATO countries, consisting not only of small bombs on aircraft, but also of field launchers deployed among ground troops at divisional levels, many now so miniaturized as to be wielded easily by one or a few men. The Soviets, naturally enough, have followed the Western lead and deployed tactical nuclear weapons of their own. As a result, it has long been assumed that should a major conflict erupt between Eastern and Western forces somewhere in Europe, both sides would be prepared to fight it at least at a tactical nuclear level.

These developments also have greatly complicated the nuclear threat. They have done so, first, by blurring the line between what any rational statesman might regard as a usable, as opposed to an unusable, weapon, i.e., one inviting unacceptable retaliation. No leader presumably would initiate a nuclear exchange that would guarantee the virtual end to his own, as well as his opponent's, society as would of course be the case if nothing but immensely destructive weapons were available to him. But when small-yield nuclear weapons are at his disposal for battlefield use, might he not take the risk that the conflict could be contained at a localized level—and never mind that the assumed battlefield would be in Central Europe rather than in North America or the Soviet Union—before it escalated into a global holocaust?

That possibility speaks volumes about the growing disenchantment of many Western Europeans with the "protection" they receive from the deployment of Cruise and Pershing II missiles on their territories. But it should also look less and less seductive even to North Americans who may secretly be willing to contemplate the destruction of other NATO populations as sacrificial lambs for their own survival. Too many factors could undermine the containment of nuclear war at a theater nuclear level. Because the difference between tactical and strategic nuclear weapons is not that between black and white, but includes all the shades of gray, the use of even the smallest, "cleanest" tactical weapons in a major conflict would raise enormously the prospect of escalation to unacceptable levels of destruction before a halt could be called. The issue cannot be resolved by the statistical measurement of a weapon's firepower and certainly not by mere labels. For in the kind of chaotic situation that would accompany a general, but still only low-level nuclear conflict, the pressures favoring escalation almost certainly would increase inexorably. Solly Zuckerman put the issue this way:

> Regardless of the care commanders might imagine they could take to confine damage to military targets, a nuclear battlefield in Europe would be a zone in which towns and villages would have been devastated; in

which all but the strongest buildings would have been utterly destroyed; in which roads would have been blocked and bridges made impassable; in which forests would have been razed; in which extensive fires would be raging; and over which vast numbers of casualties would have occurred.
. . .

    Nuclear weapons may well be classified as strategic, theatre, and tactical, but these terms are meaningless if the use of one of them may mean the use of any. . . . My experiences of generals and air marshalls in the Second World War . . . does not lead me to suppose that, if unlimited force were available, less rather than more would be used in order to secure some objective.[8]

Moreover, it also seems clear to many observers that the presence of tactical nuclear weapons in the field in Europe actually increases the threat of war. Not only are they perceived by many as usable, since exploded in small numbers they would not create an apocalypse, but also their widespread deployment would increase the probability of their accidental use through human error and because of the well-developed idea on the part of field commanders and everyone else in the military establishment that they are meant to be used. And, as already suggested, the psychopolitical implications of their deployment increasingly disturb the Western alliance. Many NATO governments claim to be assured that the presence of tactical nuclear weapons on their territories guarantees a strategic coupling of the United States to the fate of Europe. Yet common sense tells us that those in command in Washington might do everything possible to confine a nuclear battle to Europe and to prevent its escalation to the strategic or intercontinental level. The widely shared opinion of Admiral Gayler is that if U.S. tactical nuclear weapons were removed from Europe, the first consequence would be the improvement of relations within NATO.[9]

Even if we could imagine a world in which only tactical weapons and not their multimegaton big brothers existed, many of us still would have difficulty accepting them as reasonable instruments of warfare, for they too are capable of damaging human societies on a scale never experienced in our history. They should be feared and opposed for that reason alone, particularly by Europeans who would become their victims. But the alternative is even worse, for tactical and theater weapons are linked in strategies of graduated response to those weapons that can destroy our world. If our war-fighting capabilities do not merely destroy millions of our fellow humans, including friends and enemies alike, they may lead to doomsday for the earth.

THE LOGIC AND ILLOGIC OF DETERRENCE

So we are confronted with the prospect of nuclear extinction today because of the ongoing predilection of governments to regard these instruments as weapons in the traditional sense, rather than as threats to the very purposes of government and organized society.[10] That establishment outlook has been supported and maintained through military doctrines of deterrence. The idea underlying deterrence is simple enough: The purpose of the vast destructive power of nuclear arsenals is to prevent or deter one's enemy from some unacceptable foreign policy action by threatening nuclear retaliation if the opponent makes such a move. As long as that threat is perceived as credible, the enemy presumably is effectively deterred. If nuclear arsenals are not maintained in such a way as to make their threatened use frighteningly believable to one's opponent, then deterrence will fail and a major conflict will no doubt have to be fought. Such is the logic of deterrence.

The very fact that this doctrine has become the commanding one in the nuclear area is proof that nuclear explosives cannot be defended against; a revolutionary strategic doctrine responds to the revolutionary capability, although the strategy also reflects the effort to make nuclear arsenals respond to Wesphalian imperatives. Whatever is credible about nuclear deterrence flows directly from the basic premise of the Westphalian system, i.e., that its several actors are indisputably sovereign and therefore accountable in the last resort only to their own societies for which they must maintain security from encroachments. To the extent that one believes governments armed with nuclear weapons are motivated by such considerations, one may find plausible the deterrent threat. But even from this viewpoint of traditional Westphalian logic, we quickly encounter problems because the nuclear actor accountable only to its own society nevertheless must be willing to see that society destroyed (its members presumably acquiescing in their own mass deaths) if its threat to destroy the other is to be believed. We have come to an essential contradiction at the heart of deterrence theory: The nuclear actor must seek to maintain its own security by insisting upon its willingness to destroy itself, if necessary, to keep another actor from destroying it. Any commitment that does not go that final mile decreases whatever security is presumed in a doctrine of mutual assured destruction.[11]

The problem has bedeviled nuclear strategists since the early 1950s, and, more than any other factor, is responsible for the ever-upward spiraling arms race, always in the search for a more effective deterrent. In the early days, the problem was seen as one of providing a viable second-strike force, for the logic of deterrence—considered from the U.S. side—was that we had to demonstrate to the Soviets, by "hardening" missiles in underground silos, by maintaining a fearsome bomber strike force, and so on, that even if they initiated a nuclear exchange, our damaged arsenals still would have the capacity to strike back and inflict unacceptable damage on them. The elaboration and refinement of such a second-strike capability were both costly and frustrating, for technological change required continual development of new weapons and delivery systems to maintain the credibility of the deterrent. More specifically, U.S. strategists have been continually plagued by the need to bind the nuclear fate of North America to that of Western Europe if deterrence is to work on the other side of the Atlantic. That has led, as we have seen, to the added burden of tactical and theater weapons required by a graduated deterrent capability. That Sisyphean effort has been meant to convince friend and foe alike that all NATO members were, in effect, something like a single sovereign for deterrence purposes.[12] Regardless of its success, that effort has fed the arms race at an almost exponential rate.

As a result, the arms race long since took on a momentum of its own, in some ways almost unconnected to considerations of cold war and mutual deterrence, even though every new weapons system built by either side has been justified as somehow enhancing the credibility of its deterrent threat. However, the sheer number, variety, and destructive powers of the weapons in the arsenals are increasingly being viewed by many as no longer supporting, but serving to undermine, the logic of deterrence. Common sense tells us that both the superpowers have long since passed the point of having enough missiles and warheads to deter their opponent. We may not agree on precisely what that figure should be, although a mere 5 to 10 percent of the strategic missiles in each stockpile, if unleashed, clearly would provide a holocaust such as the world has never experienced. Some such number, therefore, seems a sensible estimate for a so-called minimum deterrent. President Carter perhaps inadvertently put the matter in even more extreme terms when he said in 1979 that "just one of our relatively invulnerable Poseidon submarines carries enough warheads to destroy every large and medium-size city in the Soviet Union."[13] One would think that only one such vessel in the hands of each of the superpowers might be enough to deter the other.

The difficulty today is that, in the ceaseless effort of each side to make its deterrent threat more credible, by matching the technological developments of the other side and struggling to outmatch them in numbers of weapons, the purpose of deterring one's opponent by minimal means increasingly sinks from view. Now we hear governmental officials talk of what must be done should deterrence fail, how to fight a protracted nuclear war with some assurance that at the end we might prevail.

As in all other facets of the nuclear age, the endless justification of more nuclear power in the name of deterrence has led us ever deeper into a contradiction, for it undermines the very logic of the doctrine itself. Perhaps this dynamic is inevitable, given the apparently hopeless effort to treat these explosives as if they were politically useful instruments of military capability. We have been led into this quagmire by the unresolvable problem of making deterrence credible, for it is profoundly contrary to what we hold as logical to suppose that one can threaten one's enemy endlessly when that threat is potentially suicidal. Either threats must be seen as bluffs or else they must be acted upon, perhaps not today or even tomorrow, but eventually.

The problem of the credibility of an endless bluff is joined by another now that the Soviets have the clear capacity to destroy the U.S. homeland in the process of being destroyed themselves. Until recently, one could argue that the threat of mutual suicide, while real, was decidedly asymmetrical in favor of the United States. Most of the destructive force of a Soviet first strike against the West would have been felt in Europe, while this country, damaged but surviving, could turn the Soviet Union into a wasteland in a retaliatory strike. Now, however, North America could be destroyed as completely as Soviet Russia, which makes many wonder if a U.S. administration would have the will to retaliate after a first strike against Western Europe when it would mean the destruction of the United States itself.

To counter these doubts, the cold war mentality is perpetuated. One does not believably threaten to destroy an opposing power, let alone oneself, unless that enemy is implacably hostile, utterly unlike oneself, representing, in President Reagan's phrase, "the embodiment of evil." Devil theories of one's enemies frequently have led to unspeakable evil committed in the name of righteousness; today's devil theories could lead to the destruction of most of our humanity, both physically and—what already may have progressed dangerously far— morally as well. We have scarcely begun to consider the profound immorality of basing the presumed security of our societies on the threat to kill millions upon millions of innocent people. Again the contradiction: Deterrence may keep us physically alive while leading us to our spiritual deaths.[14]

NORMATIVE RESPONSES TO THE NUCLEAR PERIL

What steps can we take to move our situation away from this most profoundly antihuman and illogical effort to achieve "security"? Has the history of these developments and the puniness of attempts to reverse them made fatalists of us all, so that we now suppose that what human purpose has created cannot be controlled and reversed by human effort? Certainly the inducements to a fatalistic acceptance of nuclear terror are all about us, from the assurances of governments that yet another weapons system will increase our security to the paucity of significant agreement by those governments to reverse the arms race.

Yet some substantial moves are possible that could dramatically improve our situation, even though none of them would provide a panacea. What follows is a look at some of the available steps, which need to be examined in light of their likely implications for our overall social and political situation as well as their immediate political feasibility. What looks wildly utopian today may become far less so once some interim measures have been accomplished upon which they can build.

A general problem needs to be addressed before we can be clear about the implications of various proposals for reducing the nuclear threat. It stems from the basic contradiction inherent in possessing a destructive capability that must never be used but whose use must continually be threatened. Should a minimum deterrent, with all its Westphalian implications for the maintenance of state sovereignty through the threat of sovereign conflict, be maintained while the wastefulness of overkill capacities is eliminated? Or is the sovereign freedom of nuclear actors to threaten mass destruction the most dangerous and immoral in the long run and would it remain so even once nuclear arsenals were radically cut back to minimum levels needed for deterrence?

The alternative we choose is basically significant for the political evolution of our species. If the goal is a restoration of a minimum deterrent, the implication is that Westphalian modes of separate sovereignties must be maintained, perhaps even shored up in some way to restore the kind of social fragmentation that the world has moved away from in recent decades. If the goal is to remove nuclear weapons from the arsenals of states, that seems most plausibly accomplished by creating an effective monopoly of control over them above and beyond existing sovereignties—in short, a world governmental authority. Presumably, few of us would be comfortable with a vision of the future in which peace would be maintained forever by the cultivation of threats, fear, and hatred (even assuming that such a mass psychological state could be forever maintained). But also, most of us would suppose that the habits of Westphalia are still too deeply ingrained for very immediate agreement on centralized control over all nuclear weapons. If we do what merely seems feasible, do we not leave Damocles's sword still dangling, only a bit less precariously, over our heads and our most hateful and destructive tendencies continually encouraged?

The best way to cut through this seemingly insoluble dilemma may be to concentrate first on restoring the minimum deterrent as the lesser evil, but to keep complete nuclear disarmament clearly in sight as the longer run goal. The two goals need not be mutually exclusive, for some, if not all, of the significant steps toward minimum deterrence should also help to create a novel political environment out of which more radical moves toward nuclear disarmament would become feasible. The social dynamics of such a scenario are admittedly tricky, for there is always the danger, among others, that measures mutually agreed upon by the superpowers to restabilize deterrence at much lower levels could also have the effect of inducing complacency, thereby removing the larger goal from public view. That is why normatively oriented attention to this issue must not lose sight of the differences in the two goals and must examine continually the movement toward either or both of them implicit in various proposals.

Building Down. As a measure to induce greater mutual confidence, the superpowers might agree that for every new weapon added to their stockpiles, they will dismantle two old or obsolete weapons, to be selected by them presumably without participation by the other side. Such a process obviously would reduce the nuclear stockpiles, though very gradually, always in the direction of some kind of minimum deterrent force. Its greatest advantage is that it would require little formal negotiation; in fact, either superpower might begin such a process unilaterally, with the announced expectation that its opponent would follow suit. Even if that did not occur, the country unilaterally engaged in building down would risk little, since the weapons it chose to eliminate would be by definition obsolete. But the political pressure on the other superpower to reciprocate would be very great, so there is a strong likelihood that if one party announced such a step, the other soon would join it.[15]

The disadvantage of the building down approach is that it would in no way address the issue of continued research and development of nuclear weapons and might even encourage ever more exotic and costly development on both sides in an ongoing effort to attain or achieve some perceived advantage. It is difficult to imagine that the decisions made in such a process would *always* enhance what both sides perceived as a strategic standoff and would *never* encourage a war-fighting or tactical capacity. In fact, this streamlining of nuclear arsenals could make nuclear war more likely precisely because bombs of the greatest megatonnage might be those each side would be inclined to view as obsolete. Clearly, then, this approach should be combined with other measures if our security is to be enhanced.

Comprehensive Test Ban. Both the United States and the Soviet Union have advocated a comprehensive test ban, and work on a draft treaty is far advanced. At this writing, however, the Reagan administration, reversing the goal of other U.S. presidents, has declined to pursue the agreement. Clearly, such a treaty is feasible, as far as the superpowers are concerned, as long as they accept the fact that their nuclear arsenals are in general parity. Were a comprehensive test ban to come into effect, it would slow the momentum of the arms race by inhibiting the development of new, and therefore untested, weapons. It would no doubt also slow further developments in the technology of delivery vehicles, although refinements to launchers that did not require tests presumably would be permitted. If such an agreement could be coupled with building down existing arsenals, the technologically induced spiral of the arms race could be seriously inhibited. Technology itself can play a positive role in encouraging a comprehensive test ban; the problem of on-site inspections for verification purposes has become less and less important as seismic technology has advanced. A politically acceptable test ban agreement now seems to depend only on the desire of the superpowers to restrain, rather than fuel, their arms race.

Nuclear Freeze. Proposals for a nuclear freeze are clearly intended to provide a dramatic commitment to the logic of a minimum deterrent capability without, in themselves, reducing stockpiles to such levels. Although some advocates (and opponents) seem to assume that a freeze would require the negotiation of a treaty, with all the prospects for prolonged delay and evisceration of the basic concept, a freeze could be arrived at just as feasibly without negotiation. Jerome B. Wiesner, science adviser to Presidents Kennedy and Johnson, has suggested one way that could be done: The president "should declare an open-ended moratorium, always subject to reversal, on the production, testing and deployment of new nuclear weapons and delivery systems. He should invite the Russians to respond with a parallel declaration of purpose. If they did, it would result in a non-negotiated freeze."[16]

To be meaningful, a nuclear freeze would have to be an initial or interim measure only, for it would only stop and not reverse the growth of nuclear arsenals. Its appeal lies in the fact that it should be possible to achieve almost literally overnight and in the hope that so dramatic a halt to the superpowers' long-standing policies would produce a climate in which more substantive agreements, perhaps in cutbacks of existing stockpiles, then could be negotiated.

Deep Cuts. Anyone who has reflected on the horrendous overkill capacities of the superpowers understands that each side has perhaps 95 percent more weapons than could conceivably be needed to deter a rational opponent. Deep cuts in these arsenals therefore are essential to reestablish a rational or minimally sufficient deterrent. The process of achieving them also would teach us what we have not yet had much opportunity to learn: how to dispose of these poisonous materials safely. Our dismal experience with the SALT and START negotiations suggests that the modest and the protracted negotiating approach is insufficient, for at the pace of these discussions, even continually successful outcomes would have to proceed for centuries to arrive at very satisfactory results. Moreover, such approaches seem to ensure the appearance of ever more intractable, but essentially technical, questions of relative equality in particular weapons systems.

One proposal for deep cuts by a distinguished U.S. statesman, George F. Kennan, suggests how it may be possible to cut through many of the complexities and thereby arrive at a relatively quick agreement.

> What I would like to see the President do, after due consultation with the Congress, would be to propose to the Soviet Government an immediate across-the-board reduction by 50 percent of the nuclear

arsenals now being maintained by the two super-Powers—a reduction affecting in equal measure all forms of the weapon, strategic, medium range, and tactical, as well as all means of their delivery—all this to be implemented at once and without further wrangling among the experts, and to be subject to such national means of verification as now lie at the disposal of the two Powers.[17]

Even a 50 percent cut should not be regarded as a final goal, in Kennan's view, for he then advocates cutting two-thirds of what remains after the first step is accomplished, thereby returning both sides to what could reasonably be called a minimum deterrent capability.

It is useful to imagine how some such ongoing process of deep cuts could be made to serve, not simply minimum deterrence, but the larger goal of the elimination of all nuclear stockpiles. When treating the serious problems that would confront those engaged in the safe dismantling and disposal of so many thousands of warheads, new cooperative measures between U.S. and Soviet scientists very likely would be feasible. Kennan suggests that a joint committee might address these issues. Media attention to these matters could be expected to make us all more aware of the incredible dangers posed by even relatively small numbers of nuclear weapons. Add to that the greater sense of what is politically possible to accomplish after a deep cuts agreement, and we can begin to imagine how the goal of minimum deterrence might be made to serve that of complete nuclear disarmament.[18]

No First Use. For years, many important national actors and private individuals have urged all nuclear powers to pledge formally that they will never use nuclear weapons first in time of conflict. Such a proposal could both strengthen the concept of deterrence, as a first step, by making clear that the only rational purpose of nuclear arsenals is to prevent some other power from using theirs, and in the longer run, delegitimize nuclear weapons more generally. If such a pledge were taken seriously over a long enough period, it would come to be viewed as a fundamental normative commitment of every nuclear actor. With that, the absurdity of maintaining any nuclear stockpiles would begin to emerge more clearly. So a no-first-use pledge has the merit of serving both deterrence and nuclear disarmament goals and, moreover, would require no complicated formulations by experts if it were drafted as a treaty. Yet if it were to avoid the fate of the Kellogg-Briand Pact, the treaty should be at least loosely tied to substantive cuts as well.

For years the Soviet Union and its allies, as well as countries without nuclear weapons, have favored a no-first-use proposal. Only the United States and its NATO allies have refused it. Why? Because the West has insisted that if it did not maintain its right to turn to tactical nuclear weapons in the event of a massive conventional attack by the Soviet bloc in Europe, it could actually make such an attack more likely because of the presumed superiority of Soviet bloc conventional forces. Clearly, this strategy is based upon the assumption that tactical nuclear warfare need not lead to general nuclear warfare; in other words, it assumes that some kinds of nuclear weapons are indeed usable. The official U.S. position is that a no-first-use policy would require massive buildups in Western conventional capability in Europe, including, presumably, a return to the peacetime draft that has been ended in the Western countries because of its unpopularity.

These assumptions have been addressed—and for many satisfactorily refuted—in a 1983 study of the issue by the Union of Concerned Scientists.[19] The study suggested that modest improvements in conventional forces alone would be needed, such as better antitank defenses, the prepositioning of supplies, and preparations for more rapid mobilization. Until the United States agrees to pledge never to use nuclear weapons first, regardless of the adjustments in its military preparations that could entail, its posture fuels the arms race, encourages its military establishment to believe in nuclear war-fighting strategies, and continually raises the spectre that this country might actually launch a nuclear attack.

STEPPING BACK FROM THE NUCLEAR BRINK

The above discussion has included a number of the proposals for reversing the nuclear arms race that have received much attention in the 1980s, although the list is obviously not exhaustive. Our attention has been focused almost exclusively on the superpowers since their arsenals are by far the largest—together they account for 60 percent of the world's military expenditures and not a day passes in which they are not constructing new nuclear warheads. Since they are not the only nuclear powers today, the other members of the nuclear club also must be made to restrain and reverse the growth of their arsenals as well. Some of the above proposals would bear directly on the policies of the nonsuperpower nuclear countries (a no-first-use pledge by all of them is an example). Others, such as various deep cuts in the existing stockpiles of the United States and the Soviet Union, could be expected to become models for the lesser nuclear countries (France and China have pledged deep cuts of their own once the United States and the Soviets begin the process), or to reinforce strictures against the proliferation of nuclear weapons to nonnuclear states far more forcefully than is possible as long as the superpower arms race continues.

The nuclear policies of the superpowers above all have established and perpetuated the myth that these instruments of mass destruction are the legitimate instruments of national power. No wonder, then, that other sovereign states also have felt they must acquire them. Perhaps the real wonder, and cause for hope, is that only four more countries have openly joined the nuclear ranks, whereas perhaps a dozen others have the clear capacity to do so. At least one or two of that group almost certainly have a nuclear bomb even though they have not publicly admitted it. Just imagine how much the hand of antinuclear forces in those countries would be strengthened by serious and substantive moves toward nuclear disarmament on the part of the superpowers!

We have seen that the world has arrived at its incredibly dangerous point today thanks to the perverse determination of those who first invented nuclear explosives to regard them as if they were traditional military weapons. The logic of Westphalia has done the rest. And the logic of Westphalia makes the mutually suicidal ride we are on so difficult to stop, even though every reasonable person must recognize its dangers. Governmental leaders so far have been so truly imprisoned by the system that they are unable to take the kind of bold initiatives common sense and human survival demand. They are the prisoners of our system of nuclear armaments in the same way that Thomas Jefferson, an otherwise virtuous man of great accomplishment, was held prisoner by the system of slavery in his time.[20] Deluded by Westphalian logic into supposing that security for the population over which they preside demands insecurity for that of the opponent, they easily pretend to be serious about arms control by putting forth proposals that can be seen in advance as unacceptable to the other side. An ill-informed public, also susceptible to Westphalian visions of "us" versus "them," is easily convinced of the righteousness of its own government's offer and the malignity of the other in refusing it.

For far too long we have drawn the wrong conclusions from this situation, supposing that our government's spokesmen must be right while wondering what is faulty in our common-sense conclusions. The relevant decision makers within governments almost certainly cannot be expected to play the disarmament game seriously until they are pushed into doing so—and pushed by the conviction that it is far too important to our security to be treated as a game. It is both sad and hopeful that the most prominent advocates today for various nuclear arms control measures are men who have held positions of great responsibility in Western countries during the nuclear period. Some of them vainly opposed their governments' nuclear policies when they were in office, although most of them no doubt were kept imprisoned by the exigencies of governmental service, the constraints on them to conform to establishment, i.e., traditional Westphalian modes of thought.[21] Once freed from those responsibilities they have been able to see and articulate the dangers more clearly.

In light of our discussion of realism versus idealism in Chapter 4, it is worth noting that one of the most eloquent recent proponents of deep cuts and a no-first-use pledge is the same George Kennan who, in the 1940s and 1950s, was a particularly influential exponent of realism in foreign policy. Kennan's fundamental outlook has not changed in the years since; rather, a careful reading of his antinuclear arguments makes clear that he has always regarded nuclear weapons as unusable instruments of foreign policy.[22] That realistic appraisal is what has led him to the "radical" positions he holds today.

Opposition to the existing nuclear status quo can only be regarded as the height of realism. Little imagination is needed to suppose that in the awful event of actual limited use of nuclear weapons, statesmen would, if they were able, rush to find the means to prevent such a catastrophe from occurring again. And almost surely they would be willing to accept "radical" or untried solutions since such solutions so clearly would be needed. Must we wait for such a disaster before we can find the will to move out of the time-honored, but potentially suicidal, approaches to our presumed security?

The nuclear issue is the most overriding of our time because it threatens our continuation as a civilized species. The structural lethargy of our international system severely inhibits meaningful action to bring it under control. We are almost surely doomed if we expect our governmental officials to solve the matter for us without constant and informed insistence from the rest of us that they do so. Such insistence requires, first, a clear understanding of the nature of the menace that confronts us, an understanding that must not be clouded by all the rhetoric about comparative strengths and weaknesses of the nuclear arsenals, about salvation through ever-greater spending on the arms race, or about nuclear war-fighting doctrines; second, a willingness to pursue the implications and test the realism of a host of measures designed to reduce the nuclear peril; and third, a realization that we must become determined to make these matters the first priority of our political lives.[23]

TOWARD NONINTERVENTIONIST FOREIGN POLICIES

The nuclear policies especially of the superpowers are the gravest threat to the security of humankind, and not until they are reversed will our very survival as a species emerge from peril. Even in that event, we should not expect military solutions to the nations' perceived security interests to disappear from the globe. Some would even argue that a world disarmed of nuclear weapons would be a world in which conventional, non-species-threatening warfare might increase. Such a possibility must be seriously addressed if our goal is to minimize the resort to violence as much as is humanly possible. An obvious model for such a goal is the stable, nonauthoritarian civil society in which there is not only an effective police power for maintaining the peace but also widespread agreement upon the values and their priorities on which social peace must rest. Yet we should not let that model blind us to as yet unrealized possibilities for minimizing violence, particularly for the shorter run; very often those who have become enamored of the goal of world government have been content to elaborate formal systems on paper and to take too little account of how informal behavioral patterns supportive of reduced violence—such as that at the intersection where the traffic light has failed—can be strengthened.

We need to recall again that the Westphalian normative system has tried to discourage any sovereign actor's interference in the affairs of fellow sovereigns. In an ideal world, the Westphalian mode would ensure the absence of violence among the separate sovereigns, because each would know precisely where the limits of its jurisdiction lay and would respect them, turning its full attention to the development of the society that lay within. In the real world, of course, such clarity and completely ordered behavior is not possible, although the Westphalian insight still can teach us much about what does and does not inhibit international conflict. When a sovereign's military capability is used strictly to defend the security of its own society, its use is legitimate and supportive of order; when it is used offensively in the effort to extend its own interests or jurisdictional sphere, it is illegitimate and initiates what is likely to be a widening circle of violence.

States that behave aggressively against their neighbors typically do not admit that that is what they are doing. Rather they insist, often sincerely, that the extension of their power is essential to thwart the unacceptable extension of some other actor's power into their sphere. In the absence of a world community police power able to act upon an authoritative interpretation of the rights and wrongs of such justifications, the self-serving and socially disruptive behavior that follows seems not only predictable and foreordained, but justified by the very nature of the system. All this is obvious when we look at the history of modern states, as is the fact that relatively great powers typically are most inclined to justify using their capabilities militarily against fellow sovereigns.

This is particularly striking in the bipolar world, where the superpowers seem to have defined their own security interests as encompassing the globe, even though each also insists that it has been forced to so sweeping a position by the limitless ambitions of its opponent. Thus, the U.S. doctrine of containment purports to make U.S. policy toward the Soviet Union strictly reactive toward Soviet would-be aggression, attempting to provide the West with the ability to respond militarily to any perceived effort by the Soviets to extend their power wherever in the world they are free to do so.[24] Conversely, the Soviets do not see their own policy as aggressive, but merely as intended to support progressive forces wherever possible in the world against the disruptive opposition of the dying capitalist system.

This habit of viewing the assertive exercise of power by one's own (or friendly) sovereign authority as benign and that of one's opponent as malicious is so deeply ingrained that we may despair of changing it. This view is even true for many who regard both countries' postures and pretensions with some measure of objectivity, because there seems no way to cut through all the issues that have made the superpowers political opponents and to get them to live in harmony. Short of that, would not the reversal of what can only be called the imperialist policies of either not lead to their sure domination by the other? The truism that seems to follow is that great powers must exercise that power, counterbalancing its exercise by their opponents, or worse disaster is sure to follow. The reality of the situation we have created seems to shut us off from behavior that would improve our situation. We dare not abrogate our power for fear that to do so would threaten many of the values that we insist upon defending.

Yet such a conclusion ignores the possibility that there may be ways of protecting those important values and interests, whatever they may be, that do not simultaneously threaten others. The poverty of the established approach is well illustrated by the U.S. experience in Southeast Asia: Even had U.S. action succeeded in "stopping communism" there, it would have had, as it did have, a brutalizing impact on the people of the area, uprooting and resettling them for their own protection, scorching the earth from which they drew their living, killing and wounding many noncombatants, and, in general, overturning rather than supporting the possibilities for orderly, peaceful life that are at the heart of the U.S. system of values. But in the end, the United States did not succeed in its military effort, and what is the result? Not a domino effect, quite clearly. Three countries—Vietnam, Laos, and Cambodia—are now under Communist rule, although deeply divided among themselves. Otherwise, U.S. influence is no doubt greater throughout the region, including China, than before we "lost" the war there.

Other, very practical reasons exist for concluding that we do not always need to be prepared to destroy a society in order to save it. Even apart from their nuclear arsenals, the military establishments of the superpowers are very costly. Perhaps because they are first in military might the superpowers rank lower than many other nations in indicators of social well-being.[25] The efforts of the Reagan administration to increase the U.S. military budget by many billions of dollars annually have for the first time raised serious questions about this country's ability to pay for such an effort, quite apart from its implications for foreign policy. At the very least, these vast increases can only be disruptive to the U.S. economy, greatly increasing the federal deficit and fueling inflation. One study published early in 1983 concluded that enactment of Reagan's original defense budget for 1984 could cause a net loss of 2.2 million jobs in the civilian economy.[26]

As a result of such considerations, suggestions that the United States should abandon its far-flung commitment to containment are beginning to receive a hearing within establishment circles in the United States. One such proposal, relying heavily on the economic argument, notes that approximately 77 percent of the U.S. military budget goes to what the author called general-purpose forces—land divisions, tactical air wings, and surface naval units—and their supporting services. He concluded that "the United States, sooner or later, must abandon containment and drastically reduce its security commitments. Both the nuclear and general-purpose forces of our defense paradigm must be redesigned to achieve a single mission: the protection of our own democratic political system and the safety and well-being of our own citizens and their domestic property."[27]

The author argued strongly for a gradual withdrawal of U.S. general-purpose forces from around the globe. That would, he acknowledged, mean an end to the U.S. undertaking to defend Western Europe, which would be the most dramatic change. He argued that the Europeans then would probably increase their defense spending, perhaps to 5 or 6 percent of their gross national products from the current average of 3.5 percent—a comparatively modest goal "that would enable them to produce more absolute military output than the Soviet Union." He conceded that such a policy might no longer make it possible for the United States to ensure its access to the Gulf; yet the current policy has even greater costs, he insisted, politically as well as economically: "The cost of preparing to defend the Gulf and the possible costs of fighting a war there exceed the possible costs of losing that oil if we fail to defend the region."[28]

This particular proposal is cited both to suggest that there are realistic alternatives to ever-increasing military budgets in the name of containment and that true realism in international politics should never depart from the principle that genuine security in the Westphalian system is rather modestly tied to the needs of the individual state; when defined in such grandiose fashion as to ensure protection for half the world, it both overextends the guarantor—with potentially ruinous costs—and deflects those whose security presumably is guaranteed from a sense of responsibility for maintaining their own place in the world. A noninterventionist orientation to the world respects the tolerance for diversity that is one of the chief hallmarks of the international system, and simultaneously encourages the adoption of nonthreatening security techniques for maintenance of individual state interests.

TOWARD CIVILIAN-BASED DEFENSE

What kinds of nonthreatening security techniques can we imagine? They include all of those that demonstrate by their very application that they cannot threaten the legitimate security interests of others, but will defend against illegitimate incursions of outside power. The posture of Switzerland has served as one model of this kind for many years. Switzerland has never sought security through the costly and probably vain attempt to match its great-power neighbors militarily. Rather, Swiss policy has clearly shown any would-be aggressor that its people would fight to defend their society, making the costs of conquest very high indeed. All Swiss males undergo training in the specific military techniques that support such a policy. They learn how to use their rugged terrain as a natural fortress and to thwart invasions by the demolition of bridges and other roadways, and they maintain an adequate state of military readiness to make any would-be attacker think more than twice.

The Swiss model cannot be duplicated exactly by other societies—geography alone would make the job more difficult for many others. But the Swiss example should remind us of the comparatively little economic cost involved in providing for the safety and well-being of a country's own citizens at home. And if well-being is measured by standard of living, the Swiss approach has served its citizens very well indeed. The crucial point is that capability must be truly defensive, designed so that it can be perceived only as such by potential adversaries. As soon as it can be interpreted as provocative, whether or not that is how it is viewed by its creators, it encourages the adversary to take exactly the kind of action that is not wanted.

A truly defensive capability is perhaps best considered as something strikingly different from most traditional military policy, i.e., as civilian-based defense. Its purpose is to prepare an entire society, not just its military arm, in the myriad techniques of resistance against an invader or would-be usurper of power. It is meant to create an ability "to make effective domination and control impossible by both massive and selective nonviolent noncooperation and defiance by the population and its institutions."[29] Its techniques are essentially nonmilitary, but vary for different groups within the society. For example, workers and managers might resist exploitation of the economy by an occupier through selective strikes, delays, and so on, whereas teachers could refuse to teach whatever "new line" was demanded by the invaders. Other groups would develop particular techniques of resistance and defiance suited to their social roles.

Many of the likely techniques of civilian-based defense have been tested successfully in a great many political conflicts from ancient times to the present. The success of Gandhi's *satyagraha* in freeing India from British colonial rule is a dramatic case in recent times.[30] Aspects of various European resistance movements to Nazi occupation also are pertinent. Lacking in virtually all these historical examples, however, has been conscious, society-wide consideration of and training for civilian-based defense *prior to* the actual domination of that society by an unwelcome power. Therefore, resistance has had to be improvised after the fact at a time when it was most difficult to make an already demoralized and frightened population understand its own potential power over the conqueror through concrete forms of resistance. Advocates of civilian-based defense suggest that we have scarcely begun to tap the possibilities inherent in resistance techniques through the kinds of advance planning that could deter attempts at conquest.

Much more attention needs to be devoted to this subject by all whose goal is noninterventionist foreign policies, for civilian-based defense can support such a goal in several ways: (1) It genuinely seeks to realign a state's policy with its basic purpose—providing security to its population—in a tangible, more effective and normatively acceptable way than is possible through interventionism. (2) It raises the cost of conquest and occupation by a foreign sovereign enormously and visibly, thereby providing a deterrent force at least as real, and very much less dangerous, than that from a nuclear threat. (3) It strongly supports democratic values and, by its example, can undermine the legitimacy of authoritarian control, because participation in civilian-based defense must be voluntary to be reliable in time of crisis, and the determination to defend the society must be widely shared. (4) Thanks to its reliance on nonviolent means, it can reduce violence and destruction and conceivably have a snowballing effect in delegitimizing traditional military applications of power.

Civilian-based defense clearly would serve the proclaimed, if not the actual, policies of great powers today, although to expect them, imprisoned as they are in their actual postures toward the world, to take the lead in this kind of training is probably unrealistic. More likely, immediate candidates may be several of the small, advanced democracies of Europe that are now hostage to the nuclear threat.[31] We should not expect any but perhaps the very smallest countries to dismantle their military capabilities while adopting civilian-based programs. Rather, these would no doubt be seen as adjuncts to them, perhaps for a very long time. We should expect, however, that once civilian-based programs were in place in several countries, confidence in their ability to deter and defend would naturally grow, thereby increasing support for them and perhaps decreasing support for the military component.

TOWARD THE LEGITIMATE USE OF FORCE

The war system survives today not only because it is encouraged by the Westphalian structure of decentralized states, but also because it has always been seen as the ultimate alternative to impotence in the face of unacceptable threats to a society.[32] If all states were to move toward noninterventionist foreign policies built upon effective civilian-based defense, then the ultimate sanction of war—its traditionally legitimate form—would no longer be needed. But we rightly regard such a prospect as utopian, for we know that too many societies are ruled by oppressive elites who maintain themselves, sometimes precariously, through the threat and use of force against their own people. Such governments need to command their own military forces to maintain themselves in power. Some of them will pursue interventionist policies against their neighbors to help maintain their control at home; none of them is in a position to support civilian-based defense programs, which of course would be used to undermine their own unpopular control. For these reasons, it is necessary to complement what are essentially the self-help strategies of noninterventionism and civilian-based defense with a global capability to use force as a sanction against unacceptable behavior by such actors.

As we have seen, recognition of this need has motivated all the efforts to create global collective security or peacekeeping arrangements in the modern period. Yet even though the twentieth century has produced novel efforts of this kind, they have so far proved to be less than adequate solutions. Our experience suggests that in some respects, the problem of an effective international police power may be unresolvable, at least for our lifetimes, if only because the creation of such power raises inevitably the divergent questions of power for whom? In support of what social values? In opposition to what legitimate wants and needs of which groups? We need only imagine a world in which the UN Security Council could function in exactly the way the Charter prescribes, with perfect harmony among the five permanent members and their complete agreement on action needed to maintain the peace. Such a world would unquestionably be a more peaceful place, although certainly many groups within it would not find it more just.

Still, we should prefer a more effective police power at the world level, even one that inhibited some of our favored social and political aspirations, as an alternative to the anarchic violence likely from utterly sovereign actors. In broadest terms, the effort to provide such police power can take two general forms: the creation of formal plans for relevant institutional change and the analysis and encouragement of patterns of behavior supporting the acceptable uses of force in the world. Clearly, the two approaches can and should be made to complement each other, for the first will necessarily emphasize ideal solutions and the second, real ones, each of which must be made to enhance the other. The possibilities for serious study are so nearly limitless that we can suggest only a very few examples.

In recent decades formal plans for an effective world police power often have taken the form of suggestions for amending the UN Charter. In keeping with the basic assumption in stable civil societies that authority should accrue to those who wield effective power, these generally have suggested weighted voting schemes, usually based upon size of populations and financial contributions to the organization. In return for weighted voting, such proposals generally would eliminate the veto power of the permanent members, thereby solidifying the concept of genuine majority rule.[33] Less far-reaching proposals would not necessarily necessitate amending the Charter, but would require agreements among the permanent members that would strengthen and regularize existing peacekeeping operations.[34]

Of course, the United Nations is not the only possible starting point on which to build an enhanced world police power. Leonard Beaton has suggested that NATO's experience with integrating the national military units of its members could become the model for a worldwide integrated force. It would be built upon the initial combination of U.S. and Soviet capabilities and proceed to incorporate additional national forces as well.[35] Such a scheme would have the merit of addressing first things first, namely, the crucial issue of how to bring the overwhelming mights of the superpowers into greater harmony with each other. But for just that reason we may be skeptical of its feasibility, at least until we have proceeded far enough down the path of nuclear disarmament to have created a more trusting, cooperative political environment than now exists.

The more far-reaching the proposal for building a more effective world police power, the more utopian it appears to be. Conversely, the more modest proposals, while perhaps realistic, may do little more than tinker ineffectively with already inadequate machinery. The great value of the more utopian suggestions is that they should force both those who conceive them and those who study them to consider all the many possibilities for political change that may or may not be realizable at the moment. In other words we should not measure their worth solely in terms of whether they might soon be adopted; rather, we should let them direct us toward the kinds of realistic policies that could eventually produce a political environment more supportive of such arrangements.

The second approach—that of encouraging those behavioral patterns that support acceptable uses of force—must always be a basic concern of any world order orientation. Balancing power has been the most time-honored of these techniques in the decentralized international system, and to the extent that the system remains decentralized, it will no doubt continue to play an important role. Yet balancing power has proved historically to be far from adequate for legitimizing the use of force because it leaves all responsibility for measuring capabilities and determining motives in the hands of those who must always base their calculations upon very imperfect information.

Two basic and recurring kinds of risks result. First, the complacent or satisfied actor may project similar motivations onto the policies of other governments that in fact have revisionist intentions instead. For example, the European democracies in the early 1930s concluded that Hitler was a reasonable statesman whose reasonable demands should be met. Second, the anxious actor may be convinced that its opponents have limitlessly revisionist designs on the world; this risk is characterized in the cold war. Every disturbance of the status quo is seen as the product of the enemy's machinations, which call for a provocative response. Our survey of the modern period suggests that when actors incorrectly view their fellow sovereigns in either of these ways, the overall configuration of world power is almost sure to be disrupted rather than stabilized, even though the disruption takes place in the name of maintaining or reestablishing a power balance.

Since the second, rather than the first, outlook leads to the most characteristic dangers of the current period, we need to consider how the risks inherent in it might be minimized. Our general goal should be to discourage the perceptions of one's opponents as unalterably malign, since such perceptions demonstrably produce self-fulfilling prophecies that themselves help maintain instability.[36] That goal can be advanced through a host of actions, all initiated on the premise that my state's positive or benign behavior should serve as an example for the other to emulate. If that emulation does not follow, my government is free to return to its previous policy with little risk to itself. But if actors are careful to indicate what kind of reciprocal action they expect, their opponents very likely will find it nearly irresistible not to follow suit. That is especially true in the area of nuclear arms control because of worldwide anxiety over the arms race (e.g., consider the likely reciprocal force of Jerome Wiesner's proposal for a nonnegotiated nuclear freeze), although many other kinds of actions could no doubt contribute to the development of a positive self-fulfilling prophecy between the nuclear antagonists. In the military field, these actions most often might take the form of an announced intention *not* to take some action that the superpower in question had the capability to take, as long as the nonaction was reciprocated; once a fair measure of mutual restraint was evident in the military sphere, more positive steps, relating to the economic or social welfare of, say, third world populations, could be taken as well.

The superpowers no doubt will continue to insist upon a right and duty to manage peace-threatening situations within their respective spheres. That fact will not always produce happy outcomes for those whose affairs are "managed." Afghan rebels and supporters of the Nicaraguan Sandinista government are examples in the early 1980s. Still, one of the striking lessons of recent decades is that the superpowers have had difficulty sustaining an effective police power in areas where they have attempted unilateral action. That difficulty does not mean that they are about to forego any future efforts to determine the shape and direction of governments wherever they think they can. Perhaps the best we can hope for is that they can be made more frequently to join in an effort to pluralize the decision-making process and the action following from it that seeks to maintain acceptable order within each of their blocs.[37] The broader the agreement within the governments of allies on the kind of police action demanded, the greater will be the clarity on what are and are not acceptable uses of force and the goals it is to serve.

This approach envisions encouragement of the kind of decision making, characteristic of pluralistic democracies, that is based upon the diversity of social interests whose values the process is not meant to destroy. That development admittedly seems to have more fertile ground for growth in the more democratic West than in the Soviet bloc, yet one of the tragedies for the West in the bipolar period has been the repeated tendency of the United States as leader of the Western bloc to emulate the authoritarian practice of its opponent in deciding when and where to intervene in the world. If supporters of greater world order would do whatever they can to place the shoe on the other foot and encourage the United States to pursue the example from its own domestic sphere of pluralistic decision making, that example might have a revolutionary impact on the Eastern bloc as well.

The vast and complex effort to reduce the threat of violence in international affairs has been dealt with only in bare outlines here. The first thrust of this discussion was to call attention to those instruments of mass destruction that are species threatening in their potential, and then to consider some of the possibilities for decoupling them from the traditional military capabilities of states with a view toward removing them from the hands of separate sovereigns. The second thrust was to suggest that we need to learn to control the use of force to the extent that it undermines, rather than supports, essential democratic values. Any stable social order is built upon its governors' ability to wield a police power for legitimate ends, its stability and its legitimacy always directly determined by the proportionality of its actual use of force. A powerful country has as much difficulty achieving the goal of social democracy in a distant nation by invading, oppressing, and killing its people as the mayor of a large city has to uphold a just social order by ordering that all strikers in an illegal job action be shot on sight. In each case, the amount of force has been disproportionate to the proclaimed policy goal.

Since, in the words of the famous aphorism, absolute power tends to corrupt absolutely, solutions for such disproportionate uses of force ideally must be sought through constitutional restraints on the exercise of force. This effort has produced generally, if not completely, satisfactory results in democratic societies. Yet although considerable progress has been made in restraining force internationally in this century, this effort has not yet gone nearly as far at the world level. Although formal, or constitutional, reforms are worth pursuing, the world is still so little integrated on the issue of the legitimate social ends force can serve that a dilemma results: If such plans are modest enough to be acceptable, they are probably too modest to do the job; if they are comprehensive enough to embody an effective global police power, they are probably not acceptable to states.

To resolve this dilemma, we must proceed simultaneously on a number of fronts. One front draws attention to the dangers to democratic values in the overreliance on force in foreign affairs. Another encourages the development of unambiguously defensive strategies in foreign policy, such as that of civilian-based defense. Another supports the widest possible international sharing of any decision to use force in an interventionary way, recognizing that what is possible in one context may not be so everywhere. Another seeks the kinds of concrete actions from antagonists that can work to minimize their mutual hostility and work to build more harmonious relationships.

There are still other fronts, of course, all of which extend from the conscious effort to further the development of community at a global level. We will turn our attention to some of these in the next several chapters.

NOTES

1. "Opposition to Nuclear Armament," *Annals*, American Academy of Political and Social Science 469 (September 1983): 14.

2. Karl von Clausewitz, *On War*, trans. J. J. Graham, rev. ed. (London: Routledge and Kegan Paul, 1966).

3. A nearly random listing of some of these might include *The Effects of Nuclear War*, 1979, U.S. Arms Control and Disarmament Agency; *Comprehensive Study on Nuclear Weapons*, 1980, Report of the Secretary-General to the General Assembly of the United Nations; *Economic and Social Consequences of Nuclear Attacks on the United States* (Washington, D.C.: Government Printing Office, 1979); Samuel Glasstone and Philip J. Dolan, eds., *The Effects of Nuclear Weapons* (Washington, D.C.: Government Printing Office, 1962); K. N. Lewis, "The Prompt and Delayed Effects of Nuclear War," *Scientific American* 241, 1 (July 1979): 27–39; Jonathan Schell, *The Fate of the Earth* (New York: Alfred A. Knopf, 1982), pt. 1; Tom Stonier, *Nuclear Disaster* (Cleveland: World Publishing Co., 1963); Norman Moss, *Men Who Play God* (New York: Harper and Row, 1968). Three books that treat the experiences of the survivors of Hiroshima and Nagasaki are Masuji Ibuse, *Black Rain* (Tokyo and Palo Alto: Kodansha International, 1969); Takashi Nagai, *We of Nagasaki* (New York: Duell, Sloan and Pearce, 1951); and Robert J. Lifton, *Death in Life* (New York: Random House, 1967).

4. As is frequently true, the artistic imagination sometimes reveals an apparent truth about what we have not yet experienced that is particularly telling. One such example is in W. B. Yeats's poem, "The Second Coming," written before the invention of atomic weapons, whose description of "mere anarchy loosed upon the world" suggests at least one of the likely consequences of a general nuclear exchange:

Turning and turning in the widening gyre
The falcon cannot hear the falconer;

Things fall apart; the center cannot hold;
Mere anarchy is loosed upon the world,
The blood-dimmed tide is loosed, and everywhere
The ceremony of innocence is drowned;
The best lack all conviction, while the worst
Are full of passionate intensity.

5. John H. Herz, *International Politics in the Atomic Age* (New York: Columbia University Press, 1959).

6. Solly Zuckerman, *Nuclear Illusion and Reality* (London: Collins, 1982), p. 50.

7. Kosta Tsipis, "The Best Nuclear Defense Is Still Negotiations," *Philadelphia Inquirer*, April 2, 1983.

8. Zuckerman, *Nuclear Illusion*, pp. 67–68.

9. Admiral Noel Gayler, address to the American Academy of Political and Social Science, Philadelphia, April 22, 1983.

10. One indication of the insidiousness of our dilemma regarding nuclear weapons is seen in the very language we have chosen to describe them. First, we must refer to them as "weapons," even though we regard them as unusable in any sense that gives meaning to concepts of military power. We regard our missiles as for "defensive" purposes only, even though they cannot defend and they are the exact equivalent of the other side's "offensive" missiles. In fact, the misuse of language confronts us at every turn, from the euphemistic jargon of military planners (who may speak of the "throwweight" needed for a missile to "lob" a "nuke") to the giving of names to missiles that are meant to reassure us (Minuteman, Peacekeeper, and so on). In the United States, all discussion of military matters is cloaked under the euphemism of "defense" (Department of Defense, defense budget, defense spending). Perhaps our founding fathers, as children of the Enlightenment, knew what they were doing when they named the relevant federal agency the Department of War. By President Truman's day, Americans apparently were squeamish at such a name, and it was changed to Department of Defense. Thus we are comforted with another euphemism. Of course, even "War Department" becomes a euphemism for an organization that may be seriously considering how to use nuclear "weapons."

11. That is the name generally given the U.S. doctrine of deterrence as it evolved under the Nixon administration, which seems not to have noticed how it fed into the paradox of deterrence with its acronym. The MAD strategy itself is now out of date as the result of the counterforce and nuclear war-fighting strategies of the Reagan administration.

12. *NATO: The Entangling Alliance*, Robert E. Osgood's 1962 book, is still valuable reading for its insight into the challenge of deterrence doctrine for the alliance in its early years. For a more recent critique, see Zuckerman's *Nuclear Illusion*, Chapter 3.

13. Quoted in Theodore Draper, "How Not to Think About Nuclear War," *New York Review of Books*, July 15, 1982, p. 42.

14. In the words of Freeman Dyson, "I do not need to spell out why it is immoral for us to base our policy upon the threat to carry out a massacre of innocent people greater than all the massacres in mankind's bloody history. But . . . an immoral concept not only is bad in itself but also has a corrosive effect upon our spirits. It deprives us of our self-respect and of the good

opinion of mankind—two things more important to our survival than invulnerable missiles." "Weapons and Hope," *New Yorker,* February 27, 1984, p. 76. See also the essay by James A. Stegenga, "The Immorality of Nuclear Deterrence," *International Studies Notes* 10, 1 (Spring 1983): 18–21, which identifies fifteen sets of moral objections to the deterrence doctrine.

15. This was the parallel case starting in March 1950, when the USSR announced that it would cease all testing of nuclear weapons in the atmosphere and would continue that policy indefinitely if the United States should follow suit. Soon thereafter, President Eisenhower announced a reciprocal U.S. moratorium on atmospheric tests. This situation lasted until September 1, 1961, when Premier Khrushchev ordered the resumption of Soviet testing, and was followed by President Kennedy's decision, in light of that action, to resume U.S. tests as well. Yet that development had unexpectedly positive results for world order: Khrushchev's announcement was widely greeted not only negatively, but as if a semiformalized normative standard had been violated. A new public value, prohibiting testing, seemingly was supported authoritatively during the period of the moratorium and the Soviet reversion to its earlier policy appeared to be a violation (albeit a perfectly "legal" action considered in terms of traditional Westphalian notions of sovereign policy-making capabilities) of a new community standard. That reaction no doubt added impetus to the willingness of both governments to move toward the creation of a formalized agreement, the Partial Nuclear Test Ban Treaty, which was negotiated rather quickly in 1963.

16. Jerome B. Wiesner, "A Way to Halt the Arms Race," *New York Times,* June 13, 1982, p. E23.

17. Statement by George F. Kennan upon receiving the international award from the Albert Einstein Peace Prize Foundation, May 19, 1981. Reprinted in *Disarmament: A Periodic Review by the United Nations* 5, 2 (October 1981): 10. See also his development of this argument in "On Nuclear War," *New York Review of Books,* January 21, 1982, pp. 8–10.

18. As Admiral Noel Gayler asked, "Can you imagine the 300 or so television correspondents and God knows how many other people would attend the first weapons turn-in with the hammer and sickle and the stars and stripes painted on them? What a change in atmosphere that would make!" ("Six Ways to Prevent Nuclear War," *Common Cause,* August 1982, p. 55).

19. *No First Use* (Union of Concerned Scientists), Vice Admiral John Marshall Lee, February 1, 1983. This study grew out of a no-first-use proposal published in *Foreign Affairs* in spring 1982, by McGeorge Bundy, George F. Kennan, Robert McNamara, and Gerard C. Smith, all of whom are former high officials in various U.S. administrations. The UCS proposal was supported by more than 500 members of the National Academy of Sciences, including forty-three U.S. Nobel laureates.

20. This comparison was made fully in a moving and provocative article by columnist Garry Wills some years ago. "If the earth lasts long enough," he said, "future generations will look back on us with the uncomprehending horror we feel for slaveholding cultures. They will ask how a nation ever thought it could justify the buildup of instruments for destroying the globe" (*Philadelphia Inquirer,* February 3, 1977).

21. Lord Solly Zuckerman, who was Harold Macmillan's chief scientific adviser and a highly informed advocate for nuclear arms control, has pointed out the kind of blindness to the implications of nuclear policy that is induced

when one is a responsible member of government: He himself was pleased with Macmillan's success at inducing the Kennedy administration to sell Britain Polaris missiles, even though such a sale was entirely inconsistent with Macmillan's "more determined fight to bring an end to the nuclear arms race." "As one of his officials in both enterprises," Zuckerman wrote some twenty years later, "the inconsistency did not strike me at the time. It does now" (*Nuclear Illusion*, p. 86).

22. In a recent book, Kennan states his view of the new weapon soon after its existence became known in World War II. If the USSR also was to acquire it, "then it had to be viewed as a suicidal weapon, devoid of rational application in warfare; in which case we ought to seek its earliest possible elimination from all national arsenals" (*Nuclear Delusion: Soviet-American Relations in the Atomic Age* [New York: Pantheon, 1982]).

23. Robert C. Johansen has provided useful advice: "The history of governmental failure to halt the arms buildup cautions us against assuming that disarmament can be achieved easily or without some major changes in attitudes and social institutions. The record of failure also suggests two wasteful tendencies of the past that citizens might do well to avoid in the future: on the one hand, the temptation to work for modest arms control measures that are achievable yet fail to lead toward disarmament; and on the other hand, the willingness to advocate directly the goal of comprehensive disarmament, yet without focusing attention and action on particular steps to begin the process that will lead to the desired destination. A more useful approach would be for citizens to set a clear policy direction by supporting proposals that are firmly linked to initiating a disarming process" (*The Disarmament Process: Where to Begin* [New York: Institute for World Order, 1977], p. 5).

24. The main author of containment, George F. Kennan, put the matter this way in the article that became the basis for the policy, little changed to this day, that the United States adopted toward the Soviets in 1959: "[Moscow's] political action is a fluid stream which moves constantly, wherever it is permitted to move, toward a given goal. Its main concern is to make sure that it has filled every nook and cranny available to it in the basin of world power" ("The Sources of Soviet Conduct," *Foreign Affairs* 25 [July 1947]:566–582).

25. For example, in the United States, one person in seven now lives below the poverty threshhold, and in the USSR, the infant mortality rate is more than twice the average for the other developed countries. See Ruth Leger Sivard, *World Military and Social Expenditures*, 8th ed. (Leesburg, Va.: WMSE Publications, 1982).

26. James R. Anderson, "Bankrupting America: The Tax Burden and Expenditures of the Pentagon by Congressional District" (Lansing, Mich.: Employment Research Associates, February 1983).

27. Earl C. Ravenal, "The Case for a Withdrawal of Our Forces," *New York Times Magazine*, March 6, 1983, p. 61.

28. Ibid., p. 75.

29. Gene Sharp, "Making the Abolition of War a Realistic Goal" (New York: Institute for World Order, 1980), p. 9. This prize-winning essay explores many of the possibilities for civilian-based defense in realistic terms.

30. In 1982, release of the film *Gandhi* provoked a new interest in many countries in the kind of nonviolent resistance practiced by the Indian leader. Some of that interest no doubt was sparked by the sense in many viewers of the ethical rightness, as well as the effectiveness, of the Gandhian approach

in a world where the military approach to security seemed increasingly bankrupt.

31. Public discussions and study of such strategies are most advanced in Sweden and the Netherlands at present. Sharp, "Abolition of War," p. 12.

32. The description of war as the alternative to impotence is that of Sharp, ibid., p. 4.

33. One of the first seriously elaborated proposals for amending the UN Charter along these lines was given in Grenville Clark and Louis B. Sohn, *World Peace through World Law*, 3d ed. enl. (Cambridge: Harvard University Press, 1966). A more recent proposal, which focuses mainly on enhancing and rationalizing the legislative powers of the General Assembly, is that of the "binding triad," which is the plan of the Center for War/Peace Studies of New York.

34. See, for example, the report of the Palme Commission, the Independent Commission on Disarmament and Security Issues, available under the title *Common Security: A Blueprint for Survival* (New York: Simon and Schuster, 1982).

35. Leonard Beaton, *The Reform of Power* (London: Chatto and Windus, 1972). See especially Chapters 5–8.

36. We all understand the sense of the self-fulfilling prophecy in our personal lives, although we do not always remember to carry its lessons over into our international behavior as well. If I have a neighbor who mistrusts me, complaining of the noise I make or of the leaves from my tree that fall onto his lawn, I will very likely develop the hostile feelings toward him that his attitude has assumed I have harbored all along. If, on the other hand, I can bring myself to offer to rake his lawn or invite him to my next party, I may see him develop into a more friendly and agreeable person. Of course, the more hostile the relationship has become, the more difficult it is for either of us to take the initiatives that might improve it. But the real point is that unilateral action by one can and very often does have dramatic, positive effects on the behavior of the other.

37. For one effort to explore the possibilities for and implications of multilateral decisions to use force within blocs in the context of the early 1970s, see Lynn H. Miller, *Organizing Mankind* (Boston: Holbrook Press, 1972), Chapters 3–4.

6

The Search for
Economic Well-Being

Our first concern is to redefine the whole purpose of
development. This should not be to develop things but to develop
man.
—The Cocoyoc Declaration, October 12, 1974

In the summer of 1983, the U.S. Congress reluctantly authorized an $8.4 billion additional appropriation to the International
Monetary Fund (IMF) in response to that agency's effort to prevent
a number of third world governments from defaulting on loans from
banks in industrialized countries. A debt of some $700 billion had
accumulated over the previous several years as the result of the North's
high interest rates, deep recession, and corresponding drop in trade
with third world countries. Many in Congress who supported the
IMF's emergency measures viewed them as necessary to keep the
entire international financial system from collapsing, whereas those
who opposed the appropriation faulted their nation's banks for having
made what they regarded as unsound loans in the 1970s when the
banks were flush with money from foreign investors suddenly rich
from oil. No doubt all members of Congress also had sharp and
painful memories of how that oil wealth had been so quickly generated
through the quadrupling of oil prices by OPEC, which had forced
significant changes in the lives of almost every American. The debt
crisis was a difficult reminder of the painfully complex consequences
that seem to have accompanied increasing economic interdependence
worldwide.

Not long before, *interdependence* was a frequent catchword to suggest
the movement toward one world, with all its implications of harmony
and peace. Only since the oil shocks of the 1970s has interdependence
begun to take on more sinister overtones for many, for we can see

the process producing conflicts and strains at the global political level that are in many cases something new under the sun. After all, the citizens of rich nations have not had to take much account of the whims of oil sheiks or the grandiose dreams of Brazilian planners before the recent past, and many no doubt still would like to think that their countries ought to reassert their independence of such interests. The centuries-old habits of Westphalia confront the dynamics of late-twentieth-century economic imperatives, and the resulting clashes are rapidly reshaping much of the agenda of world politics.

WESTPHALIA AND THE INDUSTRIAL REVOLUTION

Probably no aspect of human life has remained as constant for many centuries or has changed at such a dramatically accelerated pace in modern times as its economic base. From the origins of the earliest known societies until well past the emergence of the Westphalian international system, economic life for most people in all parts of the globe meant little more than bare subsistence. The small farmer of Elizabethan England was like his Celtic or Anglo-Saxon ancestor a thousand years before in that both were concerned primarily with sustaining themselves and their families through the fruit of their labor on the land. Like their counterparts over as many centuries in Mexico or Egypt, their lifelong expectation was that the greatest economic reward they could expect from hard work was to fulfill their basic survival needs—food, shelter, and clothing, most of which they and their families produced for themselves. When there was a tiny surplus, it could be bartered or sold for some amenity beyond their means of production, but they mostly remained poor for countless generations, malnourished, illiterate, and with a life expectancy not much beyond thirty years.

The two most compelling facts about this traditional way of life are, first, that it was everywhere accepted as the inevitable and unchanging condition for most of humanity (the rich 1 percent of the population was viewed as naturally entitled to its more exalted state), and, second, that the kinds of economic organization it produced were comparatively small scale, self-contained at local levels, and demanded very little interchange with other societies. Just as the milkmaid of Europe typically lived her whole life within sight of her village's church steeple, so her economic needs were sustained by that same tiny society, which alone knew the fruit of her labor.

By the time of the European Renaissance, larger units of economic organization began to emerge from the combination of the myriad local markets of earlier times. Greater centralization and control of economic activity from the capital became one of the fundamental features in the evolution of modern nation-states; yet the only real novelty at first was the scale of the new economic units. For the great mass of the population, material well-being still improved imperceptibly. Nonetheless, the emergence of the Westphalian system laid the foundation for profound changes in traditional economic life by creating nearly self-contained units large enough to encourage intrastate economic activity of a scope and complexity never achievable while the Middle Ages' hatchwork of barriers to economic exchange persisted.

For at least a century and a half after 1648, Westphalia served mainly to legitimize the development of separate, state-based economies. The new normative order had to treat economic exchanges across state lines and to lay down rules for the exploitation of the sea's resources, that community property of all nation-states, but these remained insignificant activities compared to those that grew within each territorial unit. The Westphalian dynamic moved states in the direction of national self-sufficiency, the economic condition of autarky, although not every state had a large enough territory or population base or the diversity of resources to make such a goal possible. Nonetheless, the political principle of laissez-faire upon which the new international system was built encouraged states to focus most of their economic and other energies upon internal development and to relegate most interstate economic activity to secondary importance.[1] Thus, economic developments in early modern Europe, like those in the political sphere, tended to reinforce the construction of comparatively impermeable or "hard-shelled" national units.

Then, at the end of the eighteenth century, the industrial revolution began in Western Europe. It was from the first a social revolution in the way it altered the traditional economic relationships of individuals, attracting huge numbers of people from the land to work for wages in city factories, demanding ever larger manufacturing enterprises, fueling the creation of an entrepreneurial class, and growing insatiable in its demands for new energy resources to drive the new modes of production. Within a few decades, industrialization also began to increase the overall wealth of a number of Western nations as they pulled away from traditional societies. It is estimated that as early as 1850, the ratio between incomes in the industrializing societies and those elsewhere may already have been about two to one—a dramatic portent of the gap between rich and poor that would widen to the present day.

As the incomes of people living in industrialized nations noticeably increased, an expectation took root for the first time in history that ever-greater economic growth and wealth was natural. However grim the working conditions in early industrial England may look to us today, most laborers viewed their own material prospects as better than they had ever been before. In fact, as average per capita income slowly rose, each generation came to expect and demand an improvement in its own economic situation over that of its predecessor, a phenomenon that has accompanied industrialization ever since.

Expectations of growth clearly create a beast with an enormous appetite. To be satisfied, it must be fed with ever greater resources, including capital and labor, which in turn help create ever larger enterprises that gain strength and generate more wealth through economies of scale. From the beginning, the industrial revolution most enhanced the place in the world of those states large enough to create formidable, diversified industrial economies—England and France led the way, followed before the end of the nineteenth century by a newly united Germany and the United States. The growth appetite could be most readily fed in states like these that commanded large and diverse resources, whether, as in the United States, in their own, largely undeveloped backyards or, as in Britain and France, in overseas territories that could supply many of the resources not available at home. The nineteenth-century period of imperialist competition was driven above all by the growth ideology. The prospect of ever greater wealth was perhaps motivation enough for many entrepreneurs, but it also carried with it greater power on the global stage than could have been imagined by earlier statesmen.

The Westphalian order adjusted to the imperialist drive, as we have seen, by creating a double standard in which vast sections of the globe simply were not deemed to be full participants in the international system. Such territories were fair game for the kind of conquest and exploitation denied the nation-states of Europe when they interacted on their home continent. Once attached to the flag of a European power, their presumed interests then were expressed for them in the distant capital. This double standard created a situation that has come to be regarded today as unjust. But as a legal fiction, it served to perpetuate the laissez-faire thrust behind the international order: Hands-off principles applied only to full-fledged sovereign states; very different principles of behavior were accepted vis-à-vis those that, by definition, were not sovereign. As a result, colonialism could rationalize the creation of larger and larger units in keeping with the new economic imperatives as long as the core territory of the original European actors was not swallowed up in the process.

Had the world at the beginning of the nineteenth century not been essentially defenseless against the more powerful industrializing countries of Europe and North America, Westphalia's impact on economic organization probably would have placed much greater restraints on the development of great industrial powers, for the growth ideology is not stopped by a sign at the nation's edge that says *hands off*. Colonialism in effect successfully masked for a century and more the artificiality of state borders from the standpoint of industrial capitalism's constant need for growth and expansion.

In addition, nineteenth-century colonialism had important economic consequences on the colonized world. The most long-lasting of these stems from the universal imperial practice of treating the overseas territories and their populations as valuable only for the supporting role they could play in feeding the growth machine at the imperial center. Thus, colonies were typically suppliers of raw materials and providers of an agricultural base to the mother country. Theories of comparative advantage were created to explain why, say, Africa's Gold Coast should grow cocoa to be produced into fine chocolate in London or Edinburgh, or why Vietnamese peasants should labor on rubber plantations so that workers at a Michelin factory in France could produce tires for Peugeots. Economic growth became a basic fact of life at the imperial center; in the colonized periphery, life remained largely at the ages-old subsistence level.

The real legacy of that practice has been its persistence even after the end of colonialism. Independence for colonized territories has not yet let them overcome, with few exceptions, their historic poverty and dependence on the North. Put slightly differently, the first industrial societies had advanced by the mid-twentieth century to the point that they were able generally to maintain a momentum in their growth that has not yet appeared in most of the once-colonized world. The 1850 income gap of about two to one, dividing industrializing Europe from the rest of the world, grew to ten to one by 1950. A mere decade later, the ratio was on the order of fifteen to one with the prospect that, if the trend continued, it could create a chasm between the wealthy and the poor of about thirty to one by the end of the century. From this one can begin to grasp the principal force underlying many current global problems and the enormous increase in attention to issues of economic development on the world's political agenda.

THE WESTERN APPROACH TO INTERNATIONAL
ECONOMIC DEVELOPMENT

The global upheavals between the two world wars were marked in the economic sphere by the Great Depression. As one advanced industrial country after another experienced the devastating effects of widespread unemployment and the collapse of capital, their governments turned to strictly protectionist policies in the effort to save their own societies. Even though the members of these governments had long shared the view that economic liberalism in the international marketplace served their mutual interests in continued growth, suddenly they had to respond to the desperate conditions of their own national constituencies. The governmental response was to ignore, regardless of the consequences, the interests of other publics as they sought to seal their own economies off from the rest of the world to save themselves.[2] Most Western leaders adopted protectionist measures reluctantly, regarding them as short-term palliatives. They almost certainly made recovery more difficult by choking back international trade instead of encouraging it. These developments remain a classic example of an ongoing dilemma in all considerations of world order: State actors, obligated to their own populations in ways they are not to the rest of the world, will always respond first to demands arising from within. If those demands are insistent or desperate enough, as they were during the depression, it matters little that they may run counter to the interests of global society, which include the long-term interests of the local society as well, even though, when basic values are at stake, these tend to be blocked from sight altogether.

Although protectionist measures generally hindered economic recovery in the 1930s, the different and more complex cure of national economic planning seemed to many in industrialized societies to produce a positive alternative to renewed growth. When the world's economy had to be rebuilt at the end of World War II, many argued in favor of international economic institutions that would allow considerable national regulation of interstate economic relations while at the same time working to minimize conflicts between and among national regulations. Nonetheless, that view lost out, and the postwar world instead was built upon the dominant U.S. vision of a return to international liberalism. Specifically, "the most significant American policy makers imagined post-war economic institutions as agencies that would aim to abolish national restrictions on the international economy rather than merely regulate them."[3] That vision guided most international economic policy for the next several decades. For example, the new international financial system created at Bretton Woods in 1945 made the U.S. dollar a kind of international currency to stabilize and facilitate investment and trade throughout the world. Another example was the long-term effort to increase trade through the gradual reduction of restrictive tariffs. To this end, the industrialized countries of the North in the 1950s formed the General Agreement on Tariffs and Trade (GATT) to work toward the gradual reduction of protectionist measures on a reciprocal basis, and in the 1960s and 1970s they engaged in the protracted negotiations of the so-called Kennedy and Tokyo Rounds that were aimed at further liberalizing trade relations. One can read the motivation behind the U.S. Marshall Plan in the same light. Because it gave the previously rich market states of Western Europe the opportunity to reconstruct their economies, it in effect ensured a more liberalized international (Western) system of work, expansion, and growth.[4]

In these and other manifestations of the liberal economic ideology, the Soviet Union and other socialist states were left largely on the sidelines. As centrally planned economies, rigorously controlled from the top, they rejected the liberal premise in both its national and international guises; they relied on neither the marketplace to determine the form and shape of their domestic economies nor the free exchange of goods and money with the West to form economic links with the outside world that might grow to become unresponsive to political control from within. As one of the two dominant powers in the world system after 1945, the Soviets did engage in economic politics as an aspect of their foreign policy. That is, they followed the example of the United States in offering foreign assistance for development projects in a number of third world countries. They also assisted selected friendly governments with large capital outlays, much as the United States did.[5] But from the beginning of the development debate, they have been largely sealed off from important participation in the international economic agenda.

The international economic regime established after World War II did not exactly turn its back on the problems of what later was to be called the third world, with its legacy of poverty and lack of development and the consequent growing disparity in well-being between its enormous population and that of the increasingly rich world of the North. Rather, the international system was built upon several general assumptions, often more implicit than explicit, in keeping with the precepts of laissez-faire liberalism.

The first assumption was that development in the poor countries would follow the revitalization of the rich, since growing demand in the North presumably would stimulate increased production in the South. Another was that states had to come to their own industrial revolutions in their own natural course, just as had occurred in nineteenth-century Europe. That assumption raised certain dilemmas: While traditional societies were encouraged to rely on the marketplace for the stimulation of capital for investment, they were also advised to take governmental action in sectors where private capital is least likely to flow. These included specifically improving the agricultural base to ensure the kinds of crop surpluses for capital that could fuel investment in industry as a second step, and increasing education, since illiterate peasants never have made successful capitalist entrepreneurs. Still another assumption stemmed from the theory of comparative advantage, suggesting that at least some poor nations—those without the resources to build diversified, self-sufficient economies on the model of the large Northern states—should expect to improve their lot by concentrating on the production of the one or two commodities they were particularly well suited to produce. In all of these assumptions, economic development throughout the South was assumed to be a positive good for everyone, but it should not be hurried for fear traumatic social upheaval would result. Nor should it be skewed through massive national planning to the detriment of the overall interests of the global economy—one integrated, that is, through liberal economic policies.

This slow-going approach to the problems of economic underdevelopment is reflected in the creation of relevant formal arrangements in the international system in the early postwar years. The International Bank for Reconstruction and Development (the World Bank) concentrated on the first, rather than the second, of its purposes in the immediate aftermath of World War II and played an important role in financing the recovery of the war-torn, but already industrialized, countries. Its weighted-voting scheme ensured that the Western states, which contributed most to its assets, would have the dominant voice in its lending policies. Since it typically made loans at conventional rates of interest, third world governments were quick to assert that it was ill equipped to deal with what they saw as their massive needs for development assistance.

As the result of continuous pressure from the underdeveloped world, new institutional arrangements and more development-oriented policies gradually were adopted over the next twenty years. In 1956, the International Finance Corporation came into being as a World Bank affiliate to promote the growth of the private sector in third world countries; that is, it largely embodied the traditional economic views of the dominant ideology while stimulating a greater flow of private capital for development purposes. In 1960, the International Development Authority was added as the "soft-loan" affiliate of the World Bank in a move that finally acknowledged the need to grant to many loan recipients the kind of concessions in interest rates and pay-back schedules unavailable before. After Robert S. McNamara assumed its presidency in 1968, the World Bank expanded its lending more than twelvefold and explicitly redirected many of its resources toward combating world poverty.[6] Even so, many of the problems of underdevelopment remained so intractable—particularly in light of that ever-deepening gap between rich and poor—that the Western approach to development and the economic system it had created came under increasing attack through much of the world. That development in turn had its origins in the vast expansion of the state system after World War II.

THE RISING VOICE OF THE THIRD WORLD

Rapid decolonization in the 1950s and 1960s brought increasing numbers of peoples who had always been voiceless in the councils of international politics into formal participation in the global system. When the United Nations was created in 1945, slightly more than half its original fifty-one members were what the United Nations later would describe euphemistically as less-developed countries. Almost none of that group of between twenty-five and thirty had more than the bare beginnings of an industrial base. Twenty years later, UN membership had more than doubled (118 in 1966), and almost all the new members were former colonies that fell into that category. Apart from the fact that they now could outvote the industrialized North in such forums as the General Assembly—a formal power that, as all would learn, could be frustratingly empty if it did not command the real financial resources of the rich minority—their participation inevitably gave them a growing voice and helped to tilt the international agenda increasingly away from the more traditional concerns of the old states.

New voices, new forums for discussions, and an ever-widening gap between rich and poor—together they have formed an ideology that now challenges the liberal vision of international economic development as outmoded and discredited by its impact on the poor. But before examining some of the specific components of that critique, it is worth noting how the global political system itself has served as a kind of catalyst in creating what can be called the New International Economic Order (NIEO) ideology.[7]

One of the early decisions of the UN Economic and Social Council (ECOSOC) was to create a number of permanently functioning regional economic commissions, which, it was thought, could attend to the economic problems of particular geographical areas of the world in ways that ECOSOC as a whole could not. On one of these, the Economic Commission for Latin America (ECLA), sat an economist whose experience there led him to develop a deep and far-ranging critique of the impact of the world's economic system on the underdeveloped countries of Latin America. In 1950 Raul Prebisch published a major work setting forth his views, which argued essentially that the international economic system was structurally biased in favor of the industrialized states and worked against the development interests of the South. The effect of economic liberalism was to maintain and strengthen the positions of the dominant industrialized countries, those at the core of the system, and to perpetuate the dependency of the underdeveloped world on their policies.[8] Prebisch's views struck responsive chords in increasing numbers of third world statesmen, who by the 1960s were in widespread agreement with him as to what was wrong with the international economic system. Just as important, third world governments were developing increasingly powerful political attacks upon it.

But the newly formed third world position first was most dramatically expressed in another international forum. In 1964, the first UN Conference on Trade and Development (UNCTAD I) saw the participating bloc of seventy-seven underdeveloped countries caucusing and voting as a unit, with the result that they succeeded through the weight of their numbers in getting many of their resolutions passed in opposition to the long-standing policies of the North. The Group of 77 (as they are still called, even though their number has nearly doubled), acting on the basis of their only strength—voting power—thus learned the importance of their own unity in the effort to implement their views. The very form of their participation in the international institutional framework has encouraged the evolution of the NIEO outlook.

THE NIEO RESPONSE TO ECONOMIC LIBERALISM

The core assumption in the NIEO critique is that the established approach to development in the post–World War II period has not succeeded and cannot succeed in eliminating the dependency of third world economies on those of the North. It does not deny that in many parts of the underdeveloped world industrialization has taken root and grown or that increases in gross national products have raised living standards in a number of countries. But it asserts that the underlying condition of dependence on economic decisions taken in the North remains and that, in effect, as a solution to one part of the problem of underdevelopment appears, a new problem arises and dependence remains. This assumption is best examined by looking briefly at several of the components in the international economic situation today.

Trade is particularly vital to developing countries as a potential source of investment capital, yet their principal trade commodities are primary products sold to industrialized countries for processing and manufacture, which then may be sold back to the developing countries as finished goods. This process presumably exemplifies notions of comparative advantage (the production of primary products—food crops, mineral extraction—is typically labor intensive, whereas that of manufactured goods, particularly those requiring high technology, is much more capital intensive). Nonetheless, it is harmful to poor countries in two ways: First, it is self-perpetuating, particularly in a world economic system dominated by private investment rather than centralized planning, for if good quality peanuts can be grown in, say, Gambia more cheaply than anywhere else, it will encourage the growing of peanuts there ad infinitum, regardless of the fact that virtually the entire crop must be exported for the survival of Gambia. Second, this dependence maintains and perhaps even increases the relative poverty of the exporting nation because of marketplace factors. In the words of a document published by the Non-Aligned Conference of states in September 1979, "the continued escalation in the prices of manufactures, capital goods, food products and services imported by the developing countries and the stagnation and fluctuations in the prices of primary products exported by them have continued to exacerbate the trade gap between the developed and developing countries and resulted in a sharp decline in the terms of trade of developing countries."[9] Although these words were describing the conditions of the late 1970s, this part of the NIEO critique insists that the ongoing tendency of the world's economic system is to maintain negative terms of trade for the producers of primary products.

Closely related is the view that major inflationary or deflationary swings in the global economy have their root cause in the practices of the industrialized countries. Wages rise in the North and the prices of goods produced there increase, making them more costly for poor countries to buy. As the purchasing power of these countries is reduced, they soon find themselves forced to enter the inflationary path themselves by raising the price of their exports in the effort to redress the growing imbalance. Northerners with memories of the leaping prices in oil exported by OPEC during the 1970s may insist that that was an example of worldwide inflation fueled from the South. Although Northern spokesmen worked assiduously at the time to convince poor countries of the treachery of their oil-exporting brothers, few third world governments were convinced. Rather, they insisted that the artificially low price of oil prior to the first OPEC action—a condition produced by the then decisive power of transnational oil companies— had in fact amounted to an ongoing subsidy by oil producers of the economic growth of the industrialized countries, where that precious resource had been used profligately. Moreover, as the North exported its inflation, oil-producing countries were forced by their declining purchasing power to correct the situation.[10]

Conversely, as we have learned in the 1980s, when the industrialized nations take drastic domestic action, such as encouraging widespread unemployment to curb their inflation, they also export their resulting recession to the rest of the world. One of the significant effects of a sharp decline in demand for the products the poor countries can export is their growing inability to repay loans granted them by Northern banks.

Nor does dependency ordinarily cease once industrialization and diversification of a poor country's economy gets underway. Societies that traditionally have been able to feed their own people, if only at subsistence levels, increasingly become food importers as their populations are drawn from traditional agricultural practices into the cities and factories. The subsistence economy is self-sufficient; advanced industrial economies typically are much less so. Even though that may explain a good deal about the development of liberal trade attitudes in advanced societies, for the country in transition today from a traditional to a modern economy one form of dependence is being exchanged for another.[11] The new dependence presents quite different problems, psychologically at least, from those faced by Europeans in the nineteenth century as they moved from the self-sufficiency of subsistence into the industrial revolution. For them, unlike third world populations today, it would be a century or more before international dependence or interdependence would become a meaningful concept.

There are many other factors in the NIEO critique. These include what is known as the transfer of technology problem, that is, the fact that most of the essential technology for development remains in the private hands of Northern entrepreneurs and managers, and so is inaccessible to those in third world countries who need it for their independent development. A related issue is that of the brain drain, which attracts intellectuals from developing countries to the better-paying jobs and higher standards of living in the North, a phenomenon that "really constitutes gratuitous and inverse transfer of technology" in the wrong direction.[12] In addition, the international monetary system and multilateral financing agencies are seen to be slanted in favor of the interests of the highly developed countries to the disadvantage of the poor.

All of these are viewed as symptoms of the third world's continuing dependency on the core industrial states, which is to say that the cause of underdevelopment problems is thought to be the system itself. As a result, NIEO advocates argue that basic structural changes are needed; more development capital, more technical assistance, and more extensive use of soft loans with low interest rates will not in themselves change the underlying condition. Although no exact blueprint exists for all the needed reforms, there is widespread agreement in the South on certain principles that should guide the effort.[13]

These principles flow from what are regarded as the inherent rights and duties of states in the modern world. The thrust of these arguments permits confrontation with the main dynamic of modern capitalism, especially in its postindustrial phase, that it is not limited by state boundaries. The invisible hand that drives laissez-faire practice cannot justifiably be limited in its operation by the artificial constraints of national borders. If the most profitable investments are halfway around the globe, capital will flow there if allowed to. If a particularly valuable resource, such as copper, exists in plentiful supply in Chile, then Chilean copper should be mined to fuel the industrial machine of the rest of the world. Free market economics does not concern itself with the effects of these practices on local polities—or rather it *would* not in a world free from pluralistic political interests and values.

In response to this tendency, the NIEO outlook places great stress on some of the traditional attributes of membership in the Westphalian political system. State sovereignty implies the inherent right of the sovereign to say yea or nay to any economic activity taking place within its borders. Not the invisible hand of the international marketplace, but the very visible hand of the local government should determine the direction of its economy. No advanced industrial country can counter with a commanding argument about that general principle, since all have turned, and still do, to the logic of sovereignty to justify their own repeated interventions in the marketplace. Liberalism, after all, has simply been one, usually dominant impulse powering Western economic growth. It has been tempered by increased governmental interventions to alleviate the worst effects of the marketplace at home. Third world leaders who argue that their own infant industries need protection to face the competition of the mature industrial sector of the North need only point to U.S. practice throughout the nineteenth century to support their case. Alexander Hamilton convinced his countrymen of the need to protect U.S. industrial development nearly two hundred years ago.

But lines tend to be drawn when sovereignty justifications for antiliberal policies go beyond any presumably encountered by the Northern societies as they were developed themselves. Such is the case in the third world claim to permanent sovereignty over their own resources. That position stems from the recognition of the great potential wealth of many such resources, of their ever-growing value because of the insatiable demand for them in advanced societies, and of the ineluctable fact that many cannot be replaced once they have been exploited. The NIEO position makes clear the potential power of the third world in this principle: "The exercise of full and effective permanent sovereignty and control over natural and other commodities and raw materials [is] a way to eliminate unequal exchange, the exercise of control over foreign capital and over the actions of transnational corporations."[14]

At least part of the reason for this focus on the rights and duties of states, then, is a quest for greater third world political power over the economic life of the world. It is natural in the Westphalian context that one of its important component arguments is that more of the binding international decisions should be made democratically, that is, on the basic principle that every state should have but one vote.[15] Some international institutions, including the General Assembly of the United Nations, operate on this principle, but the Assembly's resolutions are specifically described in the Charter as nonbinding recommendations. Institutions with true "legislative" power to command resources in the economic sphere, such as the World Bank, are exactly those whose votes are weighted in favor of the Northern countries. The democratization argument received its first major boost at UNCTAD I, which operated on the one-state, one-vote principle and saw the Group of 77 vote its policies through over the opposition of the developed countries. In the years since, that voting power has continued to enable the Group of 77 to advance its views through their formal adoption in such forums as the General Assembly, although in general the outvoted minority of Northern states still refuses to acknowledge any obligation to acquiesce in the majority will.

NEW PROBLEMS, STRATEGIES, AND GOALS

In the more than twenty years since the NIEO critique of development first began to get a hearing, many features of the world's economy have changed dramatically. Those changes naturally have produced new debates and in some cases have brought to the fore new values that are altering much of the substance of development strategies.

Curbing Population Growth

Solutions to the world's problems of poverty and underdevelopment have been made increasingly difficult over the past several decades as the result of the zooming growth in populations throughout much of the third world. In fact, it may be not so much that established development policy has failed as that the resulting overpopulation has not been adequately addressed. It took 2 million years and more before *Homo sapiens* numbered about 1 billion, which was the figure attained early in the nineteenth century at about the time the industrial revolution began. Little more than a century later, by about 1930, a second billion had been added. In only another thirty years, global population reached 3 billion, and fifteen years after that, by 1975, living human beings numbered 4 billion. Clearly, the doubling of our population in ever more telescoped periods has thrust us very far along a collision course with the planet's finite capacity to sustain human life.

Since World War II, most of this explosive growth has been within poor countries, as attention to the problems of poverty focused on the kinds of basic health and sanitation measures that can reduce the death rate. Meanwhile, as deaths per thousand persons dropped radically throughout the underdeveloped world, patterns of fertility remained largely at traditional high levels, with the result that there have been ever-growing numbers of new mouths to feed. The economic output of societies caught in explosive population growth then has to be stretched ever farther not just to feed, but otherwise to support their huge sector of dependent children. Like Alice, these societies must run ever faster just to stay in the same place. This phenomenon, vastly greater in scale and scope than anything the Northern countries had to face a century and more ago as their economic growth took off, accounts for the fact that even though productivity has increased— in many cases more than doubled—throughout the third world since World War II, it frequently has been offset by comparable growth in the population.

Although serious efforts to address the problem of high birthrates have been undertaken in a number of countries, they have been both agonizingly slow to produce the desired results—although results now are beginning to be seen—and often Draconian in their implications for the authoritarian control of governments over personal and family life. The late Indian prime minister's son, Sanjay Gandhi, became a very controversial figure before his accidental death for his direction of what allegedly were forced sterilization and contraception programs throughout the country. In China, which with India accounted for nearly 40 percent of the world's annual population growth before the end of the 1970s, Mao Tse-tung's successors have sought to achieve negative population growth through a system of increasingly severe punishments for couples who produce more than one child. Two children are permitted; if a third child is born, the parents must undergo a socially embarrassing re-education program; after that, an additional child means a forced *reduction* to the family of certain essential goods. Such drastic measures to curb population growth, however necessary they may be to the well-being of the local society immediately and the future of the entire species over the longer run, are not exactly conducive to the development of free, nonauthoritarian societies.

It is tempting for the members of rich societies to place all the blame for population problems on the poor nations whose numbers are still increasing so rapidly and to forget that the first steps of the modernization process have produced them. In its most extreme form, this kind of thinking has led to the inhuman suggestion that international assistance programs to such countries should be curtailed until famine, disease, and wholesale death have occurred on a scale massive enough to reduce substantially such populations, thus solving the problems of an increasingly crowded planet.[16] Significantly, such views assume that the rich members of the species have a right to the places in the economic lifeboat whereas the poor, because of their failure to control their growing numbers, deserve to be consigned to the sea.

Yet some third world spokesmen have turned that metaphor around by noting that the members of rich societies, not the poor, are straining the earth's carrying capacity to its limits. The typical U.S. infant will consume some fifteen to twenty times more of the globe's economic output over the course of his lifetime than will those of his generation who happen to be born in Mauritania or Sri Lanka. The United States as a whole, with barely 6 percent of the world's population, accounts for more than 30 percent of its consumption annually. So the typical American is a much more burdensome passenger in the economic lifeboat than his third world counterpart. The boat obviously can support a dozen of the world's poor more easily than it can the weight of a single North American.

Disturbing though this lifeboat metaphor may be, whomever its occupants, it is a vivid illustration of why the income gap cannot possibly be closed by increasing the wealth of the poor to something like U.S. levels, the supposition that has seemed to underlie most of the traditional efforts at development. That supposition would mean an approximately sixfold increase in the gross global economy from its current level, with none of the increase going to today's wealthiest societies. Such a goal is wrong both practically and morally: No one supposes that existing economic and political realities permit its achievement, and if by some miracle it could be done, the result would be catastrophic for the biosphere. It would be a self-defeating goal for the species.

Transnational Corporations

Meanwhile, technological momentum relevant to production has brought sweeping change in the world's economic structure. In recent decades transnational corporations (TNCs) have rapidly emerged as powerful global actors. Thanks to technological advances in communication, transportation, and management, production has been internationalized wherever these corporations have arisen. That is, TNCs operate by drawing the components necessary for modern production from more than one country. This typically means combining capital, management, and technology from an advanced industrial society and labor and raw materials from a poor country. This internationalization of production is the essential and novel feature of TNCs, for it is no longer possible to say that the goods they produce were made in the United States, Japan, or Mexico, since they may have received essential components from all three. This point bears emphasis because it is tempting to view TNCs as simply the huge offspring of the already large national corporations of an earlier day whose names they still bear. True, internationalization began when national corporations organized divisions to coordinate their overseas operations, which at first were marginal. But as the overseas component grew in size and complexity, national organization no longer was adequate. As a result, "the MNC [multinational corporation] is now moving toward a global corporate structure, organizing along functional lines—production, R&D and marketing—rather than along geographic lines. Corporate strategies are being formulated increasingly on a global scale in terms of utilizing R&D results, selection of production sites, procurement of raw materials, and marketing of products."[17]

The size alone of TNCs is staggering, suggesting their economic impact on the world. The gross annual sales of many are larger than the gross national products of a great many states. In a 1968 ranking, the annual product of General Motors was larger than that of all but the 17 richest nation-states, and 44 of the top 100 economic actors proved to be corporations and not states.[18]

These developments have some obvious implications whereas others are complex and subject to ongoing debate. It is clear from the kind of rank ordering mentioned above that the impact of transnational activities on the development strategies of many third world countries is enormous. In some cases, their economies are penetrated to the point of being overwhelmed by TNC operations within them. That situation is obvious where a largely subsistence economy becomes the locale for the production of a primary product such as coffee by a transnational corporation making use of the nation's comparative advantage in growing conditions and inexpensive labor. A huge portion of the available land and work force fall under the company's domain and, although the standard of living may rise as a result, so will all the signs of increased dependence on management and investment decisions made elsewhere. Moreover, the once self-sufficient society may be forced to import basic foodstuffs, thereby creating a new foreign exchange problem for its government. In the long run, some of the local labor force may work its way into management positions. Conceivably, as the skills of that work force grow, some aspects of coffee processing may be relocated in the territory, providing new jobs for more highly skilled workers. Yet short of a controlling interest from the local population in investment and corporate decision making, it is difficult to detect a noticeable decrease in its dependency on external economic forces.

This kind of situation also contributes to an increasingly apparent fact of global economic life—the economic gap within developing countries is widening as is that between North and South generally. A comparatively skilled, consumption-oriented, and increasingly affluent class is emerging worldwide, whose members have developed life styles more like those of their counterparts in North America or Europe than those of most of their countrymen in Pakistan, Peru, or Yemen. Although this class is also increasingly cosmopolitan, a fact that may cheer those who see in it a hopeful sign of increasing global integration, its development heightens evidence of distributive injustice that, by bringing it closer to home for millions, may further feed the flames of resentment among the still impoverished masses and thereby spread the revolution of rising expectations. Moreover, the culture of materialism and wasteful consumption spawned by this new affluence of a global class raises a growing number of questions about its moral and political acceptability in a world that must confront, not simply economic inequities, which appear to be growing more profound, but the long-term effects for the species of unbridled materialism. Transnational corporations are both the products and the agents of that culture, which is now rapidly dispersing throughout the globe.

The debate about the impact of TNCs on global integration extends beyond these concerns. Those who view them as a positive force for integration emphasize that in cutting across state lines to do their work they encourage the creation of a peaceful international environment, which is the *sine qua non* of their successful operation. Further, in this view the TNC "is by far the most effective agent yet devised for disseminating technology across national borders, dwarfing in its effectiveness other types of institutions such as the UN Special Agencies, international professional societies, private consulting firms or bilateral assistance agencies."[19] Some go so far as to argue that "by breaking the monopoly of the nation-state over international economic relations the multinational corporation [has] . . . altered the very nature of international relations,"[20] breaking down Westphalian barriers to global interaction.

A more negative assessment emphasizes how TNCs further strengthen dominant economic groups both through the stratification process already mentioned and because most of the managerial and high technological aspects of their work tend to take place only within the rich societies of the North. Although they do indeed disseminate technology across national borders, by far the greatest amount of this transnational flow occurs only among the rich countries. Furthermore, as products also of the Westphalian system, they can exacerbate its most divisive, antiglobal features. Too often they act as instruments in the foreign policy of their home governments abroad, as when, for example, the U.S. government required overseas subsidiaries of U.S.-based firms to avoid trade with centrally planned economies. Too often their powerful ability to lobby in their own interests misdirects foreign policy away from its larger public purpose, as when U.S.-based firms persuaded Congress in 1972 to violate the UN boycott of Rhodesian chromium ore. Too often their apolitical thrust works against the protection and extension of important world order values, as when profit motives alone persuade them to do business in societies with repressive or racist regimes, or when their work supports the world's military machine.

The Limits of Growth and Appropriate Technologies

Not surprisingly in light of these developments, thoughtful analysts throughout the world are viewing with increased alarm the effects of the growth imperative on all of us. Although occasional voices have objected to its moral effect on our values and priorities in the past, only within our lifetimes has it become apparent that the growth appetite must be drastically curbed; nature will do it for us if we do not take immediate steps to bring it under control ourselves. Today's environmental crisis is almost entirely the result of our failure to control the ravages of greater and greater economic development upon the planet's finite resources. That realization is only beginning to have profound implications on development strategies for poor countries.

Now that we know that the traditional Northern model of industrialization and development is an ecological threat, we have a greater sense of its irrelevance to the situation of underdeveloped societies. That model demands large infusions of capital, advanced technology, and a skilled and highly paid work force—all of which are in short supply in the South. Not only is it very costly to teach farmers on the northern Chinese plain how to use a U.S. wheat-harvesting combine, but the combine is probably inappropriate to the scale of the Chinese wheat field and if adopted would displace the jobs of several dozen harvesters, which in the aggregate causes widespread social disruption. Similarly, the destruction of traditional cottage craft industries in favor of huge manufacturing plants obviously disrupts social life, drawing millions from the land into already overcrowded cities. It may also prove counterproductive if transportation systems are inadequate to move the new manufactured products throughout the country, if housing is not available for the influx of workers at the new plant, or for a host of other reasons that may have been overlooked by the project planners. Modern industrial enterprises typically operate on a scale that increasingly is seen to be all wrong for the well-being of society, including its relationship to the natural environment.

What this means in concrete terms is that appropriate technologies need to be applied to the existing economic and social situations of poor societies. To determine appropriateness entails considerably more soul-searching about the meaning of work and production in human terms, including a concern with humanity's relationship to the natural world, than it typically receives in the more orthodox discussions of development needs and problems. One of the most influential advocates of appropriate technology, E. F. Schumacher, has proposed four essential guidelines for overcoming the evils of large-scale industrial development:

> First, that workplaces have to be created in the areas where the people are living now, and not primarily in metropolitan areas into which they tend to migrate.
> Second, that these workplaces must be, on average, cheap enough so that they can be created in large numbers without this calling for an unattainable level of capital formation and imports.
> Third, that the production methods employed must be relatively simple so that the demands for high skills are minimized, not only in the production process itself but also in matters of organization, raw material supply, financing, marketing, and so forth.
> Fourth, that production should be mainly from local materials and mainly for local use.[21]

Clearly, Schumacher wished to conserve what is soundest in the value systems of traditional societies while encouraging the development of an ability to provide greater economic well-being than they have ever known before. This concern is the common thread visible in all the counterestablishment development literature, whether criticizing the practices of advanced or postindustrial societies or the strategies for development that seek to copy them.

One not untypical result of such thinking led, for example, to the experiments with rice farming undertaken by the Japanese philosopher-farmer, Masanobu Fukuoka. Motivated by a deep reverence for nature and a conviction that modern rice-farming techniques violated nature's order far more than was necessary, he successfully attempted to grow rice without engaging in the kinds of backbreaking labor and extensive fertilization procedures that had been thought necessary for centuries. He refused to flood or weed his fields, but instead provided weed control as well as nutrients by scattering various kinds of grass seed among the plants. His experiment with natural farming succeeded, he is convinced, because it was in accordance with nature's own principles. As an admiring commentator noted, "humans work best when they work for human good, not for the 'higher production' or 'increased efficiency' which have been the nearly exclusive goals of industrial agriculture. 'The ultimate goal of farming,' Mr. Fukuoka says, 'is not the growing of crops but the cultivation and perfection of human beings.'"[22]

Fulfilling Basic Needs

Closely related to these issues has been growing attention to the fulfillment of people's basic needs as a new development strategy. As a response to the difficulty and frequently the deleterious consequences of Northern-style development, the basic needs approach deliberately relegates the process of large-scale industrialization and development of agribusiness to the background. Instead its first priorities are how to provide poor societies with adequate food, shelter, health care, and education. It responds to the problem of dependency by attempting to restore the food independence of many societies where it has been lost thanks to global specialization and the growth of transnational corporations. It is sympathetic, therefore, to the demands for greater self-reliance, although in another sense it is more modest in its goals than the schemes for autarkic development of highly diverse industrial economies. Many people associated with this approach call for an agrarian revolution oriented to home consumption, which, they think, can provide the society's basic needs and thus a platform from which to seek higher economic values.[23]

Under Robert McNamara's direction, the World Bank increasingly associated itself with basic needs strategies, although many critics argued that the World Bank has never worked more than halfheartedly in this direction because of its ongoing domination by the goals of advanced capitalist members. Such members can never encourage more than minimal self-reliance when a highly differentiated global economy, growth oriented and increasingly integrated, remains their primary vision. One critic said, "In the World Bank's view, it is essential to produce export crops so that the underdeveloped countries can pay for agricultural imports controlled by Western multinationals. The relative neglect of subsistence agriculture in the Bank's calculations is merely the transposition of its goals: generate profits for multi-nationals and hard currency for ruling elites."[24]

Now that the basic needs approach has at least received a wider hearing, a critique of its presumed effects also has been developed. This argument states that in addressing the issue of dependence and skewed efforts at industrialization, the basic needs approach is really little more than a design for keeping poor nations relatively poor. If the reinvigoration of subsistence agriculture is a principal goal, then the dramatic increases in living standards that accompany Western-style growth are forever deferred. Even if basic needs strategies succeed, so this argument goes, the result still will not be the enrichment of societies much beyond the level they attained in the past. The gap between North and South will remain, comprising now not only one of wealth, but one separating two worlds—one rich, highly skilled, and increasingly integrated; the other still poor, backward, and perpetually divided within itself.

New Industrialization in the South

For a few countries, development recently has taken off in ways that seem to defy developmental pessimists, as newly industrialized countries (NICs) have emerged from the ranks of the chronically poor. Thailand, Taiwan, South Korea, Brazil, and Mexico are among the most often cited examples. None of this group still fits the standard measurements for underdeveloped societies, although their paths out of poverty have been varied and often troublesome when examined in terms of their domestic social impact and example for other nations. Where per capita income has grown through the application of more or less orthodox development strategies, the flight to the cities has created new social problems from overcrowding and greater stratification while at the same time increasing the country's sensitivity to the growth and recession cycles of Northern economies. Where labor-intensive industrial development has produced dramatic results, as in several Asian countries, it seemingly has been made possible through the kind of discipline encouraged by highly centralized and authoritarian governmental policy.

An old lesson can be seen in the sum of these developments—that solutions to some of the problems of poverty do not solve all problems of human well-being and in fact may create new ones. The search for convergent solutions to social problems continues even when the stakes and the problems themselves change. The recently arrived laborer in Mexico City may have twice the income he knew in the countryside, even though his new environment may leave him isolated from the kind of social support he once had from his village, subjected to increased health hazards from the capital's pollution, and still malnourished and badly housed in a city that grew too fast to meet rationally everyone's needs for food and shelter.

New solutions create new problems, yet at least we are beginning to see that varied choices are possible in the search for solutions, thanks to the different road taken by the NICs. What has worked for Taiwan may not be appropriate for India for reasons that include their very different size and population, political cultures, and economic potential. The more positive face to that situation, however, is the growing availability of industrialization models other than that of the nineteenth-century West, from which a more eclectic, and perhaps more relevant, borrowing is possible than was the case in the fairly recent past. General lessons may not be apparent from the experiences of the NICs, but their more specific examples of pitfalls and possibilities should serve other poor countries in the search for their own solutions.

More negatively, the development of NICs has not solved, but globally extended, economic stratification. Their growing wealth (combined with that of the OPEC countries, most of whom became suddenly wealthy prior to their real development) has drawn them further into the dominant economic system of the North and away from a unity of interests with the poorest nations of the world. These relatively wealthy countries are able to obtain the private investment capital of the North, unlike the poorest of the poor, which have virtually no access to commercial credit. In a period when official development assistance is shrinking, these fourth world nations generally find their situations worsening while private capital flows expand to the NICs and OPEC countries.[25]

THE DIALECTICS OF GLOBAL ECONOMICS

No aspect of human life seems more fraught with dialectical tensions at every turn than the effort to provide economic well-being for all the world's people. Every set of priorities, every preferred strategy for dealing with global scarcity gives rise to its contradictory opposite. Only dimly do we yet see paths toward reconciling these opposing needs and values in ways that could help minimize the world's distributive injustice. However, a closer look at two of the conflicting configurations apparent in this chapter may reveal some of the signposts pointing to their eventual synthesis.

The first of these centers on the growth in global economic interdependence on the one hand versus greater national regulatory control to promote more autarkic conditions on the other. The substantial growth in interdependence in recent decades is the product of the ideology and practices of the dominant, free enterprise economic system of the North, which in this period has increasingly permitted the invisible hand of laissez-faire to move about the globe far more widely than Adam Smith could have imagined. Resistance to that trend in the support for national regulatory policies has become one of the hallmarks of the NIEO ideology, which is to say, of the third world generally. In crudest terms, the highly developed states of the West support a global economic ideology that cuts right through Westphalian divisions, whereas the less developed countries of the third world take strength in this debate from the rights and duties Westphalia provides them. It is no contradiction to note that the latter are strongest at the formal or institutional level of global politics, which gives fullest application to the Westphalian logic of the sovereign equality of states. On the other side, the free market industrialized states have built their economic power essentially by ignoring the logic of Westphalia, which is diametrically opposed to the creation of a global economic system. In this sense transnational corporations are viewed by some proponents of economic liberalism as potentially revolutionary actors in world politics, capable of altering the basic nature of international relations.

These highly generalized descriptions suggest that the international economic life of the West is therefore revolutionary in its impact on the Westphalian system whereas the policies of the South are conservative or even reactionary. If that conclusion seems peculiar, it is because we have not yet brought any questions regarding the *purposes* of economic activity into the equation. They all have to do with the struggle to provide greater material well-being to people; that, in turn, instantly raises issues of relative equity in the distribution of the world's material goods. These are, in short, questions of justice.

The principal argument against laissez-faire economics has always and everywhere been that its effects are unjust in two ways. First, it typically increases the wealth of those who already have more to begin with (ordinarily, those with some form of property) so that even if the energies released by economic activity at the top of the society do eventually trickle down to benefit those at the bottom, they remain relatively no better, and probably worse off, than those at the top, whose incomes have continued to soar. Second, its profit motive ensures production of salable goods for consumption but leads to deficiencies in the supply of needed public goods—health, education, public safety, and environmentally sound production policies. As a result, the phenomenon of "private affluence and public squalor" is inherent in any economic system that gives free rein to the laissez-faire impulse.[26] These issues clearly underlie the NIEO critique of today's world economic system. The argument has been fueled by evidence of a continually widening North-South gap in spite of the efforts to close it—always with the policies permitted by the dominant ideology, such as insistence on voluntarism by donor countries, emphasis on the role of private capital, nonpreferential treatment of poor countries in international trade, and so on.

As the inequities widened, the Group of 77 emerged to press for greater distributive justice with the only arrow they could find in their quiver, that of their formal equality in a system in which they were so materially unequal. In forums like the General Assembly and UNCTAD, the poor are enfranchised. That at least seems to be the point of the rules for participation in those institutions, and the Group of 77 continues to press that point in its demands upon the rich minority. Yet their enfranchisement is not as real as it appears, for these international institutions have been carefully constructed to deprive them of truly legislative power over global society. At this point the rich and powerful minority of states takes refuge in the logic of Westphalia: Their sovereignty cannot be bridged by the votes of other sovereigns; formal participation in the international institution does not confer equal rights to command the world's economic resources. By a historical and natural accident, in this view, some sovereigns are able to command more economic resources than others, but nothing in the Westphalia tradition alone can alter that fact— rather, Westphalia serves to maintain it.

If we were to imagine a world in which, say, the UN General Assembly had true legislative power, in which majority votes somehow were translated into world law, what would make its authoritative power legitimate in our eyes? For those of us from democratic political cultures, the most important would no doubt be some assurance that it functioned more or less responsively to the needs of the global population. Legitimacy in any representative institution always flows in part from a sense that it truly represents a variety of interests. We are often told that one of the chief flaws in the constitution of the General Assembly, and presumably the main reason for resisting growth in its quasi-legislative power, is the very great inequality in representativeness of the states who sit there. Even apart from considerations of how popular particular governments may be with their own people, we should be leery of legislative power accruing to an institution in which Maldives has a vote equal to that of India, China, or the United States.

Yet that argument ignores the fact that the General Assembly has long since seen the emergence of considerable bloc caucusing and voting, one result of which can be seen in the emergence of the Group of 77. Bloc votes typically come far closer to being representative of real populations and their diverse interests than is suggested by the one-state, one-vote formula. To take only the most obvious divisions, which happen to be those that hold most generally in international economic matters, third world states now number about 115 in the General Assembly, with as many votes. Western states, including European neutrals, have 24 votes, and the Soviet bloc, 8. The total population of third world states is more than 2.5 billion, that of the Western group about 775 million, and that of the Soviet bloc around 360 million. Simple division reveals that every vote cast by the third world *as a bloc* may be made to stand for some 22.5 million people. By the same measure, each Western vote reflects 37 million people, and each Soviet bloc vote about 36 million. If, as democratic theory suggests, votes in governmental institutions are meant to represent human beings and not land or trees or money, then the third world's insistence upon democratizing international economic politics takes on meaning beyond the reactionary retreat into an outmoded nationalism such as the champions of interdependence are inclined to assign it. Voting by this measure is far less biased toward the South than the one-state, one-vote analysis alone suggests. This is not to say that the General Assembly as currently structured would make a model international parliament. It simply suggests that the third world's demand for greater participation in the effective decisions about allocation of scarce resources supports in general terms notions of how a pluralistic community might be advanced at the global level.

The second major configuration of conflict is that between the growth imperative and the limits of growth. It does not break down as clearly as a debate between North and South, although unquestionably the effects of the growth reached by highly industrialized societies have forced us to question its limits. At the moment, the forces appear to be very unequal, in that the growth dynamic is still what motors virtually all development efforts, whether in the ever-expanding postindustrial economies of the North or in NIEO attempts to increase the wealth of the South. Yet it is absolutely certain that the limits to growth imposed by nature itself increasingly will shift the balance to the other side, for limitless growth is quite literally unnatural.[27] Our economic activities have not forced us to consider that fact before the recent past, for the simple reason that they did not come close to testing nature's limits.

To the extent that we have begun to discuss the limits of growth, rich and poor alike have seemed to suppose that it was not their own growth but that of the other group that had to be constrained. At least many of the world's poor have viewed with suspicion any arguments from the rich to the effect that the biosphere cannot now support the kinds of wasteful and destructive industrialization processes in the South that the North itself engaged in. If the economic pie is finite, they argue, that does not alter the need of poor countries to have a relatively larger piece of it than they now enjoy. From rich societies, the moral force of this argument for greater equity is not so much denied as ignored because of its implications for their own aspirations for still more. As Ward and Dubos said,

> Whatever their good will, most developed peoples are still affected with one type of "tunnel vision." Although they make up no more than a third of the human race, they find it exceptionally difficult to focus their minds on the two-thirds of humanity with whom they share the biosphere. Like the elephants round the water hole, they not only do not notice the other thirsty animals. It hardly crosses their minds that they may be trampling the place to ruin.[28]

Nothing in human life may be much harder than for people to curb, voluntarily and rationally, their appetites for more of the world's material goods. No society known has yet voluntarily set out to reduce its standard of living. Since any of us will naturally resist the effort to rob us of those things that we enjoy—particularly those that, through technology, provide us with a power over our personal environment such as our primitive ancestors never knew—resistance will no doubt be fierce to any antigrowth tendencies that do not provide us with alternative economic value systems to those of ever-greater consumption. In short, the challenge to the affluent today is to find the means to live better with less. That need not mean less enjoyment of our lives, but rather, learning that not every artifact produced by our technology provides greater happiness. The critical point is that if we begin seriously to think about what it means to live in greater harmony with nature's rules, we will find new ideas and relevant values. Once that has happened, the way will be much more clearly pointed toward finding the kinds of changes needed in our economic lives.

Nor do we begin that effort with an absolutely blank slate, for the traditional economic lives of societies and the increasingly insistent voice of nature already provide us with nonthreatening lessons. Our sternest critics of the growth ideology have understood since early in the industrial age that the kind of power our machine age has given us also has alienated us from nature with dehumanizing effects. When we say that the huge scale of much of our economic activity works against nature's demands, we also understand why it is dehumanizing for those caught up in it, for we are part of the natural order. From that starting point we can learn to develop technologies that have a gentler impact on the ecosystem; cultivate renewable, nonpolluting energy sources, such as wind and solar power; and learn to find greater fulfillment in the free gifts of nature that increasingly are obscured from the view of modern, highly urbanized societies. There is nothing romantic in such views, as suggested by the advocates of unchecked growth, for those who hold them do not advocate turning the clock back to a presumably simpler time. Rather, they strive, in learning from the economic lessons of our premodern history, to harness our modern technological skills in ways that can make them work for the development of people, a development in harmony with nature.

TOWARD GREATER GLOBAL WELFARE

Growing awareness of the limits to the kind and scale of growth characteristic of the industrial age can gradually build a bridge across the North-South gulf. In fact, its sketch is already being drawn from the increasingly complex facts of international economic life today.

The mere fact that opposing visions of economic development have grown to shape the international agenda is in one sense merely an indication that development concerns are receiving attention on a global scale for the first time in history. The attention and resulting conflicts are the first steps toward more effective treatment of our ills. We would do well to remember that when we long for the good old days before these issues loomed so large in international politics. Where new political conflicts exist, social injustice at last is finding expression through the political system. The interests of particular oppressed groups—whether slaves, untouchables, homosexuals, or women—are not politically relevant as long as their oppression goes unchallenged within the social order (which usually has meant, unchallenged by the oppressed groups themselves). Once significant challenges arise, what had been out of bounds to political inquiry and adjustment, perhaps for centuries, suddenly finds its place on the political agenda. What follows is typically a period of struggle between the oppressed and the dominant that gives every indication to many that the community itself is disintegrating. Certainly, a struggle is required to change the traditional social consensus about how some of its members are treated. Certainly, too, the struggle may result in bloodshed, more repression, or a revolution that brings those previously oppressed into the newly dominant position.

To say that a particular social issue, such as the impoverishment of two-thirds of the world's population, has made its way to the world's political agenda is by no means to guarantee its quick and peaceful resolution. Conflicts no doubt will continue well into the future while the plight of at least some of the world's poor worsens. Resistance to the entreaties of the poor probably will continue from the rich. Yet when we take the long view of this subject, there may be more reasons for hope than despair.

First, with the rapid decolonization of the third world after World War II, the Westphalian system was opened up in a way that gave the impoverished a new voice. Although the relevant international institutions through which these voices were heard equally did not grant them equivalent decision-making power, their growing insistence that it be given to them probably cannot be resisted forever. Increased interdependence at a multiplicity of levels all combine to make a wider sharing of economic decisions increasingly imperative. Futhermore, the quasi-parliamentary appearance of the international institutions in which economic discussions take place may itself gradually support their evolution into more truly legislative bodies. We live in a world in which most of the states of the globe have long since taken on the trappings, if not always the substance, of representative government. In this sense, most of the world lives in a political culture in which such forms of government are perceived as the norm. We may find it increasingly illogical that such comparable forms at the world level should not take on more decision-making power. Evolution is inevitably a slow, nearly imperceptible process, but most of the trends in international organization since World War II point in this direction.

Second, the liberal rhetoric of the North, with its emphasis upon free market forces as crucial to international development, should not hide the fact that these same most economically advanced states have for many decades supported widespread governmental intervention in their own economies to provide greater distributive justice. Even though some of them have experienced a reaction against the growth of the welfare state system in the 1980s, they have scarcely returned to completely laissez-faire policies. The social necessity of governmental intervention to provide greater distributive justice at home is now so widely accepted in the North that there is no very good reason why the logic that supports it should not extend to the larger social system of the world. In fact, much of the NIEO program stems from exactly such a vision: It calls for establishment of the principle of the graduated income tax at a world level in asking for official development assistance commitments from the rich based upon percentages of their GNP (currently 0.7 percent is the asked-for target). The various trade preferences, indexation of commodities, and other forms of support to the poorest sectors of the global economy that are part of the NIEO outlook all are equivalent to social programs in developed countries designed to assist the most disadvantaged members of society. Support for strong regimes to exploit and protect the global commons, particularly the oceans, stems from the same outlook.

Third, whatever the inhibitions against unlimited industrial growth on a global scale, and they will become increasingly formidable, there surely will be more of it in the South in the next decades than in the past. Other newly industrialized countries will be added to the group that has now achieved that status. Like them, they will become more fully integrated into the global economy in the process. The greatest pains of interdependence are for those countries least advanced, whose economies are least differentiated and self-sufficient. For them, the sense of helplessness in the face of economic forces beyond their control is most palpable and real. As they develop, a different quality enters their interconnectedness with the outside world; interdependence replaces mere dependence.

Once more of that kind of interdependence is present in the world, there is reason to hope that more stability and less conflict will result. With greater distributive justice, once impoverished societies not only will have more reason to be satisfied with their lot than they do at present, they also will have less incentive to stimulate conflicts with those other societies with which they are increasingly interconnected in mutually productive ways. Some have even gone so far as to posit the coming end of war as the result of such development:

> Developed states are unlikely to engage in a modern war with each other directly. The mutually reinforcing reasons are that their wars are too costly and that they need each other for the fulfillment of important interests which can be most adequately achieved by nonviolent methods. Once the developing states reach a sufficiently high level of intensity and diversification of interests, they too will experience similar constraints upon the conducting of wars.[29]

The strain of utopianism in such a view results largely because the world is currently at a stage where the political conflicts inherent in development problems and strategies are still paramount. These conflicts increasingly will be overcome if we can focus on the appalling consequences of distributive injustice. Then we must seek to overcome them, fully aware that the finiteness of nature's bounty demands a reordering of some long-standing values for the greater welfare of all the world's people.

NOTES

1. This is not to say that the new Westphalian order was solely or even primarily responsible for the development of laissez-faire economics, although a number of connections are no doubt likely. As we saw in Chapter 2, the term *laissez-faire* is just as appropriate to describe an international political system built upon the absence of a central regulatory authority as it is to label the identical ordering principle of laissez-faire economics. Nonetheless, the principle has acted on conceptually distinct spheres of social life with different consequences at different times. Until about the time of Adam Smith and the beginning of the industrial revolution, the chief *economic* thrust of laissez-faire in international *politics* was to bring to the fore mercantilist policies for the encouragement of autarky on a state-by-state basis in Europe. Smith's *Wealth of Nations* was mainly concerned with showing how intrastate economic development could be better fostered by eliminating such governmental regulations in favor of marketplace forces. But the logic of capitalism's "invisible hand" premise clearly has extended beyond national boundaries for highly developed societies. The theory of international liberalism with its espousal of free trade arose in response to that logic once intrastate development had reached a certain level in industrial societies. Today the impulse toward international laissez-faire confronts more autarkic imperatives in less advanced countries for the first time on a global level.

2. The irony of that response is apparent in the following observation: "Nationalism was in fact strengthened by the reformist orientation of modern politics: Franklin Roosevelt, a domestic reformer who tried to put the United States on the road to economic recovery after the Depression, did so at the expense of the international economic and, to some extent, political system. When governments are expected to regulate the economy to obtain maximum welfare for their citizens, they must often slight the interests of economic and political partners" (Richard Rosecrance and Arthur Stein, "Interdependence: Myth and Reality," *World Politics* 26, 1 [October 1973]:4–5).

3. Craig N. Murphy, "What the Third World Wants: An Interpretation of the Development and Meaning of the New International Economic Order Ideology," *International Studies Quarterly* 27, 1 (March 1983):6.

4. Ibid.

5. Presumably the largest of these for many years has been to the Cuban government, which by 1983 reportedly amounted to some $4 billion annually. *New York Times*, August 7, 1983, Section 4, p. 1.

6. *New York Times*, June 30, 1981.

7. The term *New International Economic Order* did not come into general usage until the Sixth Special Session of the General Assembly in 1974 when that name was attached to the program of economic reform supported by the third world, parts of which predated that session. See the Declaration of

the Establishment of a New International Economic Order (A/Res/3201 [S-VI]), and the Programme of Action on the Establishment of a New International Economic Order (A/Res/3202 [S-VI]).

8. For a sense of Prebisch's contribution, see Luis Eugenio di Marco, ed., *International Economics and Development: Essays in Honor of Raul Prebisch* (New York: Academic Press, 1972).

9. Non-Aligned Conference, NAC/CONF.6/C.2/Doc. 1/Rev. 3, p. 107. These contentions appear to many to be supported by the fact that after several decades of extensive attention to the development effort worldwide, the entire third world group of states still only accounted for some 8 percent of total world manufactured goods by the beginning of the 1980s.

10. Ibid., p. 111.

11. Great Britain has not been self-sufficient in food production since it became the first great industrial power, nor are other advanced European countries independent of the need to import food and essential raw materials. The superpowers have retained a greater measure of self-sufficiency because of their vast size and diversity of resources—the United States and Canada among major industrial powers are also principal exporters of food—although the question of self-sufficiency versus dependence is no doubt more complex than these remarks suggest. On the one hand, the diversification of the economic sector that accompanies industrialization tends to produce greater self-sufficiency in the sense that the generation of wealth is no longer entirely dependent upon one or a few economic activities. But on the other, advanced industrial countries can maintain their growth only through wider markets, increased consumption, and the search for ever more precious and far-flung resources, all of which make them increasingly dependent upon access to the outside world.

12. Non-Aligned Conference, p. 133.

13. The most fully elaborated set of such principles and policies is found in the UN Charter of Economic Rights and Duties of States, which was adopted by the General Assembly in 1974. A/Res./3281 (29).

14. Non-Aligned Conference, p. 118.

15. Murphy, "What the Third World Wants," p. 65.

16. That proposal is familiar to medical personnel on the battlefield whose resources are much too limited to treat all casualties effectively. Acting on the principle of "triage," they may then attempt to divide the wounded into three categories: first, those beyond help who must be left to die, ideally with a palliative to ease their suffering; second, those who should survive and recover with the medical assistance available; and third, those who can safely be ignored on grounds their injuries are such that they will recover even without medical attention. U.S. writers William and Paul Paddock suggested the triage concept as a policy guide to a U.S. government faced with the prospect of famine in much of the third world. See their *Famine 1975! America's Decision: Who Will Survive* (Boston: Little, Brown, 1967), Chapter 9.

17. Lester R. Brown, *World Without Borders* (New York: Random House, 1972), p. 213.

18. Ibid., pp. 214–15.

19. Ibid., p. 220.

20. Robert Gilpin, "The Politics of Transnational Economic Relations," in *Transnational Relations and World Politics*, ed. Robert O. Keohane and Joseph

S. Nye, Jr. (Cambridge, Mass.: Harvard University Press, 1970), p. 418. Gilpin makes it clear that he does not support such a view.

21. E. F. Schumacher, *Small Is Beautiful* (New York: Harper and Row, 1973), pp. 175–176.

22. Masanobu Fukuoka, *The One-Straw Revolution: An Introduction to Natural Farming* (Emmaus, Pa.: Rodale Press, 1978). The quotation is from the Introduction by Wendell Berry, p. xii.

23. See, for example, Samir Amin, "Self-Reliance and the NIEO," *Monthly Review* 29, 3 (August, 1977):1–21, and Johan Galtung, "The NIEO and the Basic Needs Approach," *Alternatives* 4, 4 (March, 1979):455–476.

24. René Dumont, interview in *African Business*, September 1982, p. 22.

25. Two sets of statistics illustrate this two-edged sword for the least developed countries. (1) In 1980, they received only 35 percent of official development assistance as against 48 percent in 1970. (2) TNC activity by the beginning of the 1980s was heavily concentrated in a relatively small number of third world states, typically the more advanced industrially, or the largest and richest in natural resources. More than 70 percent of all foreign direct investment was located in four OPEC countries, in ten of the more populous less developed countries, and in a few other places considered tax havens. "Issues Before the 36th General Assembly of the United Nations, 1981–1982" (New York: United Nations Association of the USA, 1981), pp. 87–91.

26. Barbara Ward and René Dubos, *Only One Earth* (New York: W. W. Norton, 1972), p. 20.

27. In the words of E. F. Schumacher, "Technology recognizes no self-limiting principle—in terms, for instance, of size, speed, or violence. It therefore does not possess the virtues of being self-balancing, self-adjusting, and self-cleansing. In the subtle system of nature, technology, and in particular the super-technology of the modern world, acts like a foreign body, and there are now numerous signs of rejection" (*Small Is Beautiful*, p. 147).

28. Ward and Dubos, *Only One Earth*, p. 145.

29. Werner Levi, *The Coming End of War* (Beverly Hills, Calif.: Sage Publications, 1981), p. 15.

7

The Enhancement
of Human Dignity

> The concept of human rights is a concept of world order. It is
> a proposal for structuring the world so that every individual's
> human worth is realized, every individual's human dignity is
> protected.
>
> —Patricia M. Derian
> *U.S. Department of State Bulletin*, January 1981

The logic of Westphalia suggests that the nation-state is principally what determines whether human beings shall live in dignity
and justice. Since the state is by far the most important locus of
political power in the world, it must provide security from without
and security—in all its implications for the realization of human values
beyond the basic one of mere survival—to the members of the society
within it. If civilized life requires the protections afforded by the state,
then the state must help humanity realize its higher needs and
aspirations. Nation-states can have no other justification for their
existence.

But this fundamental premise has always been built upon a disturbing
foundation of wishful thinking. Although it assumes that the state
ought to enhance the rights of human beings within its jurisdiction,
it does not ensure that they *will* do so. Worse, it fails entirely to
address the possibility, which is too often a likelihood as modern
history has shown, that governments in fact may become the greatest
violators of the rights of individuals within their control, even to the
point of denying many of them the right to life itself. What is justified
for its presumed ability to advance human welfare can become the
most dangerous enemy of humanity's well-being.

Throughout much of the Westphalian period, this wishful thinking
could be largely overlooked, for more often than not, people were

less repressed by their own governments than they were protected by them. Their human potential seemed better fulfilled by life within the sovereign state than by a struggle for survival in the hypothetical jungle outside an advanced and organized polity. Had this not been so, the nation-state system probably would not have flourished for more than three hundred years. Material realities and normative standards combined to provide a measure of well-being for individuals within the sovereign state in most times and places.

At the *material* level, even the most autocratic governments of the past did not, for the most part, have the capacity to terrorize whole populations, to choke off food supplies on a scale to make mass starvation an instrument of policy, or to peer into and control the private lives of most of their citizens. These capabilities are largely reserved for twentieth-century tyrants as the result of the insidious power available to them from various modern technologies. And at the *normative* level, the growth of the nation-state system was accompanied by continual and, in many cases, increasingly successful efforts to create domestic legal systems under which the ruler was made accountable to the ruled. The end result of that process is summed up in the postulate of democratic theory that says that sovereignty in fact resides in the people rather than in the governing elite.[1] That postulate is intended, above all, to ensure that governments shall be the servants of society rather than its capricious masters.

Yet the potential danger to human well-being always has lurked behind all claims to the absolute sovereignty of the state, as finally became abundantly clear in the terroristic and genocidal behavior of twentieth-century governments. The Nazis of Hitler's Third Reich proceeded to exterminate millions of Jews and other non-Aryan groups legally, that is, through the directives of those authorized to govern the state. The Soviet Union under Stalin institutionalized rule by terror, particularly over those members of the political elite most threatening to Stalin's rule, through political trials and the gulag system. Italian fascism produced a philosophical argument for the state's unlimited power over the individual that theoretically left *all* possibilities for realizing human potential at the whim of the state itself.[2] Out of such experiences was born totalitarianism, the most monstrous challenge to the autonomy of individual persons the world had ever seen.

THE DEVELOPMENT OF INTERNATIONAL
HUMAN RIGHTS STANDARDS

Finally there arose a horrified reaction throughout the world to atrocities committed by states that actually attempted to justify such behavior through theories of state absolutism. By the close of World War II, the Allied powers had agreed that a first order of business should be the prosecution of alleged war criminals in Germany and Japan for their violations of international law in both their planning and waging of the war, as well as for their crimes against humanity in their treatment of populations under their control.[3] The trials at Nuremburg and Tokyo that resulted were, however flawed from the standpoint of constituting victors' justice, important efforts to assert that standards did exist prohibiting the unlimited and arbitrary use of governmental power against human beings, whatever the orders of state officials. Since many of the civilized standards violated by the war criminals simply had been assumed to exist by generations of statesmen and the public, by no means all of the crimes against humanity had been codified in generally binding treaties. Prosecutors were forced to rely heavily on various national standards protecting human rights, which together, they argued, formed evidence of a customary international standard, but the ambiguity of that assertion for a determinedly legalist opponent caused many to insist that the time had come to develop treaty commitments that would define world community standards for the rights of all humanity.

Within this context the organizing conference for the United Nations, which met in San Francisco in 1945, considered the creation of an international bill of rights to be incorporated into the UN Charter, very much as an earlier such bill had been attached to the U.S. Constitution before its adoption. In the end, the framers of the Charter concluded that such a bill was too complex for quick formulation, but from almost the moment the United Nations came into being, much of its attention was turned to the issue of creating treaty standards for the protection of various human rights.

As expected, that effort has proved to be neither simple nor noncontroversial, most basically for two reasons. First, it is a clear and direct challenge to statist assumptions of sovereignty, for above all it implies the sovereignty of all members of the species above that of individual governments, reminding states that they and not human beings are the abstractions that must be made to advance human welfare. Second, the articulation of universal standards inevitably requires agreement upon specific values relevant to the advancement of human well-being, and that agreement is not easily reached in a world where competing ideologies about what is best for humankind reflect different political and social priorities, too often even serving to hide perceptions of our common humanity.

Other complications have followed from these two most basic ones. For example, the temptation is often irresistible for a government to point the finger of blame for human rights violations at its opponent and to overlook injustices to individuals within its own jurisdiction. Even governments with relatively good records in enhancing human rights may, as a result, fear that submitting to international standards will make that record something of a political football to its opponents, thus inducing them to shy away from international obligations.[4] In addition, the process can lead to cynicism when governments with little to applaud in the human rights field submit to international standards in the expectation that they will not really be called to account, except perhaps rhetorically, for their behavior. The Westphalian state remains too hard shelled for easy penetration from the world community to correct unjust treatment of individuals or groups within. The international system itself invites self-righteousness in the assertion of a government's adherence to human rights, for it knows it is unlikely to be challenged effectively, or conversely withdrawal from the fray on grounds that it will be the object of political attacks from without rather than judicious and objective judgments of its real performance.

In spite of these difficulties, the creation of international standards that articulate acceptable treatment of individuals and groups has proceeded apace over the past several decades. As a result, a sizable body of treaty law now is in existence that in toto amounts to a remarkable agreement by the representatives of world society about how human beings ought to be permitted to live their lives.

The first historic step toward consensus was the adoption by the UN General Assembly, on December 10, 1948, of the Universal Declaration of Human Rights. No member state at the time voted against the goals it espoused, and in the years since, the precepts it contains have taken on greater norm-setting importance in two ways. First, at the informal level of value formation, the Universal Declaration has remained an attractive magnet for all groups, by no means limited to governments, interested in asserting their aspirations for the decent treatment of human beings. Constant reiteration of its precepts over time has had a discernible effect, in itself, in adding to their stature, their perceived authority as obligatory standards. Over the years, too, citation of the Universal Declaration has been accompanied by numerous other declarations and resolutions, often in the General Assembly, that proclaim acceptable standards of behavior regarding specific aspects of the treatment of humans.

That informal value formation has been supported by the second kind of evidence of the growing strength of these standards. In the years since 1948, a great many states have accepted legally binding obligations through formal conventions that include the concepts of the Universal Declaration.[5] Out of the UN context have come the International Covenants on Civil and Political Rights, and on Economic and Social Rights, both of which entered into force in 1976, and which together are the explicit obligatory instruments embodying the standards of the Universal Declaration. By the early 1980s, more than sixty-five states from all parts of the world had adhered to these two covenants. Other treaties containing very broad sets of obligations are applicable to limited groups of states, most notably, the European

Convention on Human Rights (which entered into force in 1953), and the American Convention on Human Rights (which entered into force in 1978). Moreover, a great many limited-purpose conventions are now in effect to afford protection against a considerable variety of human rights issues, such as those prohibiting forced labor and racial discrimination, providing equal rights for women, and the like.

In the words of one authority assessing the results of this situation as of 1982,

> no matter what their practices, governments throughout the world have accepted the norms embodied in the many international declarations and conventions that have been adopted by international institutions as a legitimate definition of the conditions of human dignity and justice. About half of the sovereign states that comprise the global system, including within their borders more than half the world's population, have explicitly formally agreed, by signing or ratifying the relevant conventions, to be judged by the standards that have been set forth.[6]

Those facts are impressive in themselves, but the implications are greater even than that: "By according these standards legitimacy in international fora, the remaining states have implicitly accepted them as appropriate criteria for their judgment." That is, a genuine world-wide *consensus* may have emerged in recent decades on explicit and wide-ranging standards for the acceptable treatment of human beings. If that is so, its implications for the future growth of a global sense of community should be very great indeed.

WHAT ARE HUMAN RIGHTS?

As the representatives of governments have struggled to create the conventions and declarations setting forth these standards, they have been forced to probe deeply into what it means to talk about, let alone protect, such a concept as that of human rights. People reared in the Anglo-American political culture are probably inclined to suppose that rights are those human demands that no government can take from us, that are "unalienable," in Thomas Jefferson's classic description. Americans are informed by the first ten amendments to their Constitution that they have a right to free speech, to freedom from false arrest, to keep and bear arms—all of which are limitations on the powers of their government over them. So a right is likely to appear to Americans to be some kind of guaranteed freedom *from* governmental interference in our lives.

These examples suggest that when we use the term *right*, we are referring to particular human values that we regard as so fundamentally important that they must be upheld if we are to achieve what we regard as our essential aspirations within the social order. Such a conception is useful inasmuch as it need not address time-honored arguments as to *where* rights come from, i.e., from God or nature, as the natural law tradition supposes, or from their authoritative establishment by states, as strict positivism suggests. These are not trivial differences of viewpoint, as has been made dramatically clear by the horrendous deprivations of human rights in our time by state actors asserting their unaccountability to any authority higher than their own. Rather, a value-based conception of human rights helps us to focus on rights as human aspirations, and then to explore differing views as to the relative importance of various human goals, wants, and needs.

If rights are defined as those fundamentally important human values that must be secured if others are to be sought, is this definition the same as saying that they are equivalent to the base values that must be maintained for every human being simply by virtue of the fact that we are living creatures, with minimal needs of food, shelter, and clothing, if we are to keep on living?[7] Obviously, this latter description is not what seems to be assumed in the traditional U.S. conception, for nowhere in the Bill of Rights is there mentioned a right to, say, an adequate food supply for every citizen, sufficient clothing, or sound housing. Yet we know that arguing the benefits of freedom of the press is not very satisfying to a man whose family is starving to death. He will regard the need for food as more important than his ability to read uncensored news. Why then did our founding fathers fail to address these basic rights—survival values—and instead grant constitutional protection to what must be considered certain of the higher values?

Several explanations are possible. First, the U.S. republic was not created, metaphorically speaking, out of a state of nature. The level of social and economic development in the United States at the time the Constitution was adopted was such as to make it reasonable to suppose that survival needs already were generally secured, or that they could be through the creative initiative of each able-bodied citizen. That latter possibility leads directly to the second explanation, namely, that Lockean and Enlightenment precepts about the creative potential of unrestrained human beings dominated the thinking of the time; that meant that it was regarded as more important to get the government out of the way of the people, so that the people could provide for their own material needs, than to commit the government to providing them, no doubt at the expense of greater individual freedom. The third explanation for the limited content of the U.S. Bill of Rights is inherent in the second: The founding fathers were much more preoccupied with how to limit a capricious and authoritarian government from interference with the higher aspirations of its citizens than they were with giving it the kinds of commitments to intervene in the social order that, they feared, would encourage the growth of too much governmental power.

All of these arguments are familiar, but they are repeated here as a reminder of the fairly limited and special conception of human rights in the U.S. context. One additional conclusion can be drawn: The U.S. conception of rights typically sees them as the equivalent of ironclad guarantees. Since they are prohibitions upon the government, they can be secured as long as that government is committed to honoring them. Their achievement requires no outlay of governmental funds, no hiring of workers, no governmental action of any kind. Rather, they are secured specifically by nonaction from the government. Although the history of the United States makes clear that constant vigilance by private citizens, courts, and all others sworn to uphold the Constitution is needed to prevent both officials and private citizens from infringing upon these rights, the fact remains that it is almost certainly easier to secure and maintain these kinds of rights than to guarantee that no child within a polity shall suffer malnutrition, that every citizen shall be adequately housed, or that all who are capable of work shall have useful and remunerative work to do.

In many societies today, the Western conception of human rights is not fully shared. More precisely, if these are regarded as the fundamentally important values in many Western states, deserving of the name *rights,* they are not so regarded by many groups, even though they may be widely considered as desirable values for a society that has the luxury to promote them. In general, socialist ideologies tend to reverse the relative priorities, insisting upon the fundamental importance, to the point such matters should be considered as rights, of securing basic needs for all members of the society, even if this requires a large measure of governmental intervention to ensure such things as distributive justice. Indeed, all socialist thought arose as a critique of what were perceived to be the injustices and inequalities perpetuated by political liberalism. Socialism's Marxist strain, in particular, tends to regard Western-style rights as essentially serving the interests of a dominant capitalist class, since that class need not worry much about its survival needs and instead will benefit most from keeping its government from interfering in its entrepreneurial activities.

Here then is the outline of the human rights dimension to the nearly all-pervasive cold war conflict of the contemporary period. As in so much else in this era, ideological hostility has exaggerated tragically differences of viewpoint into deep, sometimes unbridgeable divisions. The most deep-seated needs and the noblest aspirations of human beings have become the object of fearful imprecations and scathing denunciations in the arena of international politics when they have seemed to support the ideology of the "enemy." We would do well to try to put these different value priorities in proper perspective.

For a start, every major Western democracy has moved to implement substantial numbers of welfare values within their societies, particularly during the twentieth century. They generally have chosen to regard these protections as matters of legislation, rather than constitutional guarantee, but no one in the democratic West seriously supposes that such matters as minimum wage standards, the right to bargain collectively, health and medical provisions, or old-age security are not now fully embedded in the fabric of protections we expect from our governments. Western democracies clearly regard governmental support of these kinds of basic values as fundamentally important, even if they do not always choose to define them as rights.

Conversely, a great many socialist governments today function within political systems in which the traditional political and civil rights associated with the West are fully protected as such. That is most obviously true where social democratic parties govern in the highly developed societies of Europe, and tends to be less often the case in societies governed by elites more or less committed to socialist tenets within the third world, although that generalization must be highly qualified for a grouping that includes such a huge number and variety of states. To take an obvious exception, poverty-stricken India's leaders have always adhered to some socialist principles in governing that vast society, but India also has managed to uphold Western-style prohibitions against the curtailment of private liberty—as evidenced dramatically when Indira Gandhi was turned out of office in March 1977, after her imposition of an antilibertarian state of emergency.

Once we consider rights as nothing more nor less than fundamentally important human values, we can also see more clearly why the relative priority given them in various societies will very likely reflect the level of a society's economic and social development. The fulfillment of basic needs no doubt should constitute a real priority for impoverished societies. Ideally, we may wish that these values would be advanced without simultaneously denigrating the higher aspirations that allow individuals to realize as much as possible of their human potential free from authoritarian restrictions. But we should at least not be surprised or unduly critical of governments that may inhibit fulfillment of some of the higher values in the interest of securing basic values for all members of their societies. In the imperfect material world in which we live, such judgments must weigh relative costs and benefits to all.

In contrast to the fact that the traditional political and civil rights of the West are essentially directives to limit governmental power, the fulfillment of basic economic and social rights typically calls for extensive use of governmental power to promote social order. That essential difference goes far to explain, if not excuse, why human rights discussions in the current period so frequently have been the victim of cold war rhetoric and conflict. The matter of balancing human freedom against governmental protection to support minimal human needs is at the very core of those social problems requiring divergent solutions, solutions that must constantly be reexamined to meet the evolving technological and desired situation.[8]

STATE NONCOMPLIANCE WITH HUMAN RIGHTS STANDARDS

In the 1980s we can easily feel cynical about the alleged progress in advancing human rights internationally over recent decades. In spite of the gradual agreement upon standards covering a host of important values, the world has been informed with shocking regularity of governmental actions involving torture, mass executions of political opponents, and even genocidal behavior in many parts of the world. Just as grave though less shocking in terms of traditional Westphalian expectations, great powers whose moral leadership of others is meant to rest mainly on the acceptability of their treatment of those they govern have conducted brutal foreign interventions with methods that too often have produced extreme violations of the human rights of others, conduct that they would not likely try to justify in the treatment of their own citizens. Do such developments suggest that efforts to define acceptable standards of conduct toward individuals throughout this period have been in vain? Before looking for an answer, we need to try to assess the characteristic causes and features of human rights violations by sovereign governments today.

We should remember that *all* government is more or less restrictive of individual freedom, that it seeks to restrain the untrammeled liberty of each one of us to do exactly as we please in the interests of the whole society. In that process, government—all governments—necessarily promotes and protects some human values and the values of some people within the society more fully than it does others. Decisions as to the allocations of values are at the very core of the political process. A society in which no arguments remained as to which should be advanced would be, by definition, a utopian society. In the real world of conflicting social interests, no such condition has been attained, except, arguably, for brief periods within very small groups of people who largely cut themselves off from the larger society, maintaining their isolation because of their prior commitment to the same values.[9]

In larger societies, such as nation-states, the justification for a pluralistic democracy is that it permits a great amount of competition for the allocation of values among diverse groups, based as pluralism is upon a conviction that no individual or group of individuals can ever be in sole or final possession of the truth about what is good for the society as a whole. The results of such competition can never be wholly satisfactory to all, or even to any, members of the society, but, in protecting the right to compete through the political process, democratic societies strive to keep repression of particular groups to a minimum and thereby to open the possibilities for human aspiration and advancement to all. To the extent democratically governed states achieve the consent of the governed, they presumably do so because of the people's confidence that value competition will be maintained through the political process, and thus potentially can be made to serve them.

The argument against authoritarian regimes is that they suppress that competition, enshrining some social values at the expense of others, maintaining social order in patterns acceptable to the governing elite at the expense of justice for those within the social system whose lives are degraded as a result. The more authoritarian a regime, the more it represses the goals of any within the society who are not themselves served by maintenance of the elite in power. Such a government's authority rests, not on consent, but upon its ability to maintain control over potentially disaffected groups.

It is therefore ominous for the global improvement of human rights that the number of repressive and authoritarian governments has been growing over the past several decades. The trend has been most evident in the growing number of militarized governments, mainly on the political right, in which members of the nations' military forces have seized and held power, often while suspending constitutional guarantees. One recent study of this trend describes nearly a tripling of militarized governments throughout the world between 1960 and 1979, from about sixteen in the earlier year to more than forty at the start of the 1980s. Add to that governments that have come under martial law or that have a civilian leadership heavily influenced by the military, and within the same period the total of more or less oppressive regimes increased from between thirty and forty to about ninety states.[10] Although the relative oppression of governments differs within this category, which comprises more than half the states of the world today, and there are obvious differences in the kind and extent of human freedoms they suppress, the trend in the direction of more militarized control seems unarguable.

This total group of states includes those ostensibly governed by very different ideologies, political histories, and social problems. The greatest increases in militarized or semimilitarized governments in this period came in Latin America and Africa; in both areas governments dependent upon the military were in a minority at the start of the 1960s, but by the end of the period, civilian-based governments were the exception rather than the rule. Only in Europe were there slight but important trends away from military authoritarianism, particularly in Spain and Portugal, and in Greece, which endured a military coup in the late 1960s that was replaced with a restored democracy in the 1970s.

MILITARIZED GOVERNMENTS IN THE THIRD WORLD

The trend of the past twenty years or so toward militarization of government has been far more striking in the third world. Within that category, Richard Falk has distinguished three kinds of regimes, each best characterized by its response to basic conditions of economic development within various societies. The first, most typical of states that are still underdeveloped politically and economically, is that of *praetorianism.* One of its basic features is that "it involves the seizure and exercise of state power by an elite that does not rest its legitimacy on any system of political accountability to the citizenry." Indeed, a characteristic of political underdevelopment is that there are "no procedures and institutions capable of legitimating government authority . . . without reliance on force."[11] Economic underdevelopment is mainly evidenced in the fact that most members of the society are largely untouched by the modern world, even though, as in Central America, the production of one or two food crops or other commodities may make the state's economy as a whole highly dependent upon the world market. Although the state does not become praetorianized because of an economic crisis connected with the industrialized world, "autocratic leadership may seek to vindicate its authority externally by a claim to provide sufficient order to assure profitable investment and steady economic growth."[12] Great inequality in wealth is characteristic of many societies where praetorianism exists, as in the still semifeudal states of Central America. In the most extreme cases, such as the now deposed regimes of Idi Amin in Uganda or the self-proclaimed Emperor Bokassa of the Central African Empire, the arbitrary exercise of naked power to terrify and destabilize potential opponents is a characteristic feature.

The second and third types of militarized governments in third world countries discerned by Falk have occurred in societies that, while still relatively underdeveloped, contain some features of economic modernity. One of these is the *Brazilianized* regime, so named for the characteristic experience of Brazil since it underwent a military coup in 1964. The Brazilianized regime is typically rightist or anticommunist in ideology and promotes a capitalist development strategy, although one strongly oriented toward state capitalism rather than unregulated free enterprise. A perceived crisis in economic development frequently precipitates the military takeover, "which is normally associated with the inability of civilian leadership to maintain order sufficient to check inflation, labor unrest, political turmoil. These societal conditions allegedly destroy investor confidence and make it difficult to attract capital from abroad in the form of private investment, bank loans, or international economic assistance."[13] A high rate of growth in the gross national product becomes a principal goal of the militarized regime with far less attention devoted to the distributive consequences than to growth itself. In such regimes, even where dramatic results in growth are evident, economic stratification within the society typically increases, with the poor considerably more squeezed by development strategies than the rich.

Finally, *Leninized* societies within the third world are built explicitly upon a reaction against capitalism. They bear the name of the founder of the Soviet state because of their emphasis on building a strong and highly centralized socialist state as a means of resisting the powerful forces of the international entrepreneur. "Leninism is associated with an insistence that armed struggle and the buildup of a strong socialist state are necessary preconditions to achieve sustainable socialism at the national level."[14] To classify a state as Leninized does not mean that it necessarily supports the international posture of the Soviet Union, any more than Brazilianized states are the unwavering allies of the United States. Within both categories are found frequent and often harsh critics of the superpower with which the third world state shares at least some tenets of economic ideology. In fact, a great many of the Brazilianized and Leninized governments of the world today also are members of the nonaligned group of states. This suggests two important conclusions: First, the fact that both these classifications spring principally from the regime's economic orientation is another illustration of the primary importance of economic development concerns within the third world today, concerns that naturally are shaped by the two dominant economic ideologies of our time. Second, the fact that many states in both categories nonetheless seek to distance themselves from the geopolitical interests of the superpower is another indication of the continued strength of nationalism, of the appeal of sovereign independence in the contemporary world. Militarization of many third world regimes is at least in part a response to the effort to establish and maintain truly independent nation-states in a world environment where many of the emerging social and economic forces make that increasingly difficult.

These trends toward the militarization of governments within the third world have threatened implications for human rights in those societies. All moves toward authoritarian control serve to constrict the political space in which diverse social groups can pursue diverse goals and values. Yet, however troubling these trends, they have been largely caused by the understandable desire to promote greater economic well-being for many if not all members of these societies. Moreover, the impulse toward tighter governmental control appears to be in part a response to perceptions of international interdependence that, from the point of view especially of the underdeveloped world, more often seems to have a pernicious than a beneficial impact on their societies. In such a context, there may be widespread agreement that many of the libertarian freedoms from governmental interference should give way to the advancement of social and economic needs through greater governmental intervention.

As usual where conflicting values are at stake, some sort of balance must be struck on the basis of priorities that themselves are formed by the real world in which a particular society finds itself. On the basis of our exploration of these issues, we might be tempted to conclude that Brazilianized and Leninized states can be differentiated in human rights terms by saying that the former type has given a higher priority to the civil liberties category of rights than to those surrounding economic and social welfare, whereas Leninized states have reversed those priorities. Unhappily, such a conclusion is unwarranted, for evidence clearly shows that a number of Brazilianized states are among the worst violators of the traditional civil and political liberties of their people. We need only consider the recent histories of Chile and Argentina for proof: The military rulers of those countries have engaged in the systematic imprisonment, torture, and murder of their regimes' opponents to the point of arousing the outrage and, far more sporadically, the effective opposition of much of the rest of the world. Even though Brazilianized states are capitalist oriented, they are untempered by dependable Enlightenment restrictions on the use of governmental power against their citizens.

Leninized states, on the other hand, justify their extensive pretensions to intervene in the lives of their citizens on grounds that only by intervention can they promote greater distributive justice. Pluralistic competition is the first victim, just as it is in an authoritarian regime of the right, although its suppression here is intended to serve the greatest good of the greatest number. Now a Brazilianized regime also may claim to espouse that goal, although evidence indicates that in such societies a minority typically is enriched at the expense of the majority. However much the socialist vision is corrupted in practice within Leninized states, it at least remains as a vision of social justice. In contrast, authoritarian regimes of the right seldom are able to conjure up a comparably attractive vision of their own, but instead must maintain order by insisting upon the fearful qualities of the socialist specter.

This observation is intended neither to excuse the oppressive features of Leninized regimes nor to argue that socialist ideologies are inherently preferable in human rights terms to nonsocialist ones. Rather, it is meant to remind those who may be predisposed to condemn severely all Marxist regimes that such a posture does not advance the effort to evaluate the actual kind and level of support for important human values around the globe today. Worldwide social integration will advance within our lifetimes only to the extent that we are able to move beyond the "we-them" labels that mainly serve to camouflage common aspirations while they simultaneously deny the legitimacy of diverse social goals. Our model for a partial transcendence of ideology might be the historic integration of European Protestants and Catholics within overarching security communities after a prolonged initial period of bitter opposition and violent warfare.[15] Our greatest challenge is to move purposefully in that direction before undergoing more of the kinds of exhausting, murderous excessess that characterized early modern Europe.

THE IMPACT ON HUMAN RIGHTS
OF GREAT POWER INTERVENTIONISM

In this spirit, what useful generalizations can be made about the treatment of human rights within the most highly developed part of the world, which includes the major adversaries in cold war terms? The first is that many and perhaps most of the states within this category have an impact on the rest of the world that is largely missing in the human rights performance of most third world states. That dimension stems from their much greater capability to make their presence felt—for good or ill—beyond their borders than is possible for most poorer, weaker states. That is most obviously true of the two superpowers with their global interests and pretensions to advance them. It is also true to a lesser extent of the advanced states of Europe and Japan, particularly and increasingly regarding their ability to penetrate other societies through the workings of the world's economic system. Power over others cannot be exercised without some measure of oppression, which insight has led to humanity's age-old struggle to make government responsive to the values of the governed. Yet at the present stage of world development, that struggle has produced far more tangible and beneficent results within certain societies than it has where governments, including those that are comparatively restrained at home, exercise power outside their own territorial scope. We would not suppose it within the realm of possibility that a U.S. president might send several thousand troops into, say, Topeka, Kansas, to topple a mayor whose policies were unacceptable to the administration in Washington; yet when, in 1983, President Reagan invaded Grenada for a comparable purpose, the public generally accepted the action as within the foreign policy prerogatives of the president.

So in considering the impact of actors within the developed world upon human rights, we must separate their domestic from their international behavior. In recent decades, both superpowers have engaged in international conduct that at its worst has been extremely destructive to basic rights within target societies. In both cases this most damaging use of power has taken place under the guise of large-scale interventions or limited wars—most notably in Southeast Asia for the United States and Afghanistan for the Soviet Union. Of course, life-sustaining rights are always threatened or destroyed in time of war, and therefore it may be that combatants cannot be judged by the same human rights standards as societies at peace—an unhappy fact with which we shall have to live as long as the international system tolerates the high violence levels that it has traditionally.

Still, it is worth thinking about these interventions in a discussion of human rights for several reasons. First, the normative trend of the contemporary period impels us to do so. Our forced attention to issues of war crimes at the end of World War II in effect directed us to consider what could be done to punish massive human rights deprivations in time of war *and* to prevent their recurrence. The rights invoked at the time were regarded as universal rights, inherent in our common humanity and supportable in time of war as well as peace. Without that assumption no case at all could be made for the justice of the Nuremburg and Tokyo tribunals. It is a measure of the continued weakness of the world's normative system that enforcement of such standards still depends upon the ability of the winning side to assume physical jurisdiction over alleged war criminals from the losing side if anything like the Nuremburg precedent is to be repeated. Nonetheless, Nuremburg standards can be demanded by an informed and critical public. In fact, they must be upheld in just that way if they are to survive and grow in authority.[16]

Second, the human rights test is an effective way to appraise the purported ends with the means used in such interventionary policy. In Vietnam, one superpower's asserted goal was to make self-determination possible for the South Vietnamese, and in Afghanistan the other superpower tried to prevent a potential counterrevolutionary movement from abandoning the country's march toward socialism. Yet in both cases, the military means used often made a mockery of the stated goal—since an army presumably does not liberate people by depriving them of their livelihood and their homes, nor by maiming and killing them. For reasons such as these a human rights test must always form an important part of the assessment of a humane society's foreign policy.[17]

Third, the ever more deadly and destructive military capability that the most advanced states have acquired makes more and more imperative the effort to constrain its use. Push-button warfare that permits the destruction of enemy soldiers without even seeing their dying faces, technology that can defoliate once fertile land, chemical combinations that bring silent, unsuspected, and agonizing deaths to defenseless civilian populations—all these and other modern capabilities threaten civilized standards in warfare in unprecedented ways. Use of this dehumanized military power tends to be less constrained by human conscience than were earlier technologies simply because of the easy distance it provides between its users and its victims. To the extent that victims are seen as abstractions rather than as flesh-and-blood human beings, human rights and responsibilities are eroded.

THE WESTERN IMPACT ON SOVIET HUMAN RIGHTS CONDUCT

Only a relative handful of authoritarian regimes remain in place over the most highly industrialized countries of the North. With the coming of democracy in the 1970s to Greece, Portugal, and Spain, those that remain at the moment are confined to the Soviet Union and its allied governments of Eastern Europe. The legacy of the Leninist insistence upon highly centralized control by a single, disciplined elite has largely determined the nature of government throughout the Soviet system down to the present day. An enormous amount has been said in the West, almost all of it negative, about the effects on human rights of the Soviet form of political control. The U.S. policy of containment of the Soviet Union has from the beginning been built upon the assumption that real liberalization of Soviet-style government would have to be generated largely from within and upon the hope that a firm but restrained containment of the Soviets might buy the kind of time needed for such liberalization to take place. What sorts of interim assessments can be made of those premises some three-and-a-half decades after they were made?

The first assessment is that, although this kind of change has been nearly indiscernible at times, the extremes of repression characteristic of much of Stalin's reign have not been matched by his successors or their allies in Eastern Europe. This is not to say that these societies are free by Western standards, or even that a clear trend is evident in that direction since about the mid-1950s, when Khrushchev's de-Stalinization campaign brought some advance toward greater governmental toleration of limited dissent, both in the Soviet Union and in Eastern Europe. Some Soviet analysts have viewed whatever trend may exist as cyclical, with brief periods of greater pluralism followed by a clamping-down process—all such moves in either direction, post-Stalin, having been fairly limited. Now that Stalin has been succeeded by five sets of leaders, the relative authoritarianism or openness with which they have ruled Soviet society bears less relationship to the personalities at the top than to the presumed imperatives of single-party control over a vast and powerful state and over the policies of its allies. Soviet-style government appears to have become a fairly predictable phenomenon in terms of the apparent boundaries to the amount of openness or repression it will tolerate. A would-be revolution in Hungary in 1956 and moves toward a more pluralistic polity in Czechoslovakia in 1968 both were ended by the military might of the Soviet Union. Yet small measures of dissent today are tolerated even in a militarized Poland, and a Hungarian government that remains subservient to Moscow nonetheless has responded fairly extensively to its own citizens' desires for greater personal freedoms.

The second generalization supports containment's original assumption that real liberalization of Soviet society must come mainly from within rather than in response to pressures from the West. Various U.S. administrations have sought to influence Soviet human rights policies in a variety of ways—for example, by attempting to tie U.S.-Soviet trade agreements to an easing of restrictions on the emigration of Soviet Jews and by insisting upon greater freedoms for prominent dissidents living within the Soviet Union. The most broad-based and highly publicized of these efforts, during the Carter presidency, evidently produced no more positive results than did earlier, more limited policies. Some would argue that such frontal assaults on the most reprehensible Soviet practices have produced a kind of paranoid defensive reaction within the Kremlin that led to even tighter control over the personal freedoms of Soviet citizens. The old dogmas of sovereignty and nationalism still are powerfully aroused and can be made to serve repressive interests whenever outside governments, and particularly those perceived as hostile, denounce another's treatment of those within its jurisdiction.

Lest that reaction be thought to apply only to such authoritarian regimes as the Soviet, consider how Americans would react to a decision by Japan to make a trade agreement with the United States conditional upon this government's consent to compensate all Japanese-Americans and their descendants for their forced internment during World War II. Or what if the Organization of African Unity were to refuse entry for all U.S. goods into Africa until such time as the government of the United States agreed to pay reparations to U.S. blacks for their history of slavery and second-class citizenship? We should no doubt regard such policies as extremely hostile, which is to say we cannot imagine them as the policies of friendly states.

A third generalization, still more a hypothetical possibility than a conclusion drawn from the record, is that Soviet conduct may be more likely to improve as the result of its increased interdependence with more pluralistic societies than as a precondition for closer ties, particularly in economic matters. Insistence that the Soviets improve their human rights record *before* the West agrees to help supply the technology, industrial goods, or commodities its economy sorely needs appears to cause counterproductive results as often as not, with the result that neither mutually beneficial goal—improved social policy or economic gain—is attained. Although this suggests a reversal of U.S. policy in recent years, the suggestion should be understood for what it intends: It does not mean that Western policy toward the Soviets should become blind to human rights considerations, nor does it mean adoption of a business-as-usual mentality that takes as the only good the turning of a profit. But it does suggest that to the extent Soviet bloc interdependence can be cultivated with the West and the rest of the world, social conditions within the USSR may gradually, if imperfectly, improve.[18]

Soviet repression of its people evidently cannot be ameliorated by strident human rights policies from its opponents. Yet we have concluded that a human rights component is important to our effort to help make a better world. What sort of role should human rights considerations have in foreign policy if there is to be any likelihood of producing progressively positive results? No easy formula is possible, although several modest considerations now seem called for, all of which should apply to democratic foreign policy generally, quite apart from the place of the Soviet Union in the world today.

First, human beings tend to improve their behavior more readily to conform to the positive example set by their friends than they do when insulted and berated by their enemies. Although exemplary behavior is not likely to be emulated by one's opponent, it at least will not be perceived as threatening to the opponent's sovereign prerogative to behave even more reprehensibly, if it chooses, and it may produce more principled behavior in one's friends. Second, since support of fundamental human rights and values is demanded by the very nature of our humanity, they are rights for every single member of the species, whether they are being realized or not.[19] This consideration should suggest to the policy maker that efforts to enhance particular rights in foreign societies will be perceived as hypocritical and insincere to the extent that they are sought selectively, by overlooking beams in the eyes of friendly governments while railing against comparative motes in the eyes of one's opponents. For a government to apply a human rights policy uniformly in its relations with all others may be an unachievable goal today, given the geopolitical considerations that are likely to work against it. Yet, since it is the only normatively acceptable goal, it must continually guide relevant foreign policy.[20]

These two considerations lead to a third, which is admittedly far easier to articulate than to implement successfully. It is that governments by their very nature can play constructive roles in advancing human rights internationally only to the extent that they are prodded by publics that are both informed and committed to the universal imperatives of human rights considerations, rather than to seeking parochial or partisan advantages. Governments will always be inclined to reach for the self-serving outcome. Private groups and individuals whose goal is the universal enhancement of human dignity need labor under no such constraint. The recent trend in awarding the Nobel Peace Prize is an interesting indicator of the implications of such a conclusion, first, because the work of several recipients in recent years has been closely tied to human rights issues, which of course says volumes about the intimate connection between the advancement of important human values and the establishment of peaceful societies. But even more significant is the fact that several Nobel awards have gone to private individuals or organizations whose efforts often have run directly counter to the practices of governments or important political parties.[21] In a world where such recognition is possible, governments and their spokesmen no longer are without effective gadflies from within their societies to push them toward the fuller enhancement of the rights of human beings.

PROTECTING HUMAN RIGHTS
THROUGH INTERNATIONAL INSTITUTIONS

The work of individuals and voluntary human rights associations is obviously and no doubt fundamentally important as a goad to acceptable action by states. Yet in this still largely Westphalian world, we have to suppose that governments themselves must make conscious choices to be bound by universal standards if humankind is to live in greater dignity in the future than in the present. We have seen that a great many standards in fact have been articulated by the international community, roughly since the end of World War II. The period of standard setting that constituted most of the human rights effort worldwide for the first two-and-a-half decades after the war now is being replaced with an era of more attention to enforcement of those standards, although this shift is still very young.

The United Nations

The last great standard-setting work of the United Nations came with the completion of the International Covenants on Civil and Political Rights and on Economic and Social Rights in 1966. Comparatively more attention since has been devoted to investigating alleged human rights violations in particular countries. Given the fact that the United Nations is a highly political body—and no doubt looks increasingly so to many in the West since the days when it tended to be much more heavily influenced by Western policies than it has more recently—its treatment of human rights issues often is highly charged, selective in its targets, and inflammatory in its results. Actually, the United Nations' human rights activity is often highly political because of two of its inherent features, its constitutional structure in which only sovereign states are represented and its nearly universal membership today. During its norm-setting phase, the facts that it spoke for governments *and* that most governments of the world were its members were crucial to its ability to create human rights treaties. Now when the General Assembly attempts to judge the relevant behavior of states, its actions often appear anything but Olympian and objective, thanks to its system of bloc caucusing, the trade-off of votes between particular interest groups, and the numerical dominance of the new, non-European member states.[22]

Since its earliest days, the intergovernmental nature of the United Nations has served to frustrate its ability to deal effectively with the policies of racial discrimination practiced by the government of South Africa. As a sovereign among sovereigns, even that government engaged in "an egregious violation" of human rights as a matter of its "fundamental national policy" could protect itself from effective penetration from the organization.[23] After more than thirty years of antiapartheid rhetoric and resolutions from the United Nations, the government of South Africa is a near pariah within the community of nations. It appears even to be facing rising if not yet overwhelming threats of revolution from within its disenfranchised black majority, but it has not bent to the will of the United Nations in any significant degree. Yet the prolonged United Nations' frustration has been expressed in the organization's continued preoccupation with racial discrimination as a human rights violation, sometimes, so it has seemed to many, to the virtual exclusion of attention to other human rights problems. When, as most notoriously in the General Assembly's 1975 resolution equating Zionism with racism, that frustration bursts out in a form that actually threatens the worldwide rejection of racism as a universal wrong, moral standards appear to risk being killed by injecting them with inflamed politics.[24]

In recent years, the General Assembly's Third Committee has focused on the human rights situation in three Latin American countries: Chile, El Salvador, and Guatemala. Few would dispute that the practices of those governments deserve international scrutiny, although many in the West bemoan the fact that the United Nations' attention is now largely limited to these cases. In the words of a Western delegate, "the easiest thing for the Third Committee to do is take up countries that are not part of any powerful voting bloc at the U.N.," and when it comes to targeting these three countries, "there is a tacit coalition among the pro-Soviet states, some of the West European countries and most of the nonaligned."[25] Bloc voting inevitably produces highly politicized outcomes.

On the other hand, inherent in everyone's view of the world is the tendency to accept votes that support the policies we espouse as not only good but just and fair minded, while branding those critical of our actions or those of our presumed friends as arbitrary and unjust. Nowhere is that tendency thrown into sharper relief than in matters relevant to human rights, which, we like to think, should, because we have defined them as such, be enshrined beyond the reach of politics. Partisan judgments here are likely to arouse us to self-righteous denunciations of the entire effort at evaluation. Yet once we have noted that Third Committee resolutions naturally express what is politically acceptable to the majority, we should acknowledge the extent to which they may reflect some legitimate objections to the policies of certain states. For example, South Africa's racist government is a reliable trading partner of the Western democracies, supplying them with needed minerals and hospitable to their investors. It is not farfetched to suggest that these economic ties have perpetuated the ruling elite and the social system it defends. Israel, in addition to its strong economic and military ties with South Africa, has been viewed by the UN majority as in open violation of a fundamentally important Westphalian standard since 1967—that of the illegitimacy of occupying by conquest the territory of other states.[26] The Latin

American governments targeted for their human rights violations all are seen to owe much of their success in gaining and maintaining themselves in power to the United States—a fact which, for many, clearly overrides whatever criticisms the U.S. government itself may make of their human rights abuses.

This does not mean that the Assembly's targets are equally culpable with respect to human rights violations, nor that those cited above are necessarily the worst offenders. But it suggests that a political body should not be expected to cease being sensitive to the competition of other important political values when it considers human rights, which is to say that the boundaries between those values and what are distinguished from them as rights tend, in the political arena, to become more or less indistinguishable. Does this serve to promote universal human rights *qua* rights? Only if men and women of good will can detach themselves sufficiently from their partisan outlooks to seek justice for all, to recognize the imperfections in their own states' treatment of human rights issues, and to fight partisanship with a quest for universally applied standards. Given the conflict-inducing imperatives of a Westphalian structure such as the UN General Assembly, that is no doubt a very large *if.*

Regional Human Rights Law

In recent decades, developing regional systems for the protection of human rights have shown the most promise of moving the subject from the realm of political partisanship to that of generally authoritative law. Here the prospect—and in the case of Western Europe, much of the reality—is the creation of a supranational body of guarantees for individuals binding upon their own states. As such goals are being realized, the member states are moving out of a purely Westphalian world.

In one sense, the fact that the states of Western Europe have moved farthest in this direction is ironic, since it probably is "the area of the world in least need of international support for human rights."[27] But that fact is, of course, also why such a system could most easily be established there, since the governments that created it felt basically unthreatened by it. In addition, they consciously chose to build a regional human rights system as yet another path toward the closer integration of their separate polities after World War II. Their widely shared common values, their friendly relations, and their general desire to demonstrate the importance of human rights to the world in the aftermath of Hitler all contributed to the building of an effective system.

Even in this area of the world where expectations for the creation of effective regional human rights law have proved most justified, it is intriguing to note the essential caution in the way the region has moved in this direction. A vast majority of the petitions from individuals that have come before the appropriate European institution have been ruled inadmissable, usually on grounds that national remedies have not yet been exhausted. Of those accepted, most find satisfactory resolution within the European Commission on Human Rights, rather than the European Court, where decisions are likely to be based upon mutually acceptable compromise as opposed to the enunciation of binding legal precedent. Thus a huge percentage of the cases, real and potential, that enter the system are resolved without contributing notably to the supranational body of relevant law, but defer to the more traditional political sensibilities of member states.

Yet this essentially slow-going process already has produced notable results. One observer has summed them up in these terms:

> It was not, in fact, idle or merely cosmetic European institutions that stood out against Greek unlawful detentions, torture, and political repression during the rule of "the Colonels." These institutions have called Great Britain to account for tolerating torture and unlawful detention in Northern Ireland. Less dramatic cases have involved challenges to criminal procedures and punishment and to limitations on freedom of expression and publication and on the scope of trade union freedom; they have involved challenges to military discipline, vagrancy legislation, and compulsory education laws. . . . A jurisprudence of substantive law and of procedure has been growing for European use and for example to others.[28]

The Latin American human rights convention has been in force only since 1978, and does not yet include among its parties any of the largest states in the region.[29] Although it is the product of discussions within the inter-American system that go back many years, it only came into force at a time when revolutionary and counter-revolutionary movements within several of the signatory states augured a growing diversity of the dominant values relevant to consensus on human rights standards. So for the short run, it seems unlikely that the convention will be able to create the kind of substantive regional law that is emerging from the European system. Yet, since the convention is in place, it retains the potential to contribute effectively, if it is taken seriously by those, including eligible governments that have not yet acceded to it, determined to make it help promote human rights within the region.

TOWARD GREATER HUMAN DIGNITY?

It is easy to be pessimistic about the prospects for enhancing human rights protections worldwide. In spite of unprecedented attention to these issues since the end of World War II, seemingly intractable problems remain in cracking the power of governments to oppress their people. Within the first decades after an international treaty prohibiting genocide entered into force, genocidal acts of governments raged largely unchecked on more than one continent. No objective observer could honestly argue that the world had begun an evident climb toward the ever-greater realization of human rights as the result of all the recent attention.

Still, the most negative observations must be balanced by a sense of what may have been accomplished and more importantly may be done in the future to increase the dignity of all members of the species. It is simple realism, first, to note that the protection of human rights is never won in any lasting sense, not even within those societies that are recognized as having the best records of achievement. The struggle is like that of Sisyphus in his eternal effort to heave his burden to the summit.[30] Without the struggle, humanity is lost, although the effort itself is endless and not necessarily obviously progressive to those engaged in it.

Part of the sense of discouragement many people feel no doubt arises from their dismay at the way in which human rights charges and countercharges fly between political opponents, poisoning the prospects for their improved relations and enhancing not one whit their human rights conduct. Sometimes including human rights issues on the global agenda appears merely to have provided states with yet another issue to divide them. But as we have seen in other matters, this politicization of human rights—i.e., bringing them into the arena where important values compete for power—appears to be an essential first step toward their advancement, however divisive and even retrogressive that process may first appear. Because we are beginning to sense for the first time in human history that we must develop the capability to correct gross injustice everywhere and not only in our own neighborhoods, the international human rights movement has arisen. That is a potentially revolutionary new perception of our real political obligations to our fellow humans, and it is only beginning to make itself felt. Little wonder that at this early stage its results have been erratic and often disappointing. More important, the kinds of concerns embodied in attention to human rights have begun to alter the ways in which both governments and informed individuals think about and evaluate international political behavior.

In considering the importance of the various human rights standards written over the past several decades, it may again be useful to consider the analogy of Magna Charta.[31] That great constitutional landmark for the Anglo-Saxon world did not have a clear and decisive impact on all British subjects until many years after the barons forced King John to sign it at Runnymede. Its legitimacy gradually emerged as the result of the long-standing determination of Englishmen to reign in the arbitrary exercise of power by the sovereign (a determination that is widely shared by human beings in all times and places when confronted with oppression). The document's existence helped clarify the purpose and, over the course of centuries, legitimize it. In much the same way we may assume that the Universal Declaration of Human Rights, the Covenants, and various treaties dealing with specific human rights issues will help to clarify and direct our worldwide task, not just within our lifetimes but conceivably for generations to come.

Evidence of this process at work already is appearing in the international legal order. In general, it is most visible at the nexus between customary and positive international law, between doctrines of consensus versus consent as the basis of international legal obligation. It is a matter of logical consistency that strict legal positivists should look at a purely Westphalian world and conclude that sovereign states may only be bound by laws to which they have specifically consented, which is most clearly done through treaty making. According to such a view, in the absence of that consent, no state can be bound by the will of others, even when an overwhelming number of them are committed to a particular multilateral treaty. Yet when that view is carried to its logical conclusion, it denies the efficacy of custom as a binding source of the law, even though a substantial amount of contemporary international law, including much that is now codified, has grown directly from the customary practices of states. At the very least, the long acceptability of a particular practice to sovereigns has always seemed tantamount to their general consent to it.

In the contemporary world, these considerations have been put into a new light, essentially for two reasons: First, a great many more sovereign actors are present in the world today than in the past, which complicates enormously the problem of securing their consent to every issue for which all of them appropriately should be bound; second, the growth of international organizations provides ongoing arenas in which governments may express their views officially, although without engaging in treaty making, through roll-call votes. As a result, one can often find the international consensus on an issue whether or not consent has been expressed through ratification of a treaty. In the General Assembly, for example, certain widely adhered to resolutions (particularly, as in the human rights area, those specifically labeled *declarations*) may serve as the basis for creation of a treaty. Others, such as the numerous condemnations of apartheid, may recur so often that they take on the general character of an international social standard on a particular issue. Because so much of the modern world is influenced by the legitimacy of representative institutions and majority rule, it seems only logical to extend that legitimacy, gradually and organically, to the international life of states. As a result, we may expect world community consensus to matter increasingly in the determination of specieswide standards in the near future.

Perhaps no area of international life is supported by the consensual view of obligation so forcefully as that of human rights. After all, if these rights apply to human beings as humans, then presumably no minority of governments should be permitted to deny their local application. As evidence, the Universal Declaration is now widely regarded as at least a quasi-obligatory set of standards, even though it is not a binding treaty,[32] and authoritative decision makers are beginning to assert the existence of relevant new norms as having emerged, at least in part, through international consensus in the human rights field. One of the most dramatic examples of the latter trend came in a 1980 decision within a U.S. Court of Appeals, when the judge held that deliberate torture engaged in by governmental authorities is a violation of the law of nations. For the principal evidence that such a standard now exists, the judge had to look to a wide variety of international statements on the subject; together these marked a clear international consensus on the unacceptability of torture, although taken singly, none would have seemed to bind relevant government officials—in this case, Paraguay's—on the basis of their overt consent to a treaty standard.[33]

In the broadest sense, this discussion focuses on the way in which a popular-based legal order develops within any society. Relevant values must be formulated before they can be agreed upon, and the process of their formation elucidates where agreements lie or may be formed. Value formation is the first step and one that, at the international level, has been entered into with considerable energy and impressive results over the past thirty to forty years. The second part of the process is to work to secure those agreed-upon values that, given the political factors inherent in Westphalia that act against such an effort, cannot be expected to be attained quickly. The mountain of injustice upon which the human rights movement labors may even grow higher before it is conquered, but every step in the direction of taming it is a victory for each of us, adding hope to our future as a species.

NOTES

1. International law also has addressed the problem of what to do in the event of unacceptable deprivations of human rights by governments over individuals within their jurisdiction. That has mainly taken the form of justifications for humanitarian intervention by other states. But Westphalia's insistence upon the hard-shell quality of the state inevitably meant that human rights violations principally had to be addressed from within through domestic law and not through the international legal order.

2. In one of his typical writings on the subject, Mussolini argued, "The keystone of the Fascist doctrine is the conception of the State, of its essence, its purposes, its ends. For Fascism the State is an absolute, before which individuals and groups are relative. . . . The Fascist State organises the Nation, but then leaves sufficient margins to the individuals; it has limited the useless and noxious liberties and has conserved the essential ones. The judge of such things cannot be the individual but only the State" (*Essay*, pt. 2, quoted in Herman Finer, *Mussolini's Italy* [Hamden, Conn.: Archon Books, 1964], pp. 204–205).

3. Crimes against humanity included murder, extermination, enslavement, deportation, and other inhuman acts committed against any civilian population, before or during the war, or persecutions on political, racial, or religious grounds in execution of or in connection with any crime within the jurisdiction of the Tribunal, whether or not in violation of the domestic law of the country where perpetrated. Article 6 of the Charter of the International Military Tribunal, 1945, reprinted in Jay W. Baird, ed., *From Nuremberg to My Lai* (Lexington, Mass.: Heath, 1972), pp. 12–13.

4. This has been characteristic of the international role of the United States. Its record of ratification of human rights conventions is one of the poorest in the world, which is particularly ironic when one considers that the standards to which the United States has been unwilling to submit through treaty obligations are very often those already established and enforced in U.S. domestic law. Those set forth in the United Nation's Convention on the Elimination of All Forms of Racial Discrimination are a case in point. The reasons for the United States' almost nonparticipation in relevant treaty law are complex, but they no doubt include, in addition to a possible residue of isolationism, constitutional jealousies over the division of legislative and treaty-making powers between Congress and the executive. See, for example, William Korey, "Human Rights Treaties: Why Is the U.S. Stalling?" *Foreign Affairs* 45, 3 (April, 1967):414–424; and Vernon Van Dyke, *Human Rights, the United States, and World Community* (New York: Oxford University Press, 1970).

5. For an imaginative early essay on the evolution of human rights law out of the general deference to the Universal Declaration, see Egon Schwelb, *Human Rights and the International Community* (Chicago: Quadrangle, 1964).

6. Harold K. Jacobson, "The Global System and the Realization of Human Dignity and Justice," *International Studies Quarterly* 26, 3 (September 1982):322–323.

7. See discussion of base values and meta needs, Chapter 1, note 8.

8. Recognition of the divergent quality of these two kinds of rights is clear in the separation of the UN Covenants into one that treats political and civil rights and another that treats economic, social, and cultural rights. The former covenant contains, in its Part 4, elaborate provisions for enforcing political rights, largely through a system of reporting to an independent, international committee of experts. Its optional protocol even permits that committee to receive petitions from individuals who wish to go over their own governments with human rights complaints. In contrast, the second covenant contains no such comparable provisions. State compliance with its standards is addressed only through the annual reports ratifying states are asked to submit to the UN's Economic and Social Council.

9. The communal movement that spread in the West during the 1960s was built upon such value agreement among the membership. So were utopian socialist communities of the nineteenth century, as formed by the followers of Robert Owen and Charles Fourier (New Harmony and Brook Farm are the two most notable efforts in the United States to establish communities based upon their principles). In this sense, too, Marx's vision of an ultimately classless or communist society as the final stage of history should be regarded as utopian, for it specifically envisions the elimination of political conflict and competition through development societywide of absolute harmony on what social values are to be advanced.

10. Richard Falk, *Human Rights and State Sovereignty* (New York: Holmes and Meier, 1981), especially Chapter 4, pp. 63–124.

11. Ibid., p. 86. Falk lists forty-nine praetorianized governments as of 1979, as follows: Afghanistan, Algeria, Bahrain, Bangladesh, Bolivia, Burma, Burundi, Central African Empire, Congo, Costa Rica, Dominican Republic, Equatorial Guinea, Gabon, Ghana, Guatemala, Guinea, Haiti, Honduras, Iraq, Jordan, Kenya, Lebanon, Lesotho, Madagascar, Malawi, Malaysia, Mali, Namibia, Nepal, Nicaragua, Niger, Oman, Paraguay, Rhodesia, Rwanda, Senegal, Seychelles, Sierra Leone, Somalia, Sudan, Swaziland, Syria, Togo, Tunisia, Uganda, United Arab Emirates, P.D.R. Yemen.

12. Ibid., p. 87.

13. Ibid., p. 73. Falk lists the following as Brazilianized as of 1979: Argentina, Brazil, Chile, Republic of China, Egypt, Indonesia, South Korea, Mexico, Nigeria, Panama, Peru, Philippines, Saudi Arabia, Singapore, South Africa, Thailand, Uruguay. Argentina returned to a democratically elected civilian government late in 1983.

14. Ibid., p. 83. Falk lists the following as Leninized states in 1979: Angola, Benin, Cuba, Ethiopia, Guinea Bissau, Guyana, Kampuchea (Cambodia), North Korea, Laos, Mongolia, Mozambique, People's Republic of China, Tibet, Vietnam, Yugoslavia.

15. See Chapter 4, especially note 15.

16. One can make a good case for arguing that it was the growth in the U.S. public during the Vietnam episode of at least an inchoate sense that U.S. behavior too often violated Nuremburg standards that led to the growing and ultimately successful domestic opposition to the war. See, for example, Telford Taylor, *Nuremberg and Vietnam: An American Tragedy* (Chicago: Quadrangle Books, 1970).

17. See David Forsythe's chapter on human rights in *American Foreign Policy in an Uncertain Age*, David Forsythe, ed. (Lincoln: University of Nebraska Press, 1984).

18. Such a possibility seems to have been supported late in 1983 when Lech Walesa, the head of Poland's banned Solidarity trade union, urged Western leaders to lift the economic sanctions imposed against the Polish government after its declaration of martial law in 1981. Walesa reportedly argued that "sanctions should be ended because what Poland needs at the moment is not losses of millions of dollars but aid of billions of dollars" (*New York Times,* December 6, 1983).

19. On this point, see Robert C. Johansen's review article, "Human Rights in the 1980's: Revolutionary Growth or Unanticipated Erosion?" *World Politics* 35, 2 (January 1983):290.

20. One significant example of the payoff of such a policy came in December 1983, when Argentina returned to democratic and civilian rule after eight years of military dictatorship whose human rights violations had become the target of President Carter's foreign policy. Carter was criticized by some Americans for alienating a friendly regime; yet more than three years after his defeat for reelection, it seemed clear that, as the *New York Times* editorialized, "Jimmy Carter's human rights policy made a crucial difference in Argentina." The junta's so-called antiterrorist campaign had claimed at least 6,000 lives. "The rampage reached its peak in 1976, the year in which Congress for the first time tied human rights strings to America's military and economic aid. It was a risky and disputed attempt to harness principle to diplomacy. But would it work? As administered by President Carter in important cases, it plainly did" (December 10, 1983).

21. Seven of the ten winners between 1975 and 1984 clearly fall within this category. They include Andrei Sakharov of the USSR (1975); Mairead Corrigan and Betty Williams (Northern Ireland, 1976); Amnesty International (1977); Mother Theresa of Calcutta (India, 1979); Adolfo Perez Esquival (Argentina, 1980); Lech Walesa (Poland, 1983); Bishop Desmond Tutu (South Africa, 1984). In 1978 Anwar Sadat of Egypt and Menachem Begin of Israel were co-winners. It is potentially significant, too, that the number of nongovernmental organizations concerned with promoting and protecting human rights has increased greatly in recent years. Conservatively estimated at several hundred today, most are Western-based. However, as two students of this subject have noted, "in Eastern Europe, the emergence of private nongovernmental human rights organizations—a Moscow-based Amnesty International Group, a Moscow Committee for Human Rights, the Charter 77 Movement in Czechoslovakia, the Polish Workers' Defense Committee—is an entirely new phenomenon in the evolution of East European Communist Development" (Laurie S. Wiseberg and Harry M. Scoble, "Recent Trends in the Expanding Universe of NGOs Dedicated to the Protection of Human Rights," in *Global Human Rights: Public Policies, Comparative Measures, and NGO Strategies,* ed. Ved P. Nanda, James R. Scarritt, and George W. Shepherd, Jr. (Boulder, Colo.: Westview Press, 1981), p. 235.

22. The United Nations treats human rights issues principally in two different arenas. The 43-member Commission on Human Rights, which includes most of the democratic states of the North, has originated most human rights treaties and in recent years has examined human rights violations in a variety of countries, including Iran and Poland. In contrast, the General Assembly's Third Committee, which includes all 158 members, is dominated by the nonaligned group. The voting power of that coalition, combined with the need to strike bargains among so vast a body, typically ensures that its investigations will be restricted to a few, universally acceptable targets.

23. The words are those of Louis Henkin, *The Rights of Man Today* (Boulder, Colo.: Westview Press, 1978), p. 107.

24. The political trade-off was clear in the Zionist resolution, when reportedly, for example, the Chilean government agreed to support it in exchange for Arab states' agreement to side with Chile in defending itself against charges of torturing political opponents. *New York Times,* October 19, 1975.

25. *New York Times,* December 7, 1983.

26. Even Israel's closest friends, including successive U.S. administrations, have given voice to such a standard in their opposition to the creation of permanent Israeli settlements in occupied Arab territory.

27. Henkin, *Rights of Man,* p. 104.

28. Ibid.

29. As of 1983, ratifying states were Colombia, Costa Rica, Dominican Republic, Ecuador, El Salvador, Guatemala, Haiti, Honduras, Nicaragua, Panama, and Venezuela.

30. See Jerome J. Shestack, "Sisyphus Endures: The International Human Rights NGO," 24 *New York Law School Law Review,* 89 (1978).

31. See Chapter 3, p. 40.

32. See Schwelb, *Human Rights.*

33. *Dolly M. E. Filartiga and Joel Filartiga, Plaintiffs-Appellants,* versus *Americo Norberto Peña-Irala, Defendant-Appellee,* No. 191, Docket 79-6090, U.S. Court of Appeals, Second Circuit, June 30, 1980 (630 F. 2d 876). See also Matthew Lippman, "The Protection of Universal Human Rights: The Problem of Torture," *Universal Human Rights* 1, 4 (October-December 1979):25–55.

8
The Closing of the World Frontier

It is [the] ratio of population to land which determines what are
the possibilities of human development or the limits of what men
can attain in civilization and comfort.
—William Graham Sumner
"Earth-Hunger or the Philosophy of Land-Grabbing"

In 1952, U.S. historian Walter Prescott Webb published an
important book exploring the political and social consequences of the
fact that the four-hundred-year period of European discovery and
exploration at the world's frontier had very recently come to a close.[1]
From the time of Columbus's discovery of the new world until about
the beginning of the twentieth century, Europe had succeeded in
dominating the globe once it entered the planet's great frontier of
the Americas, the south Pacific, and southern Africa. Together, these
lands had an area five or six times the size of Europe, they were
largely empty of people (or at least of nonnomadic populations), and
they were filled with the abundant material resources that would make
the European peoples increasingly rich and powerful in the modern
age. Webb's thesis was that this period had produced "a business
boom such as the world had never known before and probably never
can know again," for he concluded that the period of expansion then
ending was an unusual and perhaps unique phenomenon in human
history.[2]

Webb then described the way in which what for four hundred years
had been an open and expanding social system had become a closed
one, with consequences that in his day were only beginning to be
dimly perceived. We may ask, in fact, how much better we perceive
them several decades later, for many of our behavioral patterns and
values still seem to reflect the mindless habits of creatures living within

185

an expanding, largely boundless system. Reason tells us that when something is closed that has seemed always open, the resulting difference could not be greater. Yet even when we understand the facts regarding the planetary limits we have reached today, we seem to have difficulty in adjusting to them. Because we cannot yet, for the most part, sense the closing in a way that touches tangibly upon our lives, we tend still to live as if we were more or less free agents in an ever-expandable world.

HUMANITY'S IMPACT ON A SHRINKING PLANET

The facts prove dramatically the speed at which our planet is shrinking, which is simply the metaphorical way of saying that population growth in particular and the demands we make of the earth and its resources are clearly outstripping the planet's ability to sustain us in the way in which many of us, particularly in the West, have become accustomed.

At the time of the fall of Rome, some 1,500 years ago, the total human population of the world may have been about 400 million. It doubled in about another 1,000 years, and by the dawn of the Westphalian system in Europe may have reached 1 billion. Then, in one of the many factors distinguishing the modern from the medieval period, population growth began to take off, first in Europe and more recently worldwide. The globe's population reached 2 billion not in 1,000, but in a scant 300 years, by 1900. The third billion arrived a mere 50 years later, the fourth by 1980, and again the world's population doubled, but this time in the brief 80 years since 1900. Today, this vast acceleration in population growth has begun to show the slightest signs of slowing down, although almost inevitably the world's population will nearly double again before the time, perhaps early in the twenty-first century, when achieving zero population growth throughout the world may first be possible.

Although these facts are startling enough, they are only the beginning of the story of humankind's impact on the planet. That great frontier of which Webb wrote has been filled up and closed off with the booming growth in population. The nearly limitless potential abundance it once held is drying up as mineral resources are mined and otherwise exploited at a rate that surpasses even the increase in population. Each of the 2 billion people alive in 1900 on average consumed only one-sixth the amount of energy a person used in 1980—and there were twice as many people on the planet in the latter year.

This enormous increase in the consumption of nonrenewable resources now raises questions about our place in nature's scheme of things that go beyond our sheer numbers—which we conceivably can learn to limit—and ask about our social and material values. The population and energy consumption trends together suggest that some of our favorite human desires, for wealth and power over our physical universe, may yet prove suicidal for our species. We must make no mistake; these "natural" desires for wealth and mastery demand insatiable amounts of energy, which in turn generate the technology and the productivity that have so greatly enlarged our range of material goods and comforts. To have these things in the greatest possible abundance has seemed natural to us, never mind that the overwhelming number of our ancestors would have regarded acquiring them an impossible dream. For the first time in human history our generation needs to understand the dangers now inherent in the materialism most of us have taken as a good, especially since more of it became possible at the dawn of the industrial revolution.

In fact the industrial revolution was built from the beginning upon the exploitation of nonrenewable resources, specifically the fossil fuels created within the earth's surface over the course of billions of years. That they are finite is unarguable, even though some of them, notably coal, clearly exist in much greater abundance than do others, such as oil. The other chief characteristic of the fossil fuels upon which we rely so heavily is that they are never literally consumed, but are used and then passed back into the natural world in other forms, mostly as pollution.

Resource scarcity and environmental degradation—these twin dangers of our lust for power over the material world have put us on a collision course with nature itself. How well do we yet understand that our way of life, rather than nature, must ultimately give way? That is the only reasonable conclusion we can reach when we reflect that we are helpless apart from the natural world. It is a matter literally of our life or death that we learn to live in greater harmony with nature—if we are not yet too late, for clearly "technological man [is] on a course which could alter dangerously and perhaps irreversibly, the natural systems of his planet upon which his biological survival depends." As Ward and Dubos noted in the early 1970s, such dangers are already apparent "when only a third of humanity has entered the technological age."[3] Yet our development strategy has been based upon the assumption that the aspirations of the rest of our species for technological progress were as meritorious as our own and should be met. Now it seems we may have understood it backwards, that what for centuries we have regarded as our road to progress is in fact the road to ruin.

The reasons for this colossal misconception seem to lie deep within our very humanity, for as Ward and Dubos have pointed out, "man inhabits two worlds. One is the natural world of plants and animals, of soils and airs and waters which preceded him by billions of years and of which he is a part. The other is the world of social institutions and artifacts he builds for himself, using his tools and engines, his science and his dreams to fashion an environment obedient to human purpose and direction."[4] That first world of nature is appropriately named the *biosphere*, since that term reminds us that the life-sustaining component of the planet is indeed a sphere, closed and finite. The second world, made by humans, is therefore the *technosphere*, although the more general term often associated with it is *civilization*.

Traditionally, we have tended to see nature as a force to be tamed, used, and exploited for our needs. We have seen our achievements in the technosphere as a means of conquering the biosphere, bending it to our purpose. We have counted ourselves civilized to the extent we have mastered and escaped from raw nature. Such a tendency in our thinking over the course of many millenniums has given rise to our attitude that we are somehow apart from or—an attitude that may constitute our ultimate hubris—even superior to nature, which, to the extent we have succeeded in subduing it, has seemed to us a positive good. The march of human civilization has been marked by the ever-greater supremacy of the technosphere over the biosphere, and not until very recently have many of us begun to worry about the consequences of that supremacy.

The essential lesson of the biosphere is that it is neither indestructible in the face of human intervention nor replaceable by human effort. Indeed a delicate balance of nature throughout the ecology of the planet forms a life-sustaining system through an infinitely complex web of connections among the biosphere's components. Strands in the web sometimes may appear to us as inconvenient if not clearly hostile to human purpose, as seems obvious in the case of insect pests that traditionally have devoured half or more of the food crops humans have labored to produce to keep themselves alive. And with our godlike technological power, we have learned to create pesticides that work remarkably well at wiping out many of those pests. Then belatedly we have been forced to see that unasked for results have been less beneficent: Our pesticides may have eliminated the insect's natural predators as well, which in turn may have played an essential role elsewhere in the food chain; hardy survivors of the chemical may have been precisely those individuals capable of developing protective mutations for future generations that will make them impervious to the same chemical; meanwhile, the insecticide may have run off into nearby rivers and streams with potentially disastrous results for still other plant and animal species.

It may be even more disturbing to remember that the thin layer of atmosphere around the earth, which is the product of eons of development, is all that protects us from the lethal radiation of the sun. Yet much of our activity within the technosphere in the industrial age has tampered with the atmospheric layer, principally through releasing huge increases in carbon dioxide through the burning of fossil fuels. We do not know precisely how much more of this kind of tampering can take place before catastrophic changes in climate and increased penetration of the sun's ultraviolet rays occur. We do know that all extrapolations based upon population growth and energy use spell disaster sometime in the fairly near future.

Part of the hubris of the rich North today is seen in the assumption that rapidly increasing birth rates in the poor South are threatening our ecosystems with collapse. In fact, as noted in Chapter 6, those of us who are comparatively rich are a much greater burden for Mother Nature than are our poor brethren. The rich are seemingly insatiable in their demands for nature's resources and in using them are affecting the biosphere's ecology with catastrophic results. The citizen of the United States, the richest society in the world, carries around the equivalent of eleven tons of steel in cars, household appliances, and other machines, which give power over the physical universe.[5] A dozen of the world's poor demand less in the way of nonrenewable resources than does a single North American, however unpleasant the implications of that fact for Northern modes and styles of life.

Because the implications *are* so unpleasant, it is not enough to insist that the way of life rich societies have created is quite literally unnatural. Our equating that way of life with progress is too deeply ingrained for us to forego voluntarily the power over the material world that gives us pleasure. "It is a fairly general characteristic of human nature that men seek to avoid back-breaking and monotonous work, that they like comfort, are fascinated by personal possessions, and enjoy having a good time."[6] Even more fundamentally, *Homo sapiens'* creation of a technosphere more than anything else defines us as human beings. The alternative to the highly exploitative system of production that the industrialized world has produced is not a plunge into a state of nature, but rather a conscious modification of our technosphere to bring it into greater harmony with nature's laws. If we can do that, we shall truly progress. If we resist doing that, we shall have change uncomfortably, and perhaps even tragically, forced upon us by nature itself.

THE END OF LIMITLESS ABUNDANCE

If we are to understand the magnitude of the change required in many of our long-standing values, we need first to see how and why such a polar opposition has grown between our way of life in the technosphere and the demands made by our rootedness in the biosphere. Essentially, the answer lies in the fact that not until our time, to paraphrase a prominent environmentalist, has the closed circle of nature begun to redirect fundamentally the way we must live.[7] More precisely, the *planet* has become closed for all human beings today, whereas in the past it has been treated as open for some *societies* during long historical periods, whereas it seemed much more nearly closed to others. The fact that the world was open to west Europeans from the time of the Renaissance until this century has been critical in the formation of values and behavior based upon unnatural assumptions of a nearly infinitely abundant planet earth. That period of expansion and growth of course produced the Westphalian international order along with its counterparts of Lockean liberalism and laissez-faire capitalism in domestic political and economic theory. For many centuries before about 1500, Europe had been a closed and crowded place. As W. P. Webb noted, "there was not much food, and practically no means of escape for those people living in a closed world. The idea of progress had not been born. Heaven alone, which could be reached only through the portals of death, offered hope to the masses of the [European] Metropolis."[8] Then came the discovery of the nearly empty new world, with its unimaginable resources, there for the taking of any European actor with the will to exploit them.

The change in the European environment from one of scarcity to that of great abundance is what essentially defines the shift from the medieval to the modern age. Scarcity, as we saw in Chapter 2, demands more authoritarian decision making to allocate resources fairly than does enormous abundance, where a "come one, come all" spirit can be encouraged without inducing chaos. And so came the gradual shift from the hierarchical political order of the Middle Ages to the horizontal system of sovereign equals called Westphalia. Within the context of potential abundance, every diligent sovereign society could enrich itself without undermining the ability of others to do likewise, as long as each left the others largely alone and focused upon their own, internal advancement. It was also critically important that the sovereigns maintained the mutual fiction that the new territories were literally no man's lands, subject to appropriation by whichever civilized sovereign undertook to make them productive.

The world's frontier began to close to continued European exploitation at about the beginning of the present century. Meanwhile, however, the laissez-faire ordering principles of Westphalia had been exported to the entire world: European modes of economic and political organization became those of the entire planet, a phenomenon that finally became clearest in the aftermath of the colonial period when the Westphalian system covered the globe.[9] Yet another irony of our time, and a further example of the structural lethargy that inhibits complex social change, is that an international normative order based upon assumptions of limitless abundance should have become the universal order at precisely the moment when it was beginning to be ill-suited to global conditions of scarcity.

As a general principle, when the limits to abundance become evident to the members of a society, the rational political response is greater central planning for the careful and socially acceptable allocation of

scarce resources to its individual subjects. That applies for the fulfillment of economic or political values, whether the social system
involved is local or global. Within the Western world, moves away
from complete laissez-faire came first within the economic realm of
advanced industrial states, where the "dismal science" has, from the
time of Malthus, understood the underlying reality of scarcity beneath
the surface of potential abundance. The socialist critique of pure
laissez-faire capitalism assumes at a minimum that distributive justice
requires some measure of centralized intervention in the marketplace.
At the regional international level, moves toward economic integration,
as in Western Europe, have been induced partly by the lure of economies
of scale and have required centralized guidance at new, supranational
levels. At the global level, sovereigns have been disinclined to move
away from Westphalia's laissez-faire system in any formal way, and yet
in limited but important areas, they have begun to plan for the
allocation of resources along lines that reveal the new-found limits to
nature's abundance. Perhaps the most revealing of these is in the
emerging law of the sea, which departs considerably from the Grotian
laissez-faire approach.

THE CHANGING LAW OF THE SEA

When he wrote at the dawn of the modern age, at a time when
Europeans were just beginning to move about the world's frontier in
great numbers and to enrich themselves from its treasures, Grotius
took as his basic premise that the oceans of the world were limitless
in their bounty, incapable of being exhausted or destroyed by any
human activity then imaginable. He noted further that the oceans
formed the essential highway out of Europe to the world's frontier;
therefore, he built his law of the sea upon a classic laissez-faire
principle: that the oceans should be open to all capable of access to
them on a mutually reciprocal basis. Sovereigns could claim as their
own territory no more than a narrow band of the waters immediately
off their coasts—and this, presumably, in keeping with the premise
that they had a primary duty to provide security to their societies.[10]
No security argument for wider claims could outweigh the obvious
mutual benefits to be derived by all sovereigns if given easy access
to the world's great highway.

The resulting system of laws governing the seas was simplicity itself.
All the waters beyond territorial boundaries were to be regarded as
res communis or community property, much like the common grazing
lands established by many European towns and villages for their
residents' domestic animals. Any sovereign actor might travel on those
waters, fish them, and take whatever resources were available there,
which were what later generations would call free goods, supplied in
apparent endless abundance by nature itself. About all that was required

of those exploiting these resources was that their ocean-going vessels be properly licensed and regulated by appropriate sovereign authorities, since they were in effect bits of sovereign territory afloat on the high seas.

It is instructive to consider why the Grotian doctrine of an open sea came to be accepted within the Westphalian legal order. If we consider claims to sovereign and exclusive jurisdiction the chief characteristic of Westphalia, it may seem surprising that states did not extend those claims to huge chunks of the sea, effectively closing them off to rival actors. Such claims underlay the argument of one of Grotius's contemporaries, John Selden. But an effective claim to exclusive sovereignty over any piece of territory, including an expanse of water, demands an ability to control it and to keep rival claimants out with force if necessary. No doubt Europe's greatest naval powers possessed that ability by Grotius's day; yet some thirty years before he wrote, Queen Elizabeth I had proclaimed Britain's determination to enforce high seas freedom and then made good on that claim after defeating the Spanish Armada. Why had Elizabeth moved in anticipation of Grotius's argument, rather than attempting to claim vast stretches of the sea for her realm, as she no doubt now could?

The reason was that the British were beginning to see the possibilities for their own considerable enrichment through trade abroad and exploitation of the world's frontier. They above all would benefit from easy access to all the world's oceans because of their island position and lack of resources at home. They above all could be assured of winning the competition with fellow traders and explorers from other European states in the larger world. Thus, British entrepreneurs would gain less from the expensive effort by their government to maintain a credible claim to exclusive jurisdiction over a piece of the ocean than by the much cheaper policing of the oceans to ensure British access to its resources and its ports throughout the globe. What made that policing very much cheaper was that it was built upon the laissez-faire principle that requires the very *least* governance, the notion of reciprocity or equal rights for all subjects of the law. As a result, the doctrine of freedom of the seas became enshrined in the international legal order thanks to the wedding of laissez-faire economics to British gunboats.

Not until the mid-twentieth century was the Grotian system seriously challenged. That it has been both challenged and radically altered in recent years is a reflection of the closing of the circle upon the ocean's free goods. The first clear signs of change came just at the close of World War II, when President Truman issued a set of proclamations asserting the exclusive jurisdiction of the United States over the living and nonliving resources of its continental shelf, while maintaining that the traditional freedom of the seas above the shelf was not to be affected.[11] Truman's action was principally a response to pressures from U.S. oil companies, which were acquiring the technology to drill for oil under the comparatively shallow offshore waters where rich oil deposits existed.

By 1945, the United States had inherited Britain's role as the world's greatest naval and commercial power and so had no interest in claiming actual sovereignty over the continental shelf and superjacent waters, since that would have invited reciprocal claims by nonmaritime states mainly bent on restricting the access of greater sea powers to waters close to their shores. Nonetheless, the Truman Proclamation soon had exactly that effect, most notably in 1952 when Chile, Ecuador, and Peru asserted their right to claim as exclusive "conservation zones" the waters off their coasts to a distance of 200 nautical miles.[12] Significantly, these Pacific coast states had virtually no continental shelf (which, in the Americas, lies mainly on the Atlantic side of the continents) and so could not copy what must have seemed to their governments the sophistry of the Truman declarations. In fact, in the eyes of most other governments, the Latin American countries' treatment of these 200-mile zones made them virtually indistinguishable from territorial seas. In practice, therefore, a doctrine of *mare clausam* was implemented for the first time in several centuries. In spite of frequent clashes with, especially, North American fishing boats and protests by the United States, the Latin American states showed their determination to police their claims, arguing that increasing pressures upon the resources of these waters from abroad demanded their conservation.[13]

Meanwhile, other states were beginning to experience similar conflicts and to recognize the need for new multilateral agreement as the result of the ever-growing demand for the resources of the sea and its subsoil. In 1958, an eighty-six-nation conference was convened in Geneva to further codify the law of the sea. It succeeded in producing four conventions that clarified much of what previously had been customary international law, largely endorsing the traditional practices of states. Yet its Convention on the Continental Shelf, unable to define the absolute limit of the shelf area, specified that it might extend beyond 200 meters "to where the depth of the superjacent waters admit of exploitation of the natural resources of the said areas."[14] Such an expandable definition ensured that as technology capable of exploiting underseas resources increased, so would the legal limit of the continental shelf, and with increased exploitation much of the sea's subsoil would gradually be eliminated from the global commons. Sure enough, undersea technology continued to develop so rapidly that by the mid-1960s it was apparent that a more radical rethinking of the law of the sea was needed.

THE UN CONFERENCE ON THE LAW OF THE SEA

That rethinking began in earnest when Dr. Arvid Pardo, Malta's ambassador to the United Nations, proposed in 1967 that the governments of the world create a new seabed treaty based upon the premise that the seabed and its resources constituted the "common heritage of mankind." That new phrase came to be the subject of much discussion in the prolonged negotiations that followed in the Third UN Conference on the Law of the Sea.[15] The common heritage concept is in large part symbolic of the world's perceived need today to move beyond the Grotian conception of a laissez-faire order for the seas and to create real governing authority where none has existed before. Yet countries with the technologies and capital currently available for investment in deep-sea exploitation are, no doubt naturally enough, also those most enamored with continuing laissez-faire and most reluctant to acknowledge that if the sea's resources are our common heritage they should no longer be appropriated by the most powerful.

A basic division quickly formed within the conference between these highly advanced industrial states, on one hand, and most third world countries, on the other. Among the former group the most extreme view held that the seabed was effectively *terra nullius*—much like the new world in 1492—available on a first-come, first-served basis to any who could claim it. The entire Group of 77 opposed that assumption, arguing that if the common heritage principle meant anything, it should justify the greater equalization of wealth, as the world's new frontier came to be exploited, rather than a furtherance of inequality. To advance the development of the world's poor societies, they argued, an international authority must be created with the power both to license (or in effect tax) state enterprises exploiting the seabed's resources and to engage in deep-sea mining on its own, with both kinds of revenue to be distributed equitably on the basis of need.

In the effort to secure the North's agreement to that position, the third world gave away much of substance to the unilateral jurisdiction of states. The final treaty provides for the creation of 200-mile exclusive economic zones (EEZ) for every coastal state on earth. Not quite territorial seas in the traditional sense—only economic rights and not all other marks of sovereignty are granted to coastal states—this provision nonetheless legitimizes national economic expansion for most nations in a way unmatched at any previous time. The creation of EEZs excludes one-third of what traditionally have been high seas from the logic of *res communis* and, of course, from the common heritage as well. Although the two-thirds that remain do fall under the regime of the treaty's new International Seabed Authority (ISA), the overwhelming percentage of the sea's exploitable resources fall within exclusive zones. Ninety percent of the world's fisheries and at least that amount of the seabed's extremely valuable oil and gas deposits are removed from direct global competition. Moreover, most of the territory enclosed by the EEZs is gained by the world's biggest or richest countries; of the eight states that will acquire the largest EEZs, only two are not already highly industrialized.[16]

The voting framework of the International Seabed Authority will give third world states considerable voice in its activities. The Authority is governmental in a way no previous arrangement for the global commons has been; it is given the power to license and regulate the mining activities of the various state-sponsored companies at work in the form of the Enterprise, which will operate along with the private or state mining companies licensed by the Authority.[17] In effect, the Enterprise will constitute a new economic actor, created in the name of the whole global community, capable of competing in some sense with state operations in the deep-seas marketplace. It will be a public company in a new sense of the term, created by the global public. Symbolically at least, the Enterprise looks like quite a novel creation. It would be a bit like the European Coal and Steel Community (ECSC) if that were a global rather than a regional economic authority, except that the ECSC has a monopoly over Western Europe's coal and steel production whereas the ISA's Enterprise will not constitute a monopoly in seabed mining. Perhaps the nearest model is a state-run industry in a country where privately owned counterparts exist as competitors; broadcasting systems in a number of countries are examples. The result in either case is a mixed economic system, in which many of the means of production remain in private hands, there to compete with their publicly controlled counterparts.

The International Seabed Authority is the most ambitious example of functional government at the global level created to date. Yet the extent to which it will fulfill its potential remains very much an open question. This question arises first because so many of the great treasures of the sea and its subsoil are excluded from ISA jurisdiction by the creation of EEZs. For the foreseeable future, the overwhelming amount of economically significant exploitation will take place within the various EEZs rather than the area defined as high seas. Pardo, among others, was quick to understand the significance of this fact during the UNCLOS negotiations. In his view, if exclusive coastal jurisdiction had been limited to 12 miles, rather than to 200 miles, as he originally proposed, third world countries *already* would be receiving some $20 billion per year for their development purposes. As it is, poor and geographically disadvantaged countries will get less than $0.5 billion a year from the much reduced arena of the global commons and its correspondingly much less significant Authority.[18] So for the short run at least, the principal thrust of UNCLOS was to defer to the time-honored views of nation-state competition for resources, for the treaty awarded a huge majority of states handsomely with its EEZ provisions. Over the longer run, a functional international government may play a greater role in allocating scarce resources, simultaneously—through whatever deference toward its authority develops—helping to reshape values away from the competitively acquisitive ones of the separate states. The real question here is whether novel authoritative relationships can be forged at the same time the familiar and divisive ones are being encouraged to flourish on a new frontier.

The second factor that casts the future of the ISA in doubt is the reluctance of several of the most highly developed states, led by the United States, to adhere to the treaty. At the signing of the finished document at the United Nations (which signifies a state's intent rather than an irrevocable commitment), the United States was one of only four states voting against the treaty, while several of its most important European allies, as well as Warsaw Pact adversaries, abstained.[19] If the United States stays out of the treaty structure, the Enterprise will be denied 25 percent of its operating funds. More than that, the Reagan administration apparently was considering the possibility of creating a rival minitreaty to appeal to those most highly developed states with the greatest ability to engage in deep seabed mining today. Any such agreement no doubt would defer to the desires of most Western mining companies to regard the seabed as essentially *terra nullius,* whose resources are ripe for exploitation by the most powerful. Although it was by no means clear that enough other Western governments would support such a U.S. lead, the prospect at least existed that rival treaty regimes might be established, one supported by and particularly enriching to the small group of wealthy countries, the other a very much larger poor man's club largely without the technology needed to make felt a truly global capability.

The Reagan objections to the treaty centered on provisions calling for the mandatory transfer of technology from private mining companies to the Enterprise and about the possibilities for changing the treaty's mining clauses if assented to by three quarters of the ratifying states after twenty years. Both objections expressed the refusal of an administration strongly motivated by a free enterprise philosophy to acknowledge any social obligation to the wider world. In world order terms, the first objection may be taken as indicative of the general view of lobbyists from transnational corporations during UNCLOS negotiations. This view fundamentally repudiates common heritage as a legal doctrine meant to provide some distributive justice in the exploitation of the sea's resources. More than that, it confuses Grotius's assent to the technologically limited appropriation of living, renewable, and migratory resources (fish) with permission to assume property rights over the nonrenewable and fixed resources (largely manganese nodules and oil deposits) attached to or embedded in the ocean's floor.

Relevant transnationals may be able to act upon such a view of the world if they can secure the protection of, most obviously, the United States as they undertake their mining activities. Yet we know that such an interpretation of pertinent rights and duties is totally unacceptable to the 130 nations voting in favor of the UNCLOS treaty, as well, no doubt, as to most of those 15 that abstained. We can only speculate about how that opposition might be expressed in the event of unilateral and unauthorized mining activities on the high seas. Prolonged and acrimonious court tests surely could be expected; perhaps we should not even be surprised to see sporadic acts of terrorism to accompany the effort of these companies to mine the ocean depths. Such acts in turn would no doubt encourage Washington to increase its security measures for mining companies with all the attendant costs to the U.S. public and potential conflicts with other governments that such a move would produce.

The Reagan administration's stance on the UNCLOS treaty is a classic example of the temptation always faced by the strongest to suppose that its apparent ability to get what it wants for itself without any help from others is what most matters, that it can serve itself at the expense of others today oblivious to the need it may have for their cooperation tomorrow. This is clearly not the *only* conclusion one can reach today about the likely policy of a reified "America." In the decade of preparations for and participation in UNCLOS, Presidents Nixon, Ford, and Carter all supported the basic thrust of the kind of treaty that eventually emerged from the conference. Clearly, the treaty does not, and cannot, serve equally every conceivable interest group within global society. Awareness of the issues that it had to address reveals above all the effort to reconcile divergent interests in mutually acceptable ways. A mere glance at the array on each side of the final vote suggests that it succeeded for an overwhelming number of the world's governments and the social interests they represented. In this context, which includes that of ever-greater scarcity of the world's resources, it seems likely that the espousal of extremely laissez-faire policies for the world's oceans will become increasingly unacceptable.

POLLUTION AND WORLD POLITICS

From Grotius's day until the twentieth century, the doctrine of *res communis* for the high seas carried with it the assumption that individual actors had an obligation not to use that resource in ways injurious to the common interests of others. Until very recently, that meant, as a practical matter, little more than a ban against piracy—which is simply conduct unregulated by states on the high seas—and a commitment to honor the "peace of the port," and so on. The rules were few because the seas were so vast and abundant that it was nearly impossible to jeopardize them as a commons by mistakes or lack of deference to community rules by one or a few actors. At a time when human industrial wastes and use of chemicals scarcely existed, the high seas were nearly impervious to pollution on an extent that could cause obvious injury to others. Until well into this century, the oceans continued to be viewed by most as a vast, self-cleansing sewer with a limitless capacity to absorb the effluents of affluence.[20]

This attitude toward the oceans is one indication of our long-standing tendency to regard the biosphere as a bottomless storehouse of resources free to the taker willing to use and develop them. Of these, the land and the resources it holds are particularly susceptible to exclusive appropriation and private ownership, which has been the hallmark of the Western approach to land as territory. In contrast, the air and to a lesser extent the water cannot be demarcated and fenced off as neatly as the land. Both therefore have tended to be regarded as free goods, available for anyone's use. Of course, they have also always been common goods, since both air and water are essential not only to our lives but to all life on the planet. But our long-held assumption that they also were free was yet another reflection of the apparent facts that more than enough of both resources were available for everyone and that their use by some could not jeopardize the others' interests in enjoying them also in unspoiled abundance. Little attention had to be paid to the allocation of these resources since there were more than enough to go around.

Just as industrialization began the process that led to a population explosion in recent centuries, so it also began the process of exploiting the planet's free goods of air and water in ways that at last had raised questions about our long-held assumptions. We began to notice belatedly that they were not free, for social costs had to be paid for their expropriation by the industrial entrepreneur. We have usually tended until quite recently to view those costs, often in the form of polluted air or water, merely as nuisances that we could live with, as the necessary price of progress, even when we could no longer fish in our favorite stream or venture into the streets of many of our cities without experiencing stinging eyes and raspy throats. Today, however, further documentation is not needed to show that the costs are more serious than mere nuisances. They may lead directly to death as when a giant oil spill occurs in a shallow sea teeming with marine life; they may result in long-delayed death, as when a century-old slag heap from a coal mine collapsed in Wales in the 1960s, literally burying in a little school house the descendants of those who had dug the coal; they may accumulate so slowly that their impact will not be apparent for many years, as when rampant deforestation so depletes the planet's oxygen supply that increasingly it not only threatens an isolated species but all oxygen-breathing animals, including man.

Governmental authorities at various levels have begun to respond to some of the most egregious assaults on the biosphere through environmental regulations. Yet the very nature of nature itself has tended to make those responses somewhat timid, scattered, and less than fully satisfactory cures for the disease. In environmental connections a complex distance typically may exist between cause and effect. If a terrorist enters a public place and begins killing innocent people at random, the cause of their deaths is immediately and dramatically apparent, and something surely will be done to try to prevent the killer from wreaking such mayhem again. But if the same number of deaths occurs from cancer over a period of many years among the same size population of workers in a large industrial plant, not only is the effect less dramatic, but it is far more difficult to prove that the deaths resulted from a particular cause in the plant's working environment. In general, the public must see a clear and overwhelming threat to the quality of people's lives from environmental degradation before they are likely to urge action to stop it. Until the threat is dramatic, no effective constituency in favor of a clean environment is present. Meanwhile, a powerful and vocal constituency does exist on the part of the exploiters of nature's "free" goods to insist upon a continued right to use them without paying for the resulting social costs.

The biosphere, we still suppose, is there to be exploited as we create still more human products in the technosphere. After all, that is the unexamined premise of most economic development activity. When, in the late 1960s, the United Nations began to talk seriously about international action to support the environment, many third world governments reacted with suspicion. For them, this sudden concern of rich states with the added costs of environmentally sound industrial practice seemed very much like still another excuse for nonsupport of economic development programs on their behalf. Now some Northern spokesmen may have been secretly pleased to have another argument to use against pleas for their greater largess. But the interesting point here is that this conflict demonstrates how completely third world actors had embraced the classic Western attitude that humankind's material goals are in opposition to nature's own demands.

Discussions continued at the United Nations, and in 1972 the Stockholm Conference on the Human Environment brought together nearly all the world's states to determine, for the first time in history, what cooperative efforts they might make on behalf of their mutual life in the biosphere. With hindsight, the Stockholm meeting probably can be counted a modest success in terms of its tangible accomplishments. Conceivably it will one day be seen as a landmark in beginning a shift in dominant values toward greater ecological sensitivity. On a tangible level, the representatives at Stockholm agreed to create a permanent United Nations Environmental Programme (UNEP) with its own executive director, staff, governing council, and modest budget. By 1972, a number of UN agencies had undertaken environmental programs relevant to particular issues, as had several regional authorities—such as the Rhine and Danube River commissions in Europe and a great many governments in advanced industrial nations. A kind of umbrella authority therefore was needed to coordinate or oversee much of what had begun piecemeal. UNEP was created as a tiny step in that direction, although, as is typical of our Westphalian world, state governments gave it no real power to override their own policies. Still, since the relationships of nations obviously interlock on environmental problems, states might recognize the sense of a global perspective here more readily than in, say, matters of their military policies.[21]

More intangibly, what led to and followed the creation of UNEP required the kind of politicization of environmental issues that has occurred in recent decades regarding the advancement of human rights throughout the world. Such issues are no more politically controversial than motherhood until the prospect grows that they be acted upon and their relevant values protected in the political system in ways that have not been thought necessary or possible before. When a worldwide effort was launched for a cleaner environment, the issue quickly became a matter of high politics for the international community. In the course of preparing for Stockholm, governments were forced to develop policies in an area where most of them had had none before, to counter—in the case of Northern governments—the arguments of many of the poor who viewed these concerns as a subterfuge for continued social stratification, and—for many Southern governments—to try to come to grips with the implications of their own goals for the biosphere.

THE ENVIRONMENT AND GLOBAL ORDER

We clearly have not yet begun, as a planetary society, to establish an authoritative mechanism that could reasonably be expected to manage global resources and clean up our polluted environment so that our species might live in harmony with nature for centuries to come. Yet extremely modest evidence indicates that we may be beginning to make a start in that direction. Perhaps the kinds of coordinative responsibilities given UNEP can help to provide a more livable world—assuming, of course, that the very states whose policies UNEP is meant to coordinate are governed by those able to understand the global perspective and the holistic demands of environmental matters on their individual state policies. Some evidence of that kind of understanding *is* apparent today, or we should not have seen environmental concerns enter the international political agenda. Yet we know that it is characteristically human that, when confronted with the scarcity of goods, we tend to want to grab them for ourselves, to give full rein to our selfish impulses, and thereby to increase the conflicts between ourselves and others who value those same things. To prevent those conflicts from becoming ever more destructive, we almost certainly will need an ever greater authoritative allocation of relevant resources and evaluation of environmental priorities and that will require increasing departures from the global laissez-faire principles of the past.

Two contrasting images of the future may help illustrate the possibilities. The first assumes a rigid perpetuation of the decentralized sovereignties of states. In such a world, separate sovereigns, particularly those commanding the largest territories, possibly may maintain traditional policies of growth and development for quite some time. Yet even for them, such policies will only be sustained with ever greater difficulty and ever more paltry results as the costs of resource exploitation continue to rise along with pressures for more and more material goods. Increasingly harsh governmental controls may keep the local engine of production humming for a time, although with costly substitutions for resources unavailable from abroad, for the thrust of this kind of system of production is toward as much autarky as possible. We should probably expect matters of environmental quality to be the first victims. For instance, as oil became unavailable, countries like the United States with vast coal reserves almost certainly would be tempted to exploit them as cheaply as possible, regardless of the resulting scarification of the earth from strip or open pit mining. Meanwhile, embargoes and perhaps even shooting conflicts could be expected to occur with some frequency in the contest for ever more tempting resources on the ocean's floor, beneath the surface of the moon, or, more immediately, within the territory of weak and vulnerable third world countries, whose own economic status would become ever more precarious.

The second image assumes a world in which effective resource management and antipollution structures are evolving rationally. These structures almost surely would include some arrangements already in place, such as international river commissions, an effectively functioning International Seabed Authority, and many others. They might include a UNEP with the power to force polluting countries to pay to clean up the environment, national EEZs so carefully managed that they created models for marine resource and pollution management, and economic activities under way in space whose benefits were widely shared on earth particularly with those without the means of venturing onto this new frontier themselves. As such authoritative structures evolved for effective environmental management, they could no doubt be expected to breed still others as the need arose. Somewhere in the process a global network would have been produced that transcended without displacing the separate sovereign arenas for relevant decision making. New loyalties would have begun to emerge wherever new authority was effectively protecting important human values. Nor would they be identical with the acquisitive values of the industrial age, even though the quest for material wealth would scarcely have disappeared. Most important among them would be those supporting renewed understanding of our inextricable dependence upon nature, those favoring a style of human life "which accords to material things their proper, legitimate place, which is secondary and not primary."[22]

Whether one image more nearly fits the reality of the future than the other depends upon how we all behave in the effort to reconcile our technosphere more fully with the biosphere. Note that neither image assumes much chance that the laissez-faire approach to allocation of goods can continue unabated. The first, conflict-ridden scenario suggests more authoritarian control at various sovereign centers in opposition to each other, whereas the second tends to diffuse that possibility by support for a more pluralistic system of authority. As a result, even though the second image assumes more effective global centers of control than the first, it paradoxically may allow for greater choice and variation in the pursuit of localized goals.

The environmental degradation we are experiencing today is largely a rich man's disease in the sense that the material demands of rich societies have produced some of the most obvious damage. Yet poor or traditional societies are capable of assaulting the biosphere too. Such an assault is evident to any visitor to Calcutta or Peking who has witnessed how much of the pollution of those cities comes from the open cooking stoves of millions of households rather than from modern industry, or to Nepal, where the mountains have been nearly denuded by the need for fuel and building materials for a booming population. The disease is now global, the victims ourselves. The reasons for its onset, growth, and development are the strongest imaginable argument against our tendency to divide ourselves off from nature as we divide nature up among ourselves. In both respects, we must learn to replace that division with the search for greater unity.

NOTES

1. Walter Prescott Webb, *The Great Frontier* (Austin: University of Texas Press, 1964).

2. Ibid., p. 13. Webb acknowledged his intellectual debt for this thesis to that of Frederick Jackson Turner some sixty years before. Turner had addressed the impact on the United States of the closing of its own western frontier. (See Chapter 3, note 27.) Webb applied that thesis to the global level.

3. Barbara Ward and René Dubos, *Only One Earth* (New York: W. W. Norton, 1972), p. 11. This study was an unofficial report commissioned by the secretary-general of the United Nations Conference on the Human Environment, which met in Stockholm in 1972.

4. Ibid., p. 1.

5. Ibid., p. 7.

6. Ibid., p. 9.

7. Barry Commoner, *The Closing Circle* (New York: Alfred A. Knopf, 1971).

8. Webb, *The Great Frontier*, p. 9.

9. Arnold Toynbee pointed to the irony of that in an introduction he wrote to Webb's *The Great Frontier*: "The Western orientation of the leaders of the non-Western liberation movements is remarkable. Their objective in struggling so persistently to throw off the domination of the Western peoples turns out to have been to go Western, themselves, in a radical way" (p. ix).

10. Grotius's book, *Mare Liberum* (Freedom of the Sea) dates from 1609. The three-mile limit to the territorial sea is attributed to the Dutch jurist, Cornelius van Bynkershoek (1673–1743), who held that control of the sea off a nation's coast could extend only to the range of a shot from a cannon fixed on the shore. "This principle, almost universally accepted shortly after its formulation, became the basis of the three-mile limit of territorial waters when the range of coastal artillery remained fixed, for an appreciable period of time during the late eighteenth century, at about one marine league (about three miles)" (Gerhard von Glahn, *Law Among Nations* [New York: Macmillan, 1965], pp. 46–47).

11. Truman Proclamation, September 28, 1945, 59 Stat. 884.

12. Joint Declaration on Maritime Zones (Declaration of Santiago, August 18, 1952). Costa Rica later adhered to the declaration as well.

13. The United States of course had the military capability to overpower the merchant militias of these Latin states and thereby enforce its insistence on nonrecognition of their claims. But that option seems never to have been considered by any U.S. president, for the simple reason that the states in question were friendly, potentially important allies of the United States, and that fact was always more important for U.S. policy than the annoyance of these conflicts over fishing rights. The example is a good one of the frequent lack of any simple correlation between a state's potential power and its will or ability to apply it in a world where orderly relationships are also important to each actor.

14. Geneva, Convention on the Continental Shelf, 1958. Text in *American Journal of International Law* 58, Supplement (1958):858–862.

15. The Third UN Conference (UNCLOS) convened its first substantive session, after several years of preparation, on June 20, 1974. Ten additional sessions followed over a period of more than eight years.

16. The only less developed countries in this group are Indonesia and the Philippines. The United States would gain the most and largely in a temperate zone—unlike the EEZs of much of Canada, the USSR, and Denmark (Greenland): some 3 million square miles of ocean and continental shelf area.

17. This is the so-called parallel system that represents a compromise between most of the advanced Western states, who wanted only a weak Authority with little power to regulate the mining activities of state-sponsored companies, and the Group of 77's original insistence upon an Authority with a monopoly right to exploit seabed resources itself. The parallel system adopted permits both kinds of operations within the high-seas area of the Authority's jurisdiction. Under this provision, state sponsored companies are to propose two sites: One will be awarded to the company for profit (once licensing fees are paid), the other reserved for exploitation by the Authority, whose own

Enterprise might undertake operations alone or in joint venture arrangements with other corporations.

18. This conclusion is attributed to Pardo by John Logue, "Law of the Sea Will Enrich the Rich," *Philadelphia Inquirer,* December 8, 1982.

19. Those voting "no" in addition to the United States at the signing on April 30, 1982, were Israel, Turkey, and Venezuela. Abstaining were Belgium, Bulgaria, Czechoslovakia, German Democratic Republic, Federal Republic of Germany, Hungary, Italy, Luxembourg, Mongolia, Netherlands, Poland, Spain, Thailand, USSR, and United Kingdom.

20. The pun is suggested by Paul R. Ehrlich's reference to the United States as "the effluent society." *The Population Bomb* (New York: Ballantine Books, 1969), p. 140.

21. UNEP consists of (1) a small secretariat headed by an executive director, (2) a fifty-four-nation Governing Council for Environmental Programmes to provide policy guidance (which reports to the UN General Assembly through the United Nations' Economic and Social Council) and (3) an Environmental Fund of several hundred million dollars to pay for UNEP's programs.

22. E. F. Schumacher, *Small is Beautiful,* p. 294.

9
Toward Better Times

The first requisite of civilization . . . is that of justice. . . . The final outcome should be a rule of law to which all . . . have contributed by a sacrifice of their instincts, and which leaves no one . . . at the mercy of brute force.

—Sigmund Freud
Civilization and Its Discontents

For the first time in human history, the possibilities for creating a globally integrated civilization seem to be within the grasp of those of us living on the earth today. In fragmented aspects of our lives, the age-old dream of human unity has become a reality, through instantaneous communications and growing interdependence upon the products of the ongoing life of our biosphere—and in the common threat of extinction we and, thanks to our behavior, other species face. Therein lies both our best and worst of times, for that which is so clearly within our grasp can easily elude us if we allow our traditional modes of thought and behavior to comand us. Should we fail to change those habits, the result almost certainly will be unprecedented disaster.

It is easy to see the apocalyptic implications of our current condition and often much more difficult not to allow them to overwhelm us with our own sense of impotence to effect the kind of radical change that rational analysis demands. We feel powerless in the face of the most incredible power our technology has created, helpless to improve the human condition when so much in our era seems to conspire to degrade it. The "little matter" of how we get to where we would prefer to be from our present situation, which defines the sense of purpose that gives life meaning, may seem a cosmic problem when our goals encompass the globe. Few of us individually possess the kind of power that determines substantial social change and, what is worse, we must conclude that most of the politically powerful individuals in the world have, precisely because they hold it, the greatest stake in the established order and therefore resistance to change.

But each of us can try to act in accordance with Kant's categorical imperative, namely, as if we wished and expected our individual actions to become universal laws. That command remains as powerful for the ethical behavior of individuals today as in the past because it expresses the universal sense of the ends of equal justice for all members of the human family. But it has political application as well, for we measure the justness of societies by the extent to which their laws bind individuals equally, permitting and even encouraging them all to achieve the full measure of their human potential. The comparatively just society is one that has been able to make universal laws govern the behavior of those within it.

Under the name of reciprocity, this principle has formed the basis for all our efforts to advance the quality of order and justice beyond the nation-state in modern times. Reciprocity encouraged by a vision of universal justice is the expression of the Kantian categorical imperative as applied to international life. In a world with so little hierarchical allocation of socially acceptable values, the reciprocal implications of the behavior of each (especially each state) actor are especially important. To the extent that each behaves in ways acceptable to other actors, their actions are likely to be emulated, to persist, and to become predictable, i.e., to be mutually recognized as lawful. In Kantian terms, although no single actor can control the behavior of others, each can behave as it wills others to behave and thereby lead the way to a more just world order through the force of its example.[1] What follows may suggest to the reader who would try to live by the categorical imperative how that same precept might become an example to international actors for behavior that can advance justice in world order. Although most of us do not have the power to command international actors to do our bidding directly, we too can show the way by our own action, for it is men and women motivated by a vision of greater justice who have the power to improve the world. That action must no doubt take a multiplicity of forms, depending upon the particular situations of each of us. The bare suggestion of priorities and sketches for policies with which I conclude are meant to stimulate the reader to think and act upon the innumerable possibilities for improving global order.

Our basic priorities should be clear, for we are threatened with the actual possibility of our severe retrogression and conceivably even our extinction today, and not from one, but two quarters. The first and immediate peril comes from the vast stocks of thermonuclear weapons that we have created deliberately in the misguided conception that they would increase our security. The second, indirect threat is from the myriad ways in which we continue to assault our biosphere and thus endanger its capacity to sustain us. Both the direct and the indirect threats to our existence can be addressed and eliminated, and because the maintenance of life is our most basic value, these are the issues that demand the fullest attention of the current generation.

Fortunately, because of the complex interconnectedness of our values and our actions, attention to improving our chances for survival need not mean ignoring issues that may not be so immediately life threatening, such as extending economic justice and the protection of other fundamental human rights. In fact, a more benign pursuit of many of the values of self-fulfillment than dominant sectors of world society have engaged in almost certainly will help move us away from the indirect threat to extinction through environmental collapse. Advancement of our major world order values therefore is interconnected, and even as we strengthen the prospects for our survival, we must act to improve the quality of our lives globally.

A number of normative generalizations now are possible about the way we ought to live in greater planetary harmony. The first generalization can guide us in moving away from the current military peril: It is that *security for human societies is best which is defensive.* However great the risks in the prenuclear age of trying to win security for oneself by force of arms, there was at least some calculable chance of success. Even more importantly, if one lost, that typically meant losing a figurative limb and not the very life of the political actor. The certainty that our modern weapons of mass destruction will produce unprecedented devastation is undoubtedly what has prevented those with the ostensible authority to use them from doing so since 1945. Although we have taken some comfort from that fact up to now, there is ultimately nothing but discomfort in the consequences to human values should that power ever be unleashed.

The most powerful nuclear actors are the most impotent, at least in their relations with each other, because they have made themselves and their societies hostages to their own weapons. It is that counterpolitical condition that is perceived and objected to when Europeans protest the deployment of Cruise and Pershing II missiles within their territory, or when residents of the southwest United States refuse to countenance the development of a vast and sprawling "race track" basing system for the M-X missile in their region. That counterpolitical condition has been sustained and continuously reinforced by the relentless emphasis on the mutual threat from these weapons. This condition has required an almost continual need to depict the opposing forces as unalterably malign, since only the most malignant enemy would credibly require our own suicide to halt their advance. As a result, we have created the worst of all possible worlds: a global society in which the most powerful are the least secure and in which they nonetheless pursue the chimera of security by constant reinforcement of their willingness to destroy global society. This political and ethical dilemma in which we have allowed ourselves to become mired seems a nearly inviolable trap, all the more outrageous a prison when we realize how we entered it, step by step, because it seemed the only way to turn.

If we could free ourselves from this trap, might we not again be guided by time-honored precepts justifying and restraining the use of force in civilized societies? One of these precepts is that force should be used for strictly defensive purposes rather than to impose one's values on those who resist them. A second precept is that, although it may sometimes be necessary to defend oneself and even to repel and punish an aggressor who wishes to eliminate one's own freedom and autonomy, just punishment requires proportionality in the use of force, fitting the punishment to the crime, rather than the unrestrained destruction of the wrongdoer. A third, evidently unrealistic precept for the decentralized global society today is that effective force be largely monopolized through the central authority of the police. But this third precept need not be implemented fully at the global level in order to give real life to the first two. Once they are honored much more fully than in the perpetuation of a nuclear balance of terror, we may find to our surprise that moves toward a monopoly of police power at a global level begin to look possible.

Moving toward a denuclearized world is imperative to our security, and one of the most effective first steps the Western alliance might take would be to adopt a no-first-use of nuclear weapons policy. The basic argument opposing such a policy today is that it would require a considerable increase in the conventional forces available to NATO countries to counter the Soviet advantage in that regard in Eastern Europe. Although there are sound reasons for arguing against that contention,[2] those are at least the grounds on which debates about genuine security should take place, rather than over whether yet another nuclear weapons system will or will not increase our safety. For at least three reasons, the United States and its allies should join the Soviets in a no-first-use pledge and then act with them to formalize that commitment as a mark of its solemn importance to the world. First, such a pledge would move us sharply away from the ever-growing danger that nuclear war under present conditions may break out unintentionally as a result of the various tripwire mechanisms intended to make escalation from conventional to nuclear levels of conflict more or less inevitable. If we are pledged not to use nuclear weapons first, the wide dispersal of these tactical weapons among NATO troops would make no sense at all. And these weapons are dangerous, in Freeman Dyson's words, "because they are apparently benign, . . . because they allow the world to slide gradually from local squabbles into holocaust."[3]

Second, such a pledge would encourage the European members of NATO to take basic responsibility for their own security and to discredit the myth that their societies are being protected by the presence of those tactical weapons whose use would turn their soil, first and most inevitably, into a poisoned wasteland. One of the healthiest implications of the Westphalian system prior to the nuclear age was its insistence that the rights and privileges of sovereignty carried with them the responsibility for providing for one's own security. If European NATO members are enjoying something of a free ride in their perpetual tendency to spend less on their own defense than governments in Washington perennially think they should spend, then presumably the best way to end it is to remove whatever false security they may feel from their presumed protection by the U.S. first-use commitment.

Third, and most important, a no-first-use policy would create a firebreak between conventional and nuclear war with the potential to grow wide enough to become truly unbridgeable over the long run, so that nuclear weapons can begin to be eliminated from the face of the earth. If no possessor of nuclear arms ever uses them first, they are never used and cease in fact to be arms. Rather, they may become useless and dangerous artifacts, like discarded iceboxes on a playground for young children, that will increasingly be viewed as such by more and more human beings. A no-first-use policy alone speaks to tactical weapons initially; it does not dismantle strategic weapons and delivery systems unilaterally, but retains them until they can be the subject of negotiated dismantling.

A mutual policy of no-first-use acknowledges that each side *is* deterred by the other rather than, as current NATO policy says in effect, that we will *not* be deterred from going nuclear if we are sufficiently provoked. Once a real symmetry is apparent in the deterrent postures of the antagonists, it should be much easier for each side to work its way back toward a minimum deterrent, whether through negotiations, unilateral initiatives, or both. That would be a vast improvement over the current situation, yet it would not rid the nuclear powers of the immorality of their continued effort to base their security on a threat to extinguish themselves and others. Therefore, the normative goal that should emerge at this second stage is to reestablish the traditional link in the security policy of states between deterrence and defense, while moving away from species-threatening instruments of mass destruction.

Meanwhile, at this second stage, the imperial pretensions in the foreign policies of the superpowers can begin to be eliminated as we clarify the ways in which they distort, denigrate, and even nullify those humane values that a civilized social order is intended to promote. The records of the United States and the Soviet Union make clear that their efforts to control the wider world in the interests of their own attempt to dominate induces them again and again to support establishment elites in opposition to groups seeking progressive change.

Since the definition of what constitutes politically progressive or regressive forces is typically reversed from one superpower to the other, the result can be very dangerous if one's interpretation is ever forcibly challenged by the other. Even where it is not challenged directly, as in Vietnam and Afghanistan, the self-proclaimed right of each to control the political destinies of others can lead them into a morass of violence and repression that thwarts the human rights of target populations. The process can be devastating to important normative concerns and threatens always to engulf the wider world in an escalating cycle of destruction.

Even when we are able to see the inhumane impact on other people of the effort to control their destinies, we are likely to continue to insist that if we (whose motives are benign, we think) do not exercise our power in this way, other societies will fall under the more repressive sway of the Soviets. But that assumption runs counter to the reciprocal implications of the categorical imperative, which is why it is often viewed as hubristic and malign. To the extent that we can move toward a security policy that genuinely protects and defends our own home ground, leaving those functions largely to others for their own territories, we shall have restored and enhanced the most politically and ethically informed insight of the Westphalian order. We shall also, coincidentally, have moved to a world beyond bloc alliances and one therefore in which the potential has been created for a more effective collective security capability than has yet been established.

This ability to deter an enemy and defend oneself can take many more humane forms than the superpowers rely on today. That of civilian-based defense is most radically different and the most acceptable normatively. It does not threaten the survival of a would-be aggressor, but it threatens an opponent with what it expects will be an unacceptably high cost if it launches an aggression, making clear that the target population will not submit docilely to its own subjugation, but in fact will refuse to be subjugated at all. Since the only point of conquest is control—over population, resources, and therefore capabilities—it loses all meaning when it does not succeed. The effort simply becomes an unimaginable liability to the would-be conqueror. And civilian-based defense endeavors to make sure that aggression will never succeed, not without an unacceptable cost to the attacker. Its strength lies in its ability to demonstrate actively the value cohesion of the defending population, which is always and everywhere the most potent justification for taking up arms.

A substantially denuclearized world is difficult to imagine without a simultaneous increase in civilian-based defense, particularly in Western countries, where it initially should become the guiding doctrine of a third stage of security policy. As such strategies are seriously explored and adopted, cutting back more and more of the traditional offensive military components of states, even conventional ones, should become an increasingly realistic strategy. The creation of a world in which military force plays no role at all is no doubt an impossibility for human society; yet, since it has been the ideal normative vision throughout our history, we should seek always to approach it as closely as humanly possible. At a minimum, we must be guided by the standard that says that all humane use of force must be intended to advance important social values, starting most fundamentally with that of the survival of the species and moving, as we advance, up the scale of human needs to protection of the loftiest of our aspirations.

The second normative generalization deserves our consideration in connection with the indirect peril we face from the way we pursue material wealth. It is that *our material development must be bound by nature's limits*. With his usual breathtaking sense of the time frame of human development, Arnold Toynbee noted in his last major work that "the two million years that have passed since the first stone was chipped into a more useful shape by *australopithecus* is the twinkling of an eye compared with the 2,000 million years more for which, it has been estimated, the biosphere will continue to be habitable if Man permits."[4] Apparently we, the members of a single species, will decide whether life will continue on the planet, although only in this century have we begun to perceive that we held such satanic power. As we struggle to avoid the kind of apocalyptic catastrophe that could decimate advanced life forms, we also must reorder our priorities to ensure that our material development proceeds in accordance with nature's laws.

How we do that is clear enough in principle but is open to a great range of possibilities in practice. Strategies necessarily will vary from one society to another, depending upon their relative levels of economic development and many other factors. But all of them need to be informed by two more specific kinds of normative guides: (1) *All human development should proceed with the goal of conserving nonrenewable resources of the biosphere and replenishing those that can be replenished to maintain nature's balance,* and (2) *human development should be advanced in ways that maximize distributive justice and minimize social stratification throughout the globe.* For those who argue that these two guides contradict each other, there is this reply: yes, to the extent that they represent two of the kinds of values that confront us with divergent problems, forcing us to make tentative and mixed choices in particular contexts; but no, in the sense that viewing them as necessarily opposing is itself a reflection of our distorted or outmoded values. The growth mentality remains so deeply ingrained in most of us whose society first entered the industrial age nearly two hundred years ago that we still have difficulty not equating endless economic growth with human well-being. But today we must stretch ourselves to discover the many ways in which the quality of our lives can actually be enhanced, not by focusing exclusively on ever greater quantities of material goods, but by learning to live in greater harmony with nature.[5]

In the global context, the structural decentralization of the state system can play a useful role in advancing these interrelated values. From this viewpoint, much of the international effort to further economic development worldwide over the past several decades can be viewed as attempting to provide poor states with a more nearly equal footing from which to interact economically with much richer and more powerful states. That impulse, much of which is expressed in the agenda for a New International Economic Order, is an expression of the best that has always been at the heart of Westphalian organizing principles, for it supports pluralistic development and the dignity that can come only from the respect for equal rights of individual actors. More substantively, the encouragement of pluralistic development provides us with diverse and alternative models, at least some of which may support gentler technologies and more ecologically sound principles of economic activity than are available in the traditional Northern model of large-scale industrial development.

But the problem of making these positive aspects of the current developmental process prevail over its negative features is a very large one. The formal sovereignty of many more poor than rich countries has not provided them with a corresponding ability to democratize the international economic system, or even to succeed very far in providing greater distributive justice throughout the world. The structural dominance of the rich remains, as evidenced in the current stalemate in international economic negotiations intended to advance third world economic programs. Moreover, in spite of the development of alternatives to the traditional capitalist and Leninist models of economic development, both of which foster limitless growth and ecologically harmful technologies, it seems safe to say that these alternatives have not yet become established on the principal agenda of international economic development. In other words, the exploitative values encouraged by the industrial revolution in the West are still far too strongly supported in the development strategies of many third world countries today. The evidence is, first, in the existence of the unmanageable migrations from rural to urban areas with all the resulting social problems they entail; second, in the persistence of pollution havens in countries where industrial production is encouraged at the price of social well-being; and third, in the growth in size, income and, therefore, political and economic power of transnational corporations, the largest privately held economic organizations the world has ever known. Even the third world's New International Economic Order looks to many like an attempt to encourage a redistribution of wealth within the world economy without attending seriously to the impact on the biosphere of ongoing growth ideologies.

Those actors that today are in the most privileged positions within the world's economic system are no more likely to seek substantial change than are national statesmen to initiate energetic action to move away from the war system. Moreover, the illogic of traditional approaches to security must be more apparent to more informed individuals than the inequities and dangers of the world economic system, which does not, after all, appear to threaten our very lives in the same way as do multimegaton weapons. It may be that many people are beginning to see, perhaps even influence, the possibilities for reciprocal models of action for world security; yet they may have much more difficulty imagining how to influence relevant actors to move toward balanced development for our material well-being throughout the world. The economic dimension of human life apparently has too many relevant actors, too little controlled by governments, to point us toward models for action powerful enough to induce reciprocity on an effective scale.

Nonetheless, we might usefully start with the dictum that while thinking globally, we must act locally.[6] Then, from several additional generalizations about how we ought to live, we can draw a host of specific possibilities for behavior.

The next of those generalizations is that *human beings evidently take the greatest sustained pleasure of their lives from a sense of productive labor*, and *productive* is generally best defined as that which directly transforms nature's raw materials into a useful product. Clearly, as modes of production have changed with our technologies, so has our assignment of social worth to varying kinds of labor. But ever since the industrial age began, a persistent thread of criticism and concern has argued that the mechanization of labor—the interposition of powerful machines between the individual worker and the raw materials—has served to dehumanize the productive process, robbing work of much of its gratification. The same person who tends a steel mill's blast furnace by day may enjoy the weekend by cultivating a vegetable patch in the backyard. The person who earns a wage on an automobile assembly line may knit in the evening. Their hobbies are also productive work, but psychically rewarding in ways their "real" work may not be, for we do not expect to see a craftsman by trade tend a blast furnace as a hobby. The visitor to China today typically is shown through a variety of small craft factories, often rather primitively housed, with only rudimentary equipment and a small labor force. One suspects that these enterprises have become showcases for tourists not in spite of but because of their very modesty: A visitor would have difficulty not responding to such a scene with a sense that rewarding work is being done under remarkably pleasant conditions.

We should not romanticize the backbreaking toil of much of life in preindustrial societies with these observations. But we should start to acknowledge that our huge-scale and complex technologies have sometimes served to enslave our spirits even while they were liberating our bodies. Such acknowledgment can lead us to a greater respect for, and perhaps a borrowing from, modes of economic organization that do not fit the Northern industrial model; it can suggest the value in efforts to humanize our work places; and it can guide those of us moving into postindustrial societies to strive constantly to return to the human scale in our productive lives.

A further generalization is that *all the products of the biosphere are humankind's common heritage.* In recent years, a number of third world countries have asserted their permanent sovereignty over valuable natural resources within their territories in a move that some have viewed as virulently nationalistic and defiantly opposed to the larger view of the biosphere as a single natural system. Yet this assertion was a typically Westphalian reaction to the practice of distant entrepreneurs who exploited nonrenewable resources more for their private gain than for the material profit of the local society, encouraging greater social stratification. The permanent sovereignty claim is but the first, defensive step in world order policy toward recognition of the nonrenewability and therefore the preciousness to all of us, not just to the economic elites, of the earth's resources. That principle was embodied in the provisions of the 1982 Law of the Sea treaty that permits the Enterprise to engage in and license mining operations in the seabed for the economic benefit of the global community, on the basis of need. To the extent that sound and mutually reinforcing environmental policies are applied to the exclusive economic zones of coastal states, this general principle will become public policy for the world. More generally, as the world's free goods inevitably become more scarce and more susceptible to destruction through misuse, public policies at every level of society must be formulated to provide greater and greater protection over this common heritage.

From this, too, we should deduce the general behavioral principle that warns us that, whenever we are faced with any kind of development project likely to have a massive impact upon the environment, we should treat it with skepticism and try to determine if gentler alternatives are available. As usual, we must assume that such questioning will have to arise from the bottom and proceed up to relevant governmental levels, rather than the reverse.[7] Not far from my home, a project was initiated more than a decade ago to create a pumping system to remove millions of gallons of water daily from the Delaware River. The purpose of the project was to cool a nuclear generating plant and provide water for drought-prone residential areas some distance away. The utility company and the relevant county governments created an authority to undertake the project, which was well launched before grass-roots political pressure finally forced a temporary halt. As the public debate over the project's merits grew, it became clear that, as usual with policy issues, there was no way either for the proponents of the project to prove in advance that the diversion of river water would not have costly ecological effects, nor for opponents to prove that it would. Yet even though plausible arguments could be made on both sides, anyone with a sensitivity to environmental values had to argue that the risk of serious damage was present. Even if the immediate ecology of the river were not seriously affected, the diversion of the water would accelerate the suburban development of rich farmland, removing that land from the agricultural sector and contributing to the kind of urban sprawl that increases, in addition to its indirect contribution to a number of social ills, the society's assault upon the biosphere.

A final generalization about how we ought to live relates to our political as much as to our economic and social lives. It is that *the best social order would permit very great local control and autonomy in policy making, but link us in a global network of social solidarity*. As Toynbee said, "What has been needed for the last 5,000 years, and has been feasible technologically, though not yet politically, for the last hundred years, is a global body politic composed of cells on the scale of the Neolithic-Age village community—a scale on which the participants would be personally acquainted with each other, while each of them would also be a citizen of the world-state."[8] No doubt we would have to reach the height of idealism to suppose that such a vision could be reliably achieved within our lifetimes, yet with simple realism we can note that the conditions for such a social order already have been laid. We also can see realistically that the conditions for the opposite of this arrangement, the worst social order we can imagine, are lurking all about us. Those conditions would create repression and political domination at local levels without a corresponding network of authority that would bridge the globe. We may not achieve the best, but we can act every day to ensure that we shall avoid the worst.

This generalization provides an insight into why human rights issues, the enhancement of human dignity, are also at the heart of world order concerns. If, like Hobbes, we imagine a state of nature without protection for those rights, we find ourselves in a situation where might makes right, where only the strongest are afforded what all of us claim in a just social order. In asserting equal rights within civil society, whether local or global, we learn to interact on the basis of that legal fiction, our equality. Even while we develop a respect for our equal rights, we learn to develop simultaneously a toleration for our differences, which can largely be expressed within our various private spheres. The growth of our sense of communal solidarity is the other side of our respect for our separate autonomies, our sovereign capabilities as distinct creatures.

Just as that truth underlies what we regard as acceptable social order among individual human beings, so can it form the basis for acceptable global order among individual states. The Westphalian system has always been based theoretically upon that insight, but for most of its history, global sociopolitical development had not yet advanced to the point to make it drive international behavior effectively. International social and political intercourse tended to be so limited, so unconstrained by the environment of international politics, that the mutual social obligation of sovereigns could largely be ignored. Most could grow and flourish with little heed to each other. The danger in that state of affairs always has been that it hides the social obligation of each sovereign and each sovereign society from view. Each nation-state traditionally has been so isolated from others that its members have been tempted to forget that others are composed of the same species as themselves, motivated by the same biological and spiritual needs. Given the instantaneous communications possible throughout the world today, including the ability we have to wreak unspeakable damage on fellow humans across the globe in a matter of minutes, we find it increasingly impossible to forget our species sameness. A thousand traditional habits and modes of organizing our political lives conspire to try to make us forget. The challenge that we all face is to overcome them.

NOTES

1. This adaptation of the Kantian categorical imperative paraphrases Earl C. Ravenal, "The Case for Disengagement," *Foreign Affairs* 51, 3 (April 1973):521, who added, "admittedly, this is not a self-executing policy. But, at least in moral theory, it could be a self-fulfilling prophecy."

2. These arguments are cogently presented by the Union of Concerned Scientists, for example, in the February 1, 1983, study entitled "No First Use" (Union of Concerned Scientists, 26 Church Street, Cambridge, Mass.). For a summary of that study's findings, see Kurt Gottfried, Henry W. Kendall, and John M. Lee, "No First Use of Nuclear Weapons," *Scientific American* 250, 3 (March 1984):33–41.

3. Freeman Dyson, "Weapons and Hope," *New Yorker* (February 20, 1984), p. 75. See also his analysis (p. 95) of why mutual trust is *not* needed to make a no-first-use commitment effective.

4. Arnold Toynbee, *Mankind and Mother Earth* (New York and London: Oxford University Press, 1976), p. 26.

5. One pungent demonstration of the dilemmas we are led to by an overly rich way of life was made by Professor Peter Caws in his Phi Beta Kappa lecture at Temple University, on March 15, 1984. Our current mode of living, he suggested, presents two possibilities for response from poor countries. Either they will attempt to emulate the United States or they will resent our wealth, and either alternative is disastrous for us and for the world. Plato foresaw increasingly serious problems of value allocation for the rulers of "the luxurious state." See *The Republic*, Chapter 7.

6. Chadwick Alger has frequently urged students of international order today to "think globally, and act locally." See his "The Role of People in the Future Global Order," *Alternatives* 4, 2 (October 1978):232–262, and "Local, National and Global Politics in the World: A Challenge to International Studies," *International Studies Notes* 5, 1 (Spring 1978).

7. Scholars are beginning to take account of the importance of grass-roots citizens' movements in their impact on a number of local and national issues. These movements are at least instructive for extending that phenomenon much more fully to the global level. See, for example, Harry C. Boyte, *The Backyard Revolution* (Philadelphia: Temple University Press, 1980).

8. Toynbee, *Mankind and Mother Earth*, p. 593.

Index

Other Titles of Interest from Westview Press

†*International Law and a Just World Order*, edited by Richard Falk, Friedrich V. Kratochwil, and Saul H. Mendlovitz

†*The United Nations and a Just World Order*, edited by Richard Falk, Samuel S. Kim, Donald McNemar, and Saul H. Mendlovitz

†*Toward Nuclear Disarmament and Global Security: A Search for Alternatives*, edited by Burns H. Weston, with the assistance of Thomas A. Hawbaker and Christopher R. Rossi

†*Toward a Just World Order*, edited by Richard Falk, Samuel S. Kim, and Saul H. Mendlovitz

†*Culture, Ideology, and World Order*, edited by R.B.J. Walker

Global Militarization, edited by Peter Wallensteen, Johan Galtung, and Carlos Portales

†*Arms Control and International Security*, edited by Roman Kolkowicz and Neil Joeck

†*The Quest for a Just World Order*, Samuel S. Kim

†*Globalism Versus Realism: International Relations' Third Debate*, edited by Ray Maghroori and Bennett Ramberg

The Nuclear Freeze Debate: Arms Control Issues for the 1980s, edited by Paul M. Cole and William J. Taylor, Jr.

†Available in hardcover and paperback.

About the Book and Author

GLOBAL ORDER: VALUES AND POWER IN INTERNATIONAL POLITICS

Lynn H. Miller

This book examines some of the most important issues on today's international agenda. By tracing the logic of the Westphalian system of sovereign nation-states, its growth and development over the past three hundred years as the organizing mode for the entire world, and the threats to its continued ability to provide the kind of ordering framework needed today, Professor Miller provides the reader with the necessary tools to understand the chaotic universe of competing social and political forces as a world order system, one with a value structure that both shapes international behavior and makes possible its evaluation. The connections between power and values in human society, between power and authority, the relativity of both anarchy and order in the international system, and relationships between politics and law are among the subjects of his inquiry.

Professor Miller also systematically explores the principal world order problems of international warfare and the nuclear threat, global economic inequality, human rights deprivations, and planetary resource scarcity and environmental degradation. The ways in which these issues are being affected by current sociopolitical developments are investigated, as are the possibilities for implementing preferable alternatives and thus improving the human condition in all nations.

Dr. Lynn H. Miller is professor of political science at Temple University; he has also taught at the University of California, Los Angeles, and the University of Pennsylvania. He is the author of *Organizing Mankind: An Analysis of Contemporary International Organization* (1972) and coauthor (with Ronald Pruessen) of *Reflections on the Cold War* (1974).